WITH ALL
DELIBERATE SPEED

WITH ALL DELIBERATE SPEED

Segregation-Desegregation
in Southern Schools

Prepared by Staff Members and Associates of
Southern Education Reporting Service

EDITED BY
DON SHOEMAKER

BERT COLLIER
WELDON JAMES
EDGAR L. JONES
ROBERT LASCH
ROBERT A. LEFLAR

PATRICK E. MCCAULEY
JOSEPH B. PARHAM
GLEN ROBINSON
JEANNE ROGERS
WALLACE WESTFELDT

W. D. WORKMAN, JR.

HARPER & BROTHERS: NEW YORK

WITH ALL DELIBERATE SPEED

Copyright © 1957, by Harper & Brothers

Printed in the United States of America

379
S

FIRST EDITION

I-G

Library of Congress catalog card number: 57-11117

CONTENTS

EDITOR'S FOREWORD

What follows is not a documentary in the ordinary sense.

Rather, it is a summary—deliberately so—by a body of reporters. It is a journalistic summation of three turbulent years since the U. S. Supreme Court decision against segregation in the public schools.

The true "documentary" in this field, the editor and the contributors believe, is SOUTHERN SCHOOL NEWS, the paper of record. In large, though not in whole, part of this book has been drawn from SOUTHERN SCHOOL NEWS, once described as "an experiment unique in the history of journalism."

All of those who wrote the following chapters under my editorship have been identified in one way or another with this "unique" publication which, fastening on a single subject, has attempted to report in volume and without conscious bias on a matter of ultimate controversy in a great region of the United States.

SOUTHERN SCHOOL NEWS is published monthly under the sponsorship of the Southern Education Reporting Service. A word about SERS:

It was established in 1954 by six southern newspaper editors and six southern educators. As the masthead of SOUTHERN SCHOOL NEWS proclaims, SERS is "neither pro-segregation nor anti-segregation, but simply reports the facts as it finds them, state by state."

The board of directors was purposely drawn from a broad spectrum of editors and educators with a view to obtaining the widest possible representation of opinion. The group, it may be said, is agreed on one point: that the whole factual story be told in order that the southern and border region may keep informed, in one place and in detail, about a gnawing regional—and national—concern.

To be sure, it can be argued with eloquence and conviction that public school segregation-desegregation is not a regional problem at all but in reality a national one.

To treat it as such, however, is not our purpose. In this respect the record has been documented in other times and in other places. Here, we are concerned only with the impact of a court decision and a situation which has fretted and fascinated newsman and layman North, South and around the world.

About the contributors:

With two exceptions, they are staff members of SERS and SOUTHERN SCHOOL NEWS. One of the two is a prominent jurist. The other is a rising young educator. All eleven are represented in brief biographies in the back of this book.

The issue here discussed has a high emotional content North and South. It has been said that because of this passionate preoccupation the Supreme Court is beseiged by critics and back-stopped by friends to a degree without precedent in its modern history. Thus, each contributor to this symposium has a private opinion and, if his regular employment involves editorial judgment or editorial policy, perhaps a public opinion also.

As with SOUTHERN SCHOOL NEWS, I have asked only that these contributors park their opinions at some convenient curb and essay the role of reporter.

What follows, I believe, is an accurate and unimpassioned summary of three vital years' developments in the history of our times. While this recital is by no means complete, here, in the eyes of the contributors, are the events that rise above the ordinary, the day-to-day, in an era which has alternately surprised, saddened or delighted those of matching expectations or convictions. It is hoped that this will bring the whole complex subject into compact perspective.

The story begins with the Supreme Court decision of May 17, 1954. It deals with the effect on the sub-regions, the rural and urban areas, the colleges, the legislative halls and political hustings, the schoolman and the lay southerner.

On a third Monday of May a muted buzzer sounded in a marble building, a court crier rapped a gavel and intoned "oyez, oyez, oyez," and nine black-robed men filed from behind a heavy red curtain to take their places at a long mahogany bench . . .

DON SHOEMAKER

Nashville, Tennessee
August 1, 1957

WITH ALL
DELIBERATE SPEED

1.

'Law of The Land'

By Robert A. Leflar

Some lawyers were truly surprised by the U. S. Supreme Court's decision on May 17, 1954, that state-compelled racial segregation in the public schools is unconstitutional, but many were not surprised. Legal background for the decision had been gradually accumulating for several years, and students of traditional legal processes for some time foresaw that the Court would eventually hand down a determination about like that in the 1954 case. There were informed persons who thought that the decision would be postponed for a few years, or for many years, but almost none doubted that it would come in time. There were many, however, who were not ready for it in 1954.

"Separate but Equal"

The rule before 1954, that racial segregation in public schools was permissible provided the "separate" schools were "equal," went back in history to a Massachusetts case which in 1849 sustained the validity of "separate but equal" schools in Boston. True, the Massachusetts legislature had promptly enacted a statute desegregating public schools in that state, but the judicial concept lived on to dominate the South's school systems for a century.

The concept was restated by the U. S. Supreme Court in *Plessy* v. *Ferguson,* which in 1896 upheld a Louisiana statute requiring separate railroad accommodations for Negroes and whites and cited with approval the then accepted practice of public school segregation as practical precedent for the railroad rule. Reaffirmance of the approval came in a 1927 Supreme Court case which allowed Mississippi to send a Chinese child to a school maintained for Negroes.

Then came a series of cases dealing with the right of Negroes to attend state colleges. The courts of Maryland in 1936 compelled the university law school of that state to admit Negroes, rather than pay their tuition to out-of-state schools, on the theory that instruction obtained elsewhere was not "equal" to that afforded at the University of Maryland for a man who proposed to practice law in Maryland. In the *Gaines* case from Missouri, the U. S. Supreme Court in 1938 accepted the same idea, though Missouri complied with the decision by setting up a separate law school for Negroes at St. Louis. Oklahoma as a result of the *Sipuel* cases in 1948 chose to admit Negroes to its regular university law school rather than set up a separate law school. Texas established a separate law school for Negroes but the Supreme Court held that its makeshift character made it not "equal," and a Negro applicant was ordered admitted to the University of Texas law school. A Negro graduate student named McLaurin was held entitled to be seated with other students in his classes at the University of Oklahoma instead of being seated in an adjoining room where he could hear but not participate fully in class activities. Several other college cases were pending in southern state and Federal courts at the time the 1954 desegregation decision was handed down.

At that moment there were 17 American states, all in the old South or on the border of the South, plus the District of Columbia, which by law made segregated schools mandatory. Four states beyond the border—Arizona, Kansas, New Mexico and Wyoming—allowed varieties of local option on segregation. Sixteen states by law prohibited public school segregation though not all of them actually enforced their prohibitions. The 11 other states, all in the North or West, had no laws on the subject, and most of them had no reported cases in their courts.

In the southern and border states at this stage, separate schools for Negroes were universal, and they were not uncommon even in states above the border. In a few of the northern states they were maintained contrary to state law, but in general they existed under the "separate but equal" concept which was assumed to be the law.

The legal meaning of "equality" under this concept was hard to state, still harder to apply in practice. In most states the emphasis was on "separate" rather than on "equal." In any event "equality" had to be an approximation and not an exact mathematical equivalence of specific qualities and defects. Advantages and disadvantages could be weighed against each other, but in any such weighing the point of balance, or of imbalance, inevitably depended so much on discretion and individual judgment that wide variances in decision could be expected. The large number of reported cases, most of them in the Federal courts, in which equality of separate schools was at issue prior to 1954, reveal no clear formula nor consistent pattern, though it is notable that in the later years an increasing proportion of cases held that equality was lacking and must be provided by those in authority.

And the argument was being increasingly heard that compulsory separateness was itself inequality.

WHAT THE COURT SAID

That was the state of things when the five "great cases" came to the U. S. Supreme Court. All five of them were accepted by the Court in 1952 for its docket, were argued during the 1952 term, and would normally have been decided by June of 1953. But the Court was anxious that every aspect of the school segregation problem be brought out clearly before the cases were determined and therefore ordered them reargued in the fall of 1953. The order stated specific questions on which argument was requested, and invited the U. S. Attorney General and other interested persons to file briefs.

The five appealed cases presented a variety of related situations. In the *Brown* case, now famous because its name came first in the series, the lower Federal court relied on prior authority to sustain the segregated grade school system of Topeka, Kansas, though at the same time it found as a fact that segregation in itself "has a tendency to retard the education and mental development of Negro children." *Briggs* v. *Elliott* from Clarendon County, South Carolina, had held that the separate schools there were unequal and should be improved but the appellant Negroes contended for admission to white schools pending the improvement. In the Prince Edward County, Virginia, case there was a similar finding of present inequality plus a promise of improvement. The Delaware case came up from the state supreme court which found inequality in the Negro schools at Wilmington and ordered that the Negro plaintiff be admitted to the white school until the inequality was eliminated. The fifth case was from the District of Columbia and involved the validity of Federal enactments impliedly requiring separate schools in the District.

The five cases were presented to the Court again in December 1953, with briefs filed and arguments heard from the attorneys general of several of the southern states as well as the U. S. Department of Justice. Distinguished counsel for the several school districts were headed by John W. Davis, one-time Democratic Presidential nominee, and for the Negro plaintiffs by Thurgood Marshall, general counsel for the National Association for the Advancement of Colored People.

The Decision

Nearly six months passed before the Court handed down its unanimous decision broadly sustaining the plaintiffs' position. On May 17, 1954, according to the Court, "separate but equal" ceased to be law; the invalidity of state-enforced racial segregation in the public schools became the "law of the land." The decision's effect was delayed by keeping the case on the docket for further argument as to methods of enforcement. New hearings were held before the Court in April 1955, with 71 lawyers filing briefs representing various plaintiffs, 10 states, the District of Columbia, the U. S. Department of Justice and other interested intervenors. Then the implementing decision was handed down on May 31, 1955.

Basic to the Court's opinion was a recognition of the wide variety of local school problems involved. Because of this the Federal district courts were told to look at the integration plans separately submitted by the authorities of each school district against which enforcement actions should be brought, not to achieve uniformity but rather to achieve good faith implementation of the desegregation principle as applied to local facts. "Equitable principles," traditionally characterized by practical flexibility and by a facility for adjusting and reconciling public and private needs, were to be the guide. The Court called for a "prompt and reasonable start" toward compliance with the new constitutional requirement, to be then carried out "with all deliberate speed." Federal district courts were to retain jurisdiction of cases before them throughout the implementation process, as a check upon compliance.

Thus the Court not only decided the cases immediately before it, but laid down a pattern for lower courts to follow in handling the mass of anticipated future litigation.

NATURE OF THE JUDICIAL PROCESS

Some examination of relevant judicial procedures is a helpful preliminary to study of the cases that have come before the courts since May of 1955.

In general, desegregation lawsuits can be brought only by aggrieved persons. These will normally be Negro students or their parents. School boards may not in most states bring test suits for advance judicial approval of contemplated desegregation programs, but must wait until someone sues them, unless "friendly suits" can be arranged, though a school board that wants to be sued today probably can be accommodated rather readily.

Negro plaintiffs usually seek relief in Federal rather than state courts, partly because a Federal right is claimed (though the Federal right, being based on "the law of the land," is theoretically enforceable in state courts as well) but primarily because they reason Federal judges will be subject to fewer opposing political pressures than will elected state judges.

In most cases plaintiffs ask for declaratory judgments establishing their rights, on the facts proved, to attend designated schools. At the same time they pray for injunctions to restrain defendant school boards and officials from violating the rights declared to exist. Other available remedies include mandamus to compel compliance by defendants with their asserted duties under the law, taxpayers' suits to require that public funds be expended lawfully else not at all, actions for damages for harms allegedly suffered from past deprivations of legal rights, and even criminal penalties imposable under the Civil Rights acts enacted by Congress in the post-Civil War period. Such damage suits and criminal prosecutions would be against school officials personally. A third of a century and more ago, most Negroes seeking relief in school situations brought mandamus actions, but in recent years the declaratory judgment plus injunction type of proceeding has become almost standard. It affords a better setting for adjudication of all the issues usually present in school discrimination cases than do any of the other remedies, and therefore it is normally preferred by both plaintiffs and defendants.

One factor inherent in the nature of ordinary lawsuits is that they affect only the immediate parties. Thus an adjudication that one child is entitled to attend a certain school does not establish the rights of other children to attend it. The "class suit" device, under which a plaintiff or several plaintiffs undertake to represent all others similarly situated, is used in the Federal courts and most state courts to overcome this difficulty. Even this device, however, is available only for the benefit of other persons who reside in the same school district. Plaintiffs in a class suit can represent other parties only as against the same defendant, and patrons of other school districts must file their suits against different defendants.

The Procedure

Under the 1955 *Brown* decision, the defendants' answer, assuming a Federal class suit praying for declaratory judgment and injunction, could set out or at least assert steps being taken toward the formulation of a plan "to effectuate a transition to a racially non-discriminatory school system." The court is then to pass on the adequacy of the plan in terms of the Federal law, and, if the plan is inadequate, require that it be changed, either in respect to the time within which desegregation is to be achieved or in other details, to satisfy that law in the light of local conditions. Defendants who refuse to comply with the court's orders may be fined or even imprisoned for contempt. Appeal may be taken by the losing party to the Federal court of appeals for his circuit, thence to the Supreme Court itself if that Court deems the case worth hearing.

If all judicial justice were swift and sure, this presumably would end the litigation, and end it fairly soon. But other procedural steps may be called for.

One is the so-called "exhaustion of administrative remedies." Parties are not supposed to come to court until they have first pursued to a regular conclusion the administrative processes that have been set up to solve their problems without litigation. This rule makes obvious good sense. A child who wants to go to a particular school ought not to ask a court to send him there without first applying to the school officials for admission and supplying to them the information and taking the tests that will enable them to act intelligently on the application. The courts can not take over the day-to-day administration of the public schools. This patent fact suggests easy obstructive tactics to those who may wish systematically to obstruct certain types of applications. The administrative routine may be made so elaborate, so slow and so complex that it will by itself indefinitely delay access to the courts, or even hide the true reasons for denial of an application so that the record will show no ground for judicial relief.

Even more difficult to overcome are the law's traditional delays.

Astute lawyers sometimes aided by technicality-minded or even sympathetic judges may by dilatory pleas, by successive motions and objections of one kind and another, be able to drag cases along indefinitely. That is not so true today as it was a generation or two ago, nor is it as true in the Federal courts as it may be in some of the state courts.

Litigation Since 1955

The Interpretative Pattern

The five original Supreme Court cases were in 1955 all remanded to the lower courts from which they arose. In the three of them from Delaware, Kansas and the District of Columbia, compliance ensued promptly and no important new judicial developments occurred. The other two have lingered in the courts. The Prince Edward County, Virginia, case has come up recurrently, most recently in early 1957 when Federal District Judge Hutcheson refused to set a definite date by which integration must commence in the county's schools, saying:

The passage of time with apparent inaction on the part of the defendants of itself does not necessarily show non-compliance . . . Many minds are now seeking an equitable solution . . . It is imperative that additional time be allowed the defendants . . . who find themselves in a position of helplessness . . .

He then reserved to the plaintiffs the right to renew their motion for relief "at a later date after the defendants have been afforded a reasonable time to effect a solution." The Clarendon County, South Carolina, case is likewise retained on the docket under an order which merely requires obedience to the Supreme Court's decision but prescribes no details. The language of the three-judge district court which issued the order illuminatingly interprets the basic decision:

It is important that we point out exactly what the Supreme Court has decided and what it has not decided in this case. It has not decided that the Federal courts are to take over or regulate the public schools of the states. It has not decided that the states must mix persons of different races in the schools or must require them to attend schools or must deprive them of the right of choosing the schools they attend. What it has decided, and all that it has decided, is that a state may not deny to any person on account of race the right to attend any school that it maintains . . . The Constitution, in other words, does not require integration. It merely forbids discrimination. It does not forbid such segregation as occurs as the result of voluntary action. It merely forbids the use of governmental power to enforce segregation.

The statement just quoted furnishes the best key that is available to understanding of lower Federal court attitudes in the South during the last two years.

Two other Virginia cases, from Charlottesville and from Arlington County, help fill in the pattern. In class actions brought by Negroes the lower Federal courts had ordered integration to begin at once in Charlottesville and within six months in Arlington County, though the orders were suspended pending appeal. The appeals were not on the merits, but on technical legal grounds only, not alleging any existing plans for compliance. On December 31, 1956, the Fourth Circuit Court of Appeals, by Chief Judge John J. Parker, affirmed both decrees, declaring that they were reasonable in the circumstances, that plaintiffs need not first exhaust administrative remedies when it was apparent that these would be futile, and that the school authorities by doing nothing were failing to achieve that "deliberate speed" which the Supreme Court ruling requires. The Supreme Court on March 25, 1957, unanimously refused to review the two cases.

Comparable litigation, varying sometimes only in details and sometimes in major aspects, appears in several of the other southern states.

Federal Courts Aid Complying Districts

The cases arising from Clinton, Tennessee, have attracted much public attention recently. A Federal Court order issued on January 4, 1956, required that Negroes be admitted to the Clinton High School commencing the following September, and the school board proceeded to comply with the order. White citizens sought a state court injunction to restrain admission of Negroes as being contrary to state law, but the Tennessee Supreme Court sustained the chancery judge in denying the injunction on the ground that the opposing state statutes had been invalidated by the "law of the land" as announced by the U. S. Supreme Court. Then private persons including John Kasper, a resident of Washington, D.C., undertook to prevent the board from carrying out the integration program. Under fire from both sides the board in desperation sought relief from the Federal court, which obliged by enjoining Kasper and his colleagues from interfering with the board's obedience to the original order, then by sentencing Kasper for contempt when he violated the injunction. Kasper was freed on bond when he appealed the contempt sentence, and has subsequently appeared in the news by reason of similar activities in other states.*

In Hoxie, Arkansas, a local school board, complying voluntarily with the desegregation law in September 1955, also sought Federal court relief against opponents who tried to prevent integrated operation of the schools. The district court first issued a preliminary injunction, then made it permanent, a decision in turn affirmed by the Eighth Circuit Court of Appeals which held that Federal courts have jurisdiction in equity to deal with attempted deprivations of Federal rights and that the constitutionally guaranteed right of free speech does not include a right to incite disobedience to the law. An interesting corollary attack, in the state courts, on Hoxie school board members for alleged financial misconduct of district affairs was partially successful, but was generally discounted as a diversionary skirmish in the main segregation battle.

Approval and Disapproval of Plans

Several of the cases involved more or less specific plans for gradual integration, submitted by local school boards. A Nashville, Tennessee, plan was approved as to items calling for integration to begin in the first grade in September 1957, with voluntary transfers to be allowed between schools dominantly attended by one race or the other. The Federal district court held that the transfer system could stand unless it was shown to be racially discriminatory in its actual operation. Also, the district was required to submit within the year a plan for desegregation of the system beyond the first grade. A Little Rock,

---

* Still later, Kasper and six Clinton residents were convicted of criminal contempt by a jury in Federal court at Knoxville, because of their activities interfering with performance of the court's integration order. Defense counsel asked for a rehearing and said the case would be carried to the higher courts, if necessary. The Knoxville trial, which lasted 16 days, was the first of its kind and its outcome was said to have had a bearing on Civil Rights legislation then before Congress.—Editor

Arkansas, plan calling for integration over a six-year period beginning in September 1957 at the high school level, then in the junior high school, then in the grammar school, was approved by the Federal district court and by the Eighth Circuit Court of Appeals. A plan submitted in Hopkins County, Kentucky, to integrate one grade at a time, beginning with the first grade, over a twelve-year period, was held not to satisfy the requirement of "all deliberate speed." On the same ground the Court of Appeals of the Sixth Circuit reversed a district court which had sustained a Memphis State College five-year plan for integrating first at the graduate level then one year at a time down through the four regular college classes. The U. S. Supreme Court in May 1957 refused to review the Circuit Court decision.

Open Resistance

Though state courts have consistently accepted the principle that the U. S. Supreme Court desegregation decisions are binding on them, and most state and lower Federal courts have at least tried to go through the motions of obedience to the "law of the land" so laid down, there have been a few instances of almost deliberate resistance.

Among these the University of Florida law school case is the most spectacular. Virgil Hawkins, a Negro, brought mandamus to compel his admission to the law school in the early '50's, and the Florida Supreme Court decided against him on racial grounds in 1952. In 1954, at once after adjudicating the public school segregation cases, the U. S. Supreme Court reversed and remanded the Florida decision for reconsideration "in the light of" those cases. The Florida Supreme Court in 1955 again denied admission, saying that (1) "all deliberate speed" did not require action so soon, and (2) mandamus is a discretionary writ that should not be issued if public disturbances would ensue from it. The U.S. Supreme Court again reversed and remanded, pointing out that under the pre-1954 cases the delays of "all deliberate speed" do not apply to admission to graduate and professional schools. On March 8, 1957, the Florida Supreme Court once more denied admission, accepting the higher court's conclusion concerning "all deliberate speed" but asserting " . . . it is unthinkable that the Supreme Court of the United States would attempt to convert into a writ of right that which has for centuries at common law been considered a discretionary writ; nor can we conceive that the Court would hold that the highest court of a sovereign state does not have the right to control the effective date of its own discretionary process." So the case is now made to turn on the technical nature of mandamus, and once more it will go up to the Supreme Court at Washington.

Federal District Judge William H. Atwell was more abrupt in throwing out a proceeding to require integration in the Dallas, Texas schools, after the Court of Appeals had ordered him to hear the case. He first criticized the Supreme Court decision (" . . . the Court based its decision on no law but rather on what the Court regarded as more authoritative, modern psychological knowledge . . . "), then added " . . . the white schools are hardly sufficient to hold the present number of white students; . . . it would be unthinkably and unbearably wrong to require the white students to get out so that the colored students could come in," and dismissed the suit "without prejudice in order that the School Board may have ample time, as it appears to be doing, to work out this problem."

The practical result has so far been little different in the case of the Mansfield school district, also from Texas, in which the Court of Appeals held the Negro applicants were entitled to a prompt start toward integration, "uninfluenced by private and public opinion as to the desirability of desegregation in the community." Federal Judge Joe Estes issued an order accordingly, but Governor Shivers sent in the Texas Rangers to "maintain law and order" and directed the school board to transfer dissident persons out of the district.

The Validity of Evasive Legislation

The prospect of judicial success with legislative devices for superficial compliance or evasive delay has so far depended on whether the new laws appear on their face to have been enacted in good faith. Thus, Federal district courts have invalidated two 1956 Louisiana acts which (1) required each applicant for admission to a state college to present a certificate of eligibility signed by his parish school superintendent but (2) provided for removal from office of any teacher "performing any act toward bringing about integration of the races" in state schools. The companion enactments were described as "a transparent device" to continue segregated schools.

The judicial approach is well illustrated by decisions on the validity of Virginia and North Carolina "pupil placement" or "assignment" laws. Nine of the southern states have enacted such laws. In general they authorize school officials to assign each individual student to the school which he is to attend, the assignment to be based on numerous relevant factors such as the health and welfare of the child and of other children, type of curriculum offered, physical closeness of residence to the school, availability of transportation, and the like. Appeal to higher adminstrative authorities is regularly allowed.

Federal District Judge Walter E. Hoffman held the Virginia Pupil Placement Act invalid, since on its face it was designed to preserve segregation. This design appeared not only from the legislative debates, but from a provision in an accompanying statute that the pupil's race was one of the factors to be considered in assigning him to a school, plus a companion provision that if white and Negro children be assigned to the same school, that school shall be "closed and removed from the public school system." The Fourth Circuit Court of Appeals subsequently upheld Judge Hoffman's determination.

The North Carolina pupil placement law, on the other hand, has been judicially sustained. It differs from the Virginia enactments in that race is not one of the factors specified as controlling the assignment of pupils, and it does not penalize desegregation. Legislative debates may have shown an expectation that the North Carolina act would aid in preserving segregation, but the act at least did not say so openly and, declared Judge John J. Parker for the Federal Court of Appeals, "It is to be presumed that [school officials] will obey the law, observe the standards prescribed by the legislature, and avoid the discrimination on account of race which the Constitution forbids." Negro pupils must first pursue the administrative procedures prescribed by the law, then, held the court, if the law is administered discriminatorily against them, they can come back and secure Federal relief. An admissions procedure that is fair on its face will stand unless discrimination under it is proved.

Another evasive device that has been suggested is that the states turn their schools over to private agencies, such as charitable corporations or even churches, for segregated operation. The theory of this would be that such privately enforced segregation would not run afoul of the Fourteenth Amendment's requirement that no "State" shall deny to any person the equal protection of the laws. This possibility is now minimized by the Girard College case, from Pennsylvania. Stephen Girard by will 125 years ago set up a trust fund to establish and maintain a school for "poor male white orphan children," with the City of Philadelphia as trustee, and the school has since been operated according to the trust. On April 29, 1957, the U. S. Supreme Court, unanimously overturning a Pennsylvania Supreme Court decision, held that this constituted "state action" and that Negroes should be admitted to the school even though the racial restriction was privately prescribed.

EXTRA-JUDICIAL INFLUENCES

Law does not exist in a social vacuum, nor do courts. Everyone knows that social policy affects judicial law-making, especially the making of constitutional law. It follows inevitably, since social policy is seldom agreed to unanimously, that some will disagree with the law when it is announced by the courts.

If the relevant social policy is backed up by a strong political majority, judicial decisions in accordance with it are readily accepted. It is only when public opinion is closely divided on matters fundamental to a society's way of life that so-called "judicial legislation" produces violent public reactions.

Only twice in America's history have there been reactions of the first magnitude against U. S. Supreme Court holdings. One was against the Dred Scott decision which in 1857 declared that Negro slaves were not citizens within the Constitution's meaning. The other is the subject of this chapter. The first produced threats of nullification from William Lloyd Garrison and his confreres in the North. The present one brings interposition resolutions from the legislatures of the South. Neither then nor now do courts ignore such voices, especially when they are strong where the court sits.

In the school cases the U. S. Supreme Court localized the implementation problem by requiring school districts to initiate plans for integration and by directing the Federal district courts to supervise the process, all in the light of local facts. The resultant judicial pattern has varied with geography. In northern and border areas "all deliberate speed" has come to mean "today" or within time limits firmly set. Further south it means "soon" or within time limits yet to be fixed. In the Deep South time limits have not been seriously discussed. Local opinion does not change the rule of law which the

Supreme Court has found in the Constitution and which lower courts must accept as the high court has stated it, but public opinion does affect the local administrative factors which the district courts have been directed to consider in applying the rule.

Matched against these local variables are the imponderables of Federal power—executive and legislative more than judicial. So far the national effort for racial integration in the public schools has been left almost solely to the judiciary, traditionally weakest of the three departments of government. President Eisenhower has made public statements generally approving the Supreme Court's decision and urging its gradual acceptance. Attorney General Herbert Brownell has been somewhat more explicit in calling for obedience to the Court's mandate, and the Department of Justice has actively aided the integrationists in the Hoxie, Arkansas, and Clinton, Tennessee, litigation. The Congress is considering enactment of "civil rights" legislation designed to afford added remedies to those seeking desegregation. Vastly greater exercises of power by the executive and legislative branches could occur, but unless they do the role of the courts is a lonely one.

There are times when the solitary district judge cannot but ask himself: "Is 'law' what the courts say it is, or is it what the people do?"

2.

The South's Own Civil War

BY WELDON JAMES

The battle for the schools—and for the mind and the future of the South—was not confined to the chartable plains of politics, courts and legislatures. The 1954-57 period saw a mushrooming of pressure groups and propaganda groups of varied hue. Their tactics varied from the frontal assault and the flank attack to the postponement of immediate conflict. Their forces skirmished in the swamplands of economic pressure and counterpressure, in trade unions, in industry, in the press, in every aspect of community life.

And in the high mountain passes of conscience there was the clash of Christian steel on Christian steel, of one man's concept of civic virtue against that of his neighbor.

In this new and unfinished civil war there were volunteers from the North, and there were outposts that saw action there. But the main battlefield, as of old, was in the South. And native to the South, this time, were the great majority of the contestants, white and Negro, not all of them in any one camp, not even by races. But the major antagonists among them, whatever their flag, warred for a conformity and unity of thought, from white man and black man alike, that would bring triumph to their cause.

Among organized segregationists, fighting for a unity in the white South unknown since The War Between the States, the chief aim was to convince white and Negro alike that desegregation could never work, that it must be postponed indefinitely or preferably forever, that segregation was best for the self-interest of both races.

Among organized and unorganized integrationists, with their de-

15

mands varying from militant insistence on quick desegregation to cautious counsel of long-range adjustment to "the inevitable," there were wry admissions that their opponents had indeed forced the "temporary silencing" of many who quietly disagreed with them.

PRESSURES FOR SEGREGATION

The three-year period following the Court's 1954 decision saw a phenomenal growth of groups organized for the primary purpose of maintaining segregation. Some 50 have been in existence at one time or another. Their claimed membership, running into the hundreds of thousands, far outstrips their opposition. And it ranges from prominent politicians and "solid" business and professional leaders in certain groups to what some segregationists themselves condemn as rabble-rousers, publicity seekers, and fastbuck boys who never had it so good before, what with selling five-dollar memberships and keeping their books to themselves.

The splintered and minuscule groups of the old Ku Klux Klan had some resurgence, too, despite anti-masking or specifically anti-Klan laws in several of the southern states, and despite Federal condemnation of four of the older groups as subversive or un-American.

This background, stemming from the Klans' ancient history of violence and terroristic tactics, dimmed its appeal to the segregationist majority in organizations pledged to non-violence. New Klan organizers fought this with an apparent attempt to gain "respectability" as just another organization, foreswearing violence and, in at least one city, joining with "other civic organizations" to sponsor a softball team (the city league blew up, though, after a broadside from *The Chattanooga Times* in May 1957 at the great national corporations whose Chattanooga branches were "playing ball" with the Klan).

In April 1957 the state of South Carolina refused to grant a charter to the "South Carolina Knights of the Ku Klux Klan, Inc." No state in the Deep South is more officially and unofficially resistant to integration, but such organizations as the KKK, Attorney General T. C. Callison held, "are in ill repute throughout the country."

In the same month northern newspapers and national magazines reported how a variety of new Klan groups were bringing "new terror to the South." But in a book review in *The New York Times* of April 21, George Barrett, discussing some aspects of Carl T. Rowan's *Go*

South to Sorrow (Random House, 1957) had this to say:

For this reviewer, who has covered some of the battles, Mr. Rowan speaks too awesomely of the power of the race-monger. He cries out against the Ku Klux Klan—but, indeed, so do all but an absurdly small number of white southern-ers. He cries out against the 'forces of darkness'—but, indeed, few in the Deep South do not; rather, the occasional break-out of racist fury shocks so many southerners by its stupidity that each time it happens the segregationist cause loses many of its supporters. He lists 25 white supremacy organizations of ominous coloring that have sprung up suddenly—but at least half of them (a fact Mr. Rowan does not point out) are pip-squeak outfits or, in some cases, have had their members literally run out of Southern towns.

White Citizens Councils

Among the many post-decision groups organized for the primary purposes of opposing the Supreme Court's ruling and to preserve the racial status quo in the South are the white Citizens Councils, not all under the same leadership, but the largest in the region; the States' Rights Councils in Florida and Georgia; the Patriots of North Carolina, Inc.; the Defenders of State Sovereignty and Individual Liberties, in Virginia; the National Association for the Advancement of White People in Delaware; the Tennessee Federation for Constitutional Government, the Pro-Southerners, and the Tennessee Society to Maintain Segregation, in Tennessee; Southern Gentlemen, Inc., chiefly in Louisiana; and a wide variety of smaller organizations such as the Virginia Citizens Committee for Better Schools, the Grass Roots League, American Education, Inc., North Carolina Association for the Preservation of the White Race, Inc., We, the People, Knights of the White Christians, and the Pond Hollow Segregation Club.

The first of the white Citizens Councils was organized in Indianola, Mississippi, on July 11, 1954, by 14 men who "met and counseled together on the terrible crisis precipitated by the U. S. Supreme Court in its Black Monday decision of May 17, 1954." Its offshoots spread rapidly to Virginia, South Carolina, Georgia, Florida, Alabama, Louisiana, Texas, Tennessee, Arkansas, and, in fragmentary fashion, to several of the border states.

By mid-1957 the increasing membership claims of the various state associations of Citizens Councils (embracing a wide variety of individual units) indicated that, as several other organizations diminished in size, the Councils were emerging as the preponderant chain for the segregationists of the region. Mississippi claimed 80,000 members, Alabama 100,000, South Carolina 40,000, Texas 20,000. And their numbers were increasing in Louisiana, despite competition with the "Southern Gentlemen," and in some other states, though in North Carolina, Georgia and Virginia native-grown groups were still tops with claims of 15,000 to 20,000 members.

An effort to coordinate the activities of all segregationist organizations was called for early in 1955 by U. S. Senator James O. Eastland of Mississippi, and led to quick interstate organization of the Federation for Constitutional Government, headed by John U. Barr, a New Orleans industrialist.

The new group invited "all patriotic organizations" throughout the nation "to cooperate in a united movement for the preservation of America under a constitutional form of government." Whatever the degree of coordination achieved, the organization from the beginning has had on its executive and advisory committees a large number of the officials of other segregationist groups, as well as many participants in the 1948 States' Rights movement.

On these committees also are 49 members holding either state or national public offices (including U. S. Senators Strom Thurmond of South Carolina, Herman Talmadge of Georgia, and Eastland of Mississippi, and Georgia's Governor Marvin Griffin). They range from circuit judges and state legislative leaders to several U. S. congressmen. And among the total membership are several retired army officers, two doctors and one professor.

The non-violent aims and methods of the great majority of the segregationist organizations are best described by a brochure, "The Citizens Council," published by the Mississippi Association of Citizens Councils. The brochure calls the Citizens Council "the modern version of the old-time town meeting," which "simply provides the machinery for mobilizing, concerting and expressing public opinion."

To do this job each Citizens Council, the brochure explains, has four basic committees: Information and Education, "to convince all of our people of the advantages of segregation and the dangers of integration"; Political and Elections, which "studies candidates for local and state elections and presents their qualifications to the voters"; Membership and Finance, which "enlists all patriotic white citizens for membership"; and Legal Advisory, which "provides the legal knowledge that will aid us to achieve our aims by constitutional, lawful means" and "anticipates moves by agitators and devises legal means for solving any racial problems that might arise locally."

Such group activities are also, as the chapter on "Segregation and Politics" indicates, a springboard into politics for some of the Citizens Council leaders, and they are credited with forcing some erstwhile "moderate" politicians more firmly into the segregationist mold. But since virtually all the Deep South's elected officials are segregationists anyway, the Citizens Councils and similar groups—though they broadcast their literature to all the 48 states—are chiefly significant as the community-action arm of all segregationists, in and out of office. Tactics and leaders differ from community to community. And their numbers are small compared to the total population of the South. But in many a community they have demonstrated considerable power to achieve at least the appearance of unity or conformity by methods that include not merely the "educational" equation of school desegregation with the inevitability of racial inter-marriage and "mongrelization", but also by economic boycott and harassment of whites or Negroes who "get out of line," and sometimes by applying the formidable weapon of social ostracism to the former.

PRESSURES FOR INTEGRATION

Arrayed solidly against the organized segregationists, and one of their favorite targets, is the National Association for the Advancement of Colored People, the interracial organization behind nearly every one of the 100-odd school integration suits filed since 1954, the legal victor in most of the decisions, and, before 1955, the motive force behind 36 of 39 Supreme Court decisions affecting long-established racial customs—including, of course, the school desegregation ruling.

When the first white Citizens Council was formed in 1954, a spokesman identified four forces that must be fought if segregation were to be preserved. The list included politicians and political parties "who cater to a concentrated Negro minority vote," "the considerable leadership in the Protestant and Catholic churches," and "large segments of the press and many so-called liberals who insist that integration of our democratic society is the next logical step toward our achievement of democracy in America." But Target Number One was listed as the NAACP—and in the three years since, outside the Federal courts, its road in the South has been a rocky one.

By organized and unorganized segregationists it has been denounced as "Communist," "a bunch of outside agitators" sustained by "powerful forces" ranging from the misled northern press and communications industries to "Jewish bankers."

Georgia's Attorney General Eugene Cook summed up such attacks in a speech entitled "The Ugly Truth About the NAACP" before the 55th annual convention of the Peace Officers Association of Georgia— a speech subsequently reprinted and distributed by the thousands by the white Citizens Councils. On the basis of innumerable "citations" of un-American activities from a variety of sources against individuals connected with it, he concluded that the NAACP, "either knowingly or unwittingly, has allowed itself to become part and parcel of the Communist conspiracy to overthrow the democratic governments of this nation and its sovereign states."

Milder charges from other quarters were that the NAACP since 1954 had been "too aggressive," "needlessly insulting" and "possessed of a self-defeating passion for speed." And in late 1956 Superintendent Omer Carmichael of the desegregated Louisville school system, while voicing no complaints about NAACP branches in Kentucky, held the national organization responsible for much of "the chaos and confusion" farther South. (In a rejoinder, NAACP headquarters in New York disclaimed such credit in favor of groups and politicians "defying" the Supreme Court ruling.)

Weapons of War

Economic reprisals and counter-reprisals, charges of fraud or intimidation, and economic aid to the "casualties" distinguished the community in-fighting between supporters and opponents of the NAACP. (See the chapter, "The Deep South.")

Decrying legislative and other assaults against the NAACP as "restricting freedom of speech, assembly, petition, redress of grievances in the courts, and even freedom of thought," Roy Wilkins, the Association's executive secretary, said they showed that "the attempt to enforce racial inequality has entered dangerously into the area of civil liberties, in violation of the Bill of Rights"—and that "this invasion of individual liberties has extended [to] Southern white citizens."

In March 1957 at a Washington hearing, U. S. Senator Sam J. Ervin, Jr., of North Carolina said, " . . . I was glad to state that I had never heard of the NAACP being charged with being listed as a subversive organization, and that I for one would stand and fight to the last ditch to see the NAACP or any other organization have the right of freedom of speech, even though I might disagree with many of their views and with many of their activities . . ." An NAACP press release subsequently titled the Ervin statement, "Quotation of the Week."

Self-Portrait

From published statements of its top officials and from its own publications, here is the NAACP's portrait of itself:

Race riots in Springfield, Illinois, in 1908 sparked its formation in 1909 as an interracial organization "pledged to a nation-wide work for justice to the Negro race." Among its white founders were lineal as well as spiritual descendants of the old Abolitionists. Its top leadership, then and since, has included eminent leaders of both races. Its policies are not "charted by a handful of northerners, mostly New Yorkers, who have taken it upon themselves to dictate to the rest of the nation concerning rights of Negroes," but by an annual convention representing all its 350,000 members in 43 states, the District of Columbia, and Alaska—60 per cent of them in the southern and border states.

The organization maintains that it does not have a war-chest of millions of dollars, "contributed to it by trade unions, foundations and wealthy white radicals," but instead operates on a modest annual budget of about $600,000, 85 per cent of which comes from members who pay fees of $2 to $10, and more from special fund-raising projects staged by local branches.

In the view of the NAACP, it is a "vicious lie," one "widely circulated by Attorney General Eugene Cook of Georgia and by the white Citizens Councils," to say that the policies, program and goals of the NAACP are inspired by Communists and their fellow travelers and that the organization is dominated by left-wing elements. The truth is that the NAACP is strictly an American organization with the basic American goals of freedom, equality and justice for all. Were its anti-Communist record not clearly established, it would not have won the acclaim of such distinguished Americans as J. Edgar Hoover, Robert

F. Wagner, Dr. Ralph J. Bunche, Mrs. Eleanor Roosevelt, Francis Cardinal Spellman and others, nor would Presidents Harry S. Truman and Dwight D. Eisenhower and Vice President Richard M. Nixon have addressed its meetings.

With a look at recent events and with a promise for the future, Thurgood Marshall, the NAACP's veteran special counsel, had this to say:

"As we enter the year of 1957, we do so with full realization that everything possible, lawful and unlawful, has been done to stop progress toward desegregation. Our record insofar as legal work is concerned will show that we have not only not been stopped, we have not even been slowed down . . .

"Despite open opposition, sophisticated laws of harassment and unheard of legal gimmicks, we shall continue the steady drive toward desegregation in the South. We will not be prodded to move more rapidly than wisdom requires us to do. On the other hand, we shall not be slowed down one iota from the steady program which has been adopted by our membership in the 17 southern states."

Of its continuing battle with its chief antagonist, the white Citizens Councils, Marshall has said: "We have lost ground in the area of public opinion." The Councils, he told a Nashville audience, though their actions constituted "no more and no less than open rebellion," have succeeded in convincing a large group of the public that there are only two "extreme" sides—that of the Councils on one end and that of the NAACP on the other—whereas "the true white southerner" need not go along with either, but "can go along with the Supreme Court as he sees it."

INTERRACIAL GROUPS

Lesser targets for the ire of organized segregationists, as Attorney General Cook of Georgia had intimated, were several interracial organizations. Some of those worked openly but not exclusively for integration of the schools, some only for improvement of the Negro's economic and social lot, some simply for "better human relations."

Chief among them was the Southern Regional Council and its state affiliates, varying in name from interracial committees to human relations councils, and including among their members throughout the South, as Mr. Cook had noted was the case in Georgia, "distinguished clergymen and prominent civic and social leaders."

The SRC, itself the successor to older organizations, was organized in 1943 with the declared purpose "to attain through research and action the ideals and practices of equal opportunity for all peoples in the region." Among its stated functions: to serve as a meeting ground for citizens of all races and religious persuasions; to present the facts about the South, "and their implications"; to counteract appeals to prejudice and violence; "to stimulate local initiative to work for local solutions in full democracy, so that legislation and judicial rulings may be translated into justice for the individual in his everyday life."

Aside from a spate of segregationist charges that such organizations were either "dupes" or controlled by "more sinister elements," their members could read in a full-page red-and-black ad of the Citizens Councils (in the *Montgomery Advertiser* of May 12, 1957) that: "There are only two sides in the Southern fight—those who want to maintain the Southern way of life or those who want to mix the races . . . Whites must stand by whites just as negroes are standing by negroes . . . There is no middle ground for moderation . . . that middle ground has been washed away by the actions of the NAACP in seeking to destroy the freedoms of the Southern white man."

The ad proclaimed, above the signature of State Senator Sam Engelhardt, Jr., executive secretary of the Citizens Councils of Alabama, that "there is no hate or animosity in this organization—only the positive approach that if we are to have segregation we must take steps to preserve it."

Two months earlier someone practiced dissuasion of a different kind in Mississippi, firing a bullet into the home of a woman member of the Mississippi Council on Human Relations. Mrs. D. S. Wheatley, Sr., wife of a cotton buyer in Greenwood, linked the bullet with her membership in the council. The organization, she said, "is entirely a Mississippi group and has no Communist connections whatever," its purpose being "to work for better human relations."

IN THE CHURCHES

In the South itself the 1954-57 period demonstrated that perhaps the greatest threat to the unity sought by organized segregationists came from the churches, themselves entangled in all but continuous debate. Top-level pronouncements of virtually every denomination, in varying language, endorsed the Supreme Court's desegregation decision as consonant with Christian doctrine, and bespoke orderly compliance with the law.

One exception was the United Lutheran Church, which at its biennial convention late in 1956, at the wish of southern ministers hoping to "save some scars," deleted a statement that the Court's decision was "in harmony with Christian convictions." The statement actually adopted at the convention in Pennsylvania asked church members to work with "Christian patience and understanding" for the removal of prejudice and discrimination in human relations, and declared that, in the church's "deep involvement in the moral crisis," Christians "have moral responsibilities to keep open the channels of communication and understanding among the different groups in this controversy."

And there were other churchly statements that fell short of outright endorsement. But representative of the expressions of the larger southern Protestant denominations (Baptist, Methodist, Presbyterian, Episcopalian) was the position taken by the Southern Baptist Convention at St. Louis in 1954: "We recognize that this Supreme Court decision is in harmony with the constitutional guarantees of equal freedom to all citizens and with the Christian principles of equal justice and love for all men . . . We urge our people and all Christians to conduct themselves in this period of adjustment in the spirit of Christ."

Most publicized of all, perhaps, was the 1957 pronouncement of the 97th General Asssembly of the Presbyterian Church in the U. S. (Southern) at Birmingham. Backing up and strengthening earlier statements, it indicted all forms of racial segregation. The 4,000-word statement, approved with a scattering of negative votes, strongly defended the controversial interracial Koinonia community in Georgia, warned church-goers against joining Klans and Councils, and condemned discrimination in education, employment, religion and politics.

Local Dissent

In Protestant denominations top-level resolutions of representative bodies are not always binding on individual congregations or ministers. And the three-year period saw enough localized dissent throughout the South to revive the ancient jest that "the assembly or the convention proposes—but the congregation back home disposes."

Individual pastors sharing the conscientious segregation beliefs of their flocks denounced the integrationist resolutions. Some who didn't were moved to move on to other pulpits. Some state groups refused to add their endorsement. The Georgia Baptist Convention in 1956, for instance, turned down by a 3 to 1 vote its social service commission's endorsement of the Court decision and the suggestion that "our churches seek to create an atmosphere that would make it possible for those who administer our public schools to comply with the instructions of the courts." The Convention instead approved appeals to "exercise Christian grace and patience with one another" and to "faithfully teach and proclaim the basic principles."

Early in 1955 Methodist students from 15 Alabama colleges commended the Supreme Court's desegregation decision and unanimously held that they "should accept the implications set forth by this decision with the poise, calmness and courage of Christian students." Three months later 300 pro-segregation Methodists from four southern states, meeting in Birmingham, heard Dr. Stanley Frazer, pastor of Montgomery's St. James Methodist Church, speak against "a sort of brainwashing" of Methodist youth groups by integration supporters and "radical" church newspapers. The group adopted a resolution denouncing the policy of church newspapers and urging that church publications "open their columns to both sides of the discussion of racial customs and practices."

A Methodist educator, Montgomery School Superintendent Clarence M. Dannelly, in 1956 said "a climate of circumstances" had made it "seem necessary" for him to resign the second highest position open to a layman in the Methodist Church, vice president of the church's judicial council. In the same election at the General Conference in Minneapolis a Negro official in Washington, Assistant Secretary of Labor J. Ernest Wilkins, had been named president.

In March 1956 the Woman's Auxiliary of St. Andrew's Protestant Episcopal Church, Mount Pleasant, South Carolina, adopted a resolution "opposing integration as advocated in the booklet, 'Just, Right and Necessary'"—a booklet prepared by the National Council of the Episcopal Church. The following month the Protestant Episcopal Diocese of South Carolina, at its 166th annual convention, declared by a 94 to 43 vote that "there is nothing morally wrong in a voluntary recognition of racial differences and that voluntary alignments can be both natural and Christian."

Subsequently the Protestant Episcopal Church's magazine, *The Living Church,* commented that the resolution "gives expression to the agony and tension of soul that faces men of good will in many parts of the South today," but said it had been "put through under a gag rule" and should have been defeated: "for it is one thing to be gentle and understanding about sin; it is another thing to pass resolutions commending sin on a 'voluntary' basis."

In the spring of 1957 the Reverend Doctor Frederick H. Olert, president of the Virginia Council of Churches (highly critical of the state's segregationist politicians) and pastor of Richmond's Second Presbyterian Church, acknowledged that dissension over racial views had prompted his surprise resignation. "I could stay here and weather the storm," he said, "but I wish to do nothing to hurt this church." His new pastorate was in Kansas City, Missouri.

Despite all dissent at the more local levels, however, the top-level declarations of the major Protestant churches in one of the great "Bible Belts" of the nation kept the issue debatably alive. The pronouncements may have led to no overnight integration in the Methodist Church, as called for in 1956—and echoed by a Kentucky interracial Methodist workshop that fall, the first of more projected for areas farther South. But they ended the hope of the organized segregationists that only the segregationist conscience would be mirrored in the unity sought for the white South. And they led to more Bible reading and searching than at any time in the South's history, one minister estimated, as troubled persons in both camps sought scriptural justification for their attitudes on race.

Catholics in the South

Though small in numbers in the South outside the New Orleans and Louisville areas, and in Texas, the Catholic Church, with its long-established policy of integrating wherever the law permitted, lent powerful support to those made integrationist by "Christian conscience"—and issued the stern warning to Catholics that segregation was "morally wrong and sinful," and that though the Church had tolerated it simply to avoid greater evils, such toleration could not be permanent.

That warning came from Archbishop Rummel of New Orleans, whose announced plans to start general integration of the archdiocese's 75,000 parochial school pupils set no date, despite some press reports that he had "backed down" by not specifying the start in September 1956. Catholic spokesmen denied any back-down and pointed to a pastoral letter of August 5 in which the archbishop announced that he would postpone integration in his schools "until at least September of 1957." The Commission on Human Rights of the Catholic Committee of the South branded "organized racism as anti-American, anti-Catholic, anti-Southern and irreligious," which drew blasts from Citizens Council spokesmen who said there were Catholics—and Jews as well—among their members. Another point of view led to organization of the Association of Catholic Laymen, headed by Emile Wagner, an attorney and Orleans Parish (county) school board member. The group, formed in opposition to parochial school desegregation, was quashed in May of 1956 by the Archbishop's order.

Critical of Government

Early in 1957 the interracial Richmond Ministerial Association adopted a "Statement of Conviction" criticizing Governor Stanley and the General Assembly for their "exceedingly inept handling of the current racial situation" and opposing enactment of registration laws for those trying to influence legislation on racial matters. The president, Dr. Joseph S. Johnston, said that each minister spoke for himself, not for his church or his congregation, and that about 150 ministers usually attend the association's meetings. The *Richmond Times-Dispatch* then polled more than 350 Richmond area ministers, reported 104 favored the statement, 39 opposed it, 150 declined to comment, and 50 others gave qualified or restricted answers.

And a Virginia legislator warned that the ministers "may criticize all they want, but if they are urging legislation to foster integration or segregation they would be getting themselves into trouble" (under new laws regulating organizations involved in racial activities).

Earlier the Virginia Council of Churches had pledged support of ministers who might be penalized for pulpit discussion of issues stemming from the Court's decision. And the Norfolk Ministers' Association, by a 53 to 8 vote, had condemned the Gray Plan to avoid segregated schools—as had the press of the Baptist, Methodist and Presbyterian churches in the state.

In April 1957 300 southern church leaders—out of 4,500 invited—attended an interracial three-day Conference on Christian Faith and Human Relations in Nashville. President Eisenhower had been invited to address the conference, but was represented only by a telegram. His non-appearance and the "neutral" tone of his telegram were said to be the reasons for a return telegram asking him to come South and "add a personal word of encouragement" to churchmen working "to establish a more democratic order" in their communities.

A North Carolina preacher commented wryly on the 300 delegates who came and the 4,200 who didn't: "I always felt there were many others in the South that felt as I did, but I was never sure. Now I know that there are at least 299 others."

LABOR AND INDUSTRY

Some difficult-to-measure pressure-factors, cutting both ways, affected southern labor and industry in the 1954-57 period.

Relatively weak compared to union strength elsewhere in the nation, the South's labor unions generally reflected the region's majority opposition to integration of any sort. This collided, of course, with the strong integrationist stand taken by the merged American Federation of Labor-Congress of Industrial Organizations, and led to largely ineffective attempts to replace the AFL-CIO unions with independent segregated organizations.

Commenting on this in the October 4, 1956, issue of *The Reporter*, Henry Trewhitt observed:

Whether or not an independent movement ever gains a secure foothold, organized labor already has suffered serious losses. There is no way of knowing how many potential members have been frightened away or not reached. Certainly there have been many.

And there has been a weakening to some extent of every local in which the issue has arisen. Added to the suspicion always displayed toward union labor in the South and to the unsettled differences between AFL and CIO unions, the controversy has proved a debilitating factor.

In 1957 national spokesmen (quoted by the Associated Press) did not quibble with such conclusions. In non-South states they rated their proportion of organized workers at 40 to 60 per cent of the total force. In the South (excluding United Mine Workers and railway unions) they gave these estimates:

North and South Carolina, each 9 per cent; Mississippi 15; Georgia 16; Texas and Virginia, each 17; Florida 18; Louisiana 20; Arkansas 21; Tennessee 22; and Kentucky and Alabama, each 24 per cent.

Spokesmen admitted, too, that "support of most unions for racial equality among workers is unpopular among many of the workers the unions are trying to organize."

Among labor's own skirmishes on the racial front during this period was that involving segregated teachers' unions. Eight locals in Georgia, Louisiana and Tennessee—four all-white, four all-Negro—were ordered by the American Federation of Teachers in 1956 to drop their race barriers by December 31, 1957, or get out of the union. A spokesman for an Atlanta local retorted: "We want to keep our union segregated, at least as long as the community is segregated . . . If the AFT ousts us, we can stand on our own." A Chattanooga local has taken a similar position.

In May 1957 Emanuel Muravchik, chairman of the anti-discrimination department of the Jewish Labor Committee, reported to his organization that "an overwhelming majority" of white union members in the South oppose school integration and show "considerable support" for the white Citizens Councils—but that they remain "consistently loyal to the AFL-CIO and will not disaffiliate."

This, he said, was "in sharp contrast to the position taken by the northern labor leadership, who regard white Citizens Councils as anti-labor organizations."

Whatever their status as anti-labor organizations, Citizens Councils in a number of communities had backed municipal ordinances charging as high as $2,000 for local licenses to solicit members in dues-paying organizations. In mid-1957, organized labor was already moving to challenge such ordinances in the courts.

Question for Industry

The generally recognized anti-mixing sentiments of southern unionists, coupled with headline stories of racial trouble in the last three years, posed a large question for southern industry: Are "foreign" industries now refusing to move South but moving instead, if they move at all, into areas less afflicted with racial tensions?

There have been published reports of a few such instances—met in some cases by published denials. In statistical fact, the boom in 1954-57 netted several of the Deep South states bigger industrial gains than some of the "quieter" border states—but since moving plans are not made overnight, it might be premature to predict that this pattern would continue.

The promise of "stability," some segregationists insist, is as likely to be maintained in the Deep South as anywhere else, no matter what "exaggerated talk" of racial tensions may be spread by businessmen in other sections. But where racial trouble has actually occurred, the experience of Birmingham suggested to observers that some temporary "bypassing," at least, may be expected.

The *Birmingham Post-Herald* in 1957 quoted two leading executives as saying that "expanding industry is bypassing Birmingham and other sections of Alabama in location of branch plants, sales offices and warehouses."

William P. Engel, former chairman of the Birmingham Chamber of Commerce Committee of 100, told the *Post-Herald:*

"We must face up to our own deficiencies. The hoodlumism here has hit headlines throughout the nation. As a result, we have lost one major plant in Birmingham and several smaller installations. Place yourself in the shoes of a man who wants to bring a plant to Birmingham. Would you, under the circumstances, do it? If we object to interference from outside interests we should object to interference from within."

And Cooper Green, vice president in charge of industrial development for the Alabama Power Company, told the newspaper that he had personal knowledge of "two major and two minor installations" that have shelved "temporarily" plans to move into Alabama.

"The [racial] publicity has hurt Birmingham and Montgomery," he said. "Prospects on whom we call in an effort to get them to locate in the state have asked us about the trouble we are having here. No industry wants to move into a troubled area. I am not alarmed at the moment. I think we will continue to grow when the situation calms down and many prospects have indicated interest when the trouble subsides."

In editorial comment the *Post-Herald* observed:

Now, Birmingham can see the price which must be paid for the racial out-breaks and the resulting hoodlumism . . . We must live with our racial prob-lems for years to come. But violence will only make them greater and will injure the whole community.

In Charlotte, North Carolina, syndicated Columnist Sylvia Porter thought she had discovered a similar loss-of-industry fear. But North Carolina spokesmen pooh-poohed the idea, satisfied that the Tar Heel state (thanks perhaps in part to Governor Hodges' moderation policy, one businessman thought) "continues to be one of the most rapidly growing states in the Southeast."

And South Carolina for 1956 reported a net gain of $142 million in new industries, while Georgia in the same year broke its old 1955 record for welcoming business firms—more than 2,000—and for the fourth consecutive year led the Southeast in the new or expanded in-dustries field: 179 plants, with a total new investment of $121 million, excluding a host of smaller plants having less than $50,000 capital investments.

COVERING DIXIE

In May 1955 when the Supreme Court handed down its decision on how the ruling of a year earlier was to be carried out, the Greenville (Miss.) *Delta Democrat-Times* said editorially: "There is no solid South in the wake of this decision."

Three years have passed since the original decision. A close read-ing of the newspapers of the region will show that in the first year, at least, there was a tendency to "play down" the story, either for fear of offending readers, or for lack of interest in the issue—or for both reasons. Today the volume of press coverage is great—and growing. The newspaper reference library of the Southern Education Report-ing Service now contains some 50,000 clippings on school segregation-desegregation and allied matters, with the greatest volume catalogued for the years 1955 and 1956.

(Bem Price, southern-born feature writer for the Associated Press, who has the "segregation beat" for that news service, says that south-ern client newspapers more often use his stories than do northern ones. A survey of the AP "log" [showing story usage], which samples 60 newspapers with about one-third of them in the South, indicated that 44 per cent used a general segregation story in 1954, 25 per cent used another of similar nature in August 1955, 35 per cent used one on the white Citizens Council movement written from Jackson, Mississippi, 35 per cent used one on Louisville school desegregation in November 1956 and 38 per cent carried another on "what the South thinks" in December 1956. Since these are "competitive" papers, it may be assumed that they also used features of this kind from other news services and syndicates.)

Today, also, there is no unanimity of opinion in the editorial columns of newspapers of the southern and border states. Yet a study of the press in the "solid South" itself indicates that, of the some 30 newspapers of largest circulation, less than a dozen might be described as "not hostile" to integration. These papers are in Arkansas, Georgia, North Carolina and Tennessee.

Exceptions to any rule of journalistic interpretation must be made, of course, if we consider the whole blanket of daily and weekly newspapers covering Dixie. In nearly every instance, Negro newspapers of the region (in which there is only one Negro daily) favor compliance with all dispatch. Some white weeklies and smaller dailies, usually in the upper South, have counseled desegregation. Buford Boone, publisher of the *Tuscaloosa News*, won a Pulitzer Prize in 1957 for editorials which decried violence in the Autherine Lucy incident. Editor P. D. East of the *Petal* (Miss.) *Paper,* a weekly, attracted attention for his satirical treatment of segregationist groups (which he admitted had cost him both readers and advertising).

Negro weeklies are located in most large southern cities and in some of medium size. Their voice is all but unanimous, an exception being that of Percy Greene's *Jackson* (Miss.) *Advocate,* which called in 1957 for more "Uncle Toms" to keep Negroes from being "led over a precipice." A critic of white legislatures and pro-segregation groups, the *Atlanta Daily World,* remarked of the Negro press: "In spite of its handicaps, its trials, its mistakes and those hidden enemies who would do hurt, harm and danger, the Negro press marches on. It is the sure arm of Democracy . . ." In defending the NAACP against criticism by a white editor, Publisher P. B. Young, Sr., of the widely-circulated *Norfolk Journal and Guide,* said: "The Negro press has believed from its beginning in 1827 that its mission was to create public opinion where none existed, favorable to freedom and democracy . . . it is proud of the part it has played in supporting every legal effort the NAACP has made in the direction of removing barriers to Negro advancement."

Generally speaking, the individual white dailies have been consistent in their editorial opinion—for the most part segregationist—since 1954. Those voicing opposition to the Court ruling at the outset are just as much against it today. The papers calling for gradualism still caution "go-slow," though in a few instances there is a tendency for this gradualism to veer toward "don't-go."

Quote, Unquote

In the border states a number of influential newspapers in cities such as Louisville, St. Louis, Baltimore, Charleston, West Virginia, Wilmington, Delaware and Washington asked for prompt compliance at the beginning, and today continue to urge that steps be taken to comply with the spirit of the Court's opinion. Typical, perhaps, of the comment of the border state papers was that of the *St. Louis Post-Dispatch* when it said:

In the friendliest possible way . . . we would advise southern leaders that the time has come to stop explaining why they do not like the Supreme Court decision, and to start building public acceptance in the South for carrying out that decision. And we know of no better way to build public acceptance than to do what many communities have done—to begin integration.

Once away from the border states no single large newspaper has emerged as enthusiastically integrationist. Where newspapers divide at all, they divide into two camps: one large, one relatively small; one for rigid segregation, the other for gradual or eventual desegregation. Somewhere in between but closer to the latter position, perhaps, are newspapers critical of state pro-segregation policies as voiced by legislatures or governors. When, for example, the Pearsall Plan was broached in North Carolina, four of the largest dailies, including the *Charlotte Observer*, the *Raleigh News and Observer*, the *Charlotte News* and the *Winston-Salem Journal*, opposed it. The nearly unanimous voice of the Virginia press, led in part by the *Richmond Times-Dispatch* and the *Richmond News Leader*, for state pro-segregation policies and plans in 1955 and 1956 was broken only by the questioning of the *Norfolk Virginian-Pilot*.

Perhaps no newspaper has been as vocal in adamant opposition to the Court and all its works as the *Jackson* (Miss.) *Daily News*. The Jackson daily said in 1955:

The Supreme Court tells the Federal tribunals in the various states to require school boards to make a prompt and reasonable start toward full compliance. It won't happen in Mississippi.

We are slow starters, and this is one time we won't start at all.

Any attempt toward a start in this state is going to be met with stern resistance right at the beginning.

In the traditional South the most outspoken voice insisting that the Court's decision is the law of the land and must be obeyed has been the *Nashville Tennessean*, which has repeatedly called for ending of racial discrimination on a gradual basis, but one that will conform with the Court's decision. It said in early 1957:

The fact is that the decision of the Supreme Court, as the highest court of our own state has twice pointed out, has made a dead letter of compulsory segregation in Tennessee. The sooner that fact is accepted, the better it will be for all concerned. For the Supreme Court's decision is not going to be reversed by "manifesto" or circumvented by legislation, no matter how cleverly contrived.

Again without notable exception, the southern press has spoken out against violence of the Klan-fostered type. A considerable body of it has been critical of the NAACP; a lesser part, of the white Citizens Councils. And the press campaigns within the war itself have not been without their scars. In Florence, South Carolina, Editor Jack O'Dowd found his editorials so unappreciated by his readers that he moved North. Hodding Carter of the *Delta Democrat-Times*, who first editorially tagged the Citizens Councils as "uptown Klans," found his "gradualism" cost circulation and advertising income, too. By the spring of 1957 he was convinced, he told members of a Unitarian Church conference in Nashville, that the Court desegregation rulings were changing the easy-going southern climate for tolerance into a demand for conformity of thought—a demand coming from both races.

"Because of this," he said, "the First Amendment to our Constitution is probably in more danger in the South today than are either our white or Negro children."

It was quite a civil war among its own people the South staged in 1954-57. The inner conflict for some, as Robert Penn Warren called it, torn between custom and conscience and the need to reconcile the two, manifestly was as strenuous as the battle in the open.

Nobody thought it would end soon. And some thought it might be another Thirty Years' War.

3.

Communities in Strife

BY WALLACE WESTFELDT

The night was hot, but the 2,000 men and women on the south side of the square didn't seem to mind being jammed together. They were there for a meeting and they had no intention of leaving before it started.

The women, some with babies in arms, wore sleeveless dresses. The men wore work or sports clothes. Their voices melded into a steady hum, punctuated now and then by the sharp cry "Hey! Nigger! Get him!" as boisterous teenagers, encouraged by adults, tossed firecrackers at automobiles driving on Main Street and attempted to tip over cars driven by Negroes.

The town's police, augmented by specially deputized residents of the county, had arrested six men on charges of breach of the peace since seven o'clock.

The hour of eight neared—meeting time. Suddenly, the police disappeared from the sidewalks they had been patrolling and regrouped in front of the white painted court house. Their commander for the night, a lawyer by trade, wore a blue suit, white shirt and blue tie with white polka dots. He carried a submachine gun.

The crowd, now concentrated at the southeast corner of the square, spilled over into the court yard. The police moved toward them in a skirmish line. Abruptly, police and crowd met at a monument to the community's World War II dead inscribed with the admonition "Lest We Forget."

The crowd was told to step back. It refused.

"Pfft! Sissss!"

A cloud of acrid, grey-white smoke spewed out of a can dropped at the feet of the crowd. A news photographer, standing on top of the monument, disappeared momentarily, enveloped in the smoke. "Gas!" a voice screamed, and the crowd broke. Men close to the point of impact ran blindly, shouting angrily, tears streaming down their faces. Within minutes, five more tear gas grenades were exploded by police to keep the crowd from reorganizing.

A high-pitched wail suddenly cut through the roar of the crowd. Sirens. Thirty-nine state highway patrol cars whipped into the square. A burly, six-foot-seven, 290-pound patrol commander stepped from the lead car. Peace was restored to the town after five days of tension and turbulence. The next day 650 National Guardsmen rolled into town behind tanks to keep the peace.

This was Clinton, the east Tennessee mill town of 4,000 where 12 Negro children were attending class with 800 white children in Anderson County's Clinton High School.

This was an illustration of how one community was resisting desegregation at school-opening time in September 1956, the first real time of decision in some areas. But many communities of like size and makeup—that is, rural and rural-urban with relatively small Negro student populations—adjusted from segregated to desegregated school systems without incident.

Although less than 50 per cent of southerners now live on farms, the region is still largely rural and rural-urban. And it is a land of paradoxes. Communities almost next door to one another have reacted to the school segregation-desegregation issue as though they might be a continent apart. Some of these implications are discussed in the chapter "The Deep South." For the main, we are concerned here with the incidents that leaped into bold headlines the country over when the issue first was joined.

Nothing New

Resistance to desegregation was not new. Back in the fall of 1954, just four months after the U. S. Supreme Court delivered its ruling in the school segregation cases, demonstrations of students and adults broke out in Washington, D.C., in Baltimore, at Milford, Delaware, and in White Sulphur Springs, West Virginia. The disturbances in Washington and Baltimore were brief and did not affect desegregation. In White Sulphur Springs, resistance delayed desegregation for a year.

The resistance of 1956 as contrasted with that of 1954, however, seemed to have in it a different temper. For one thing, there was more organization. And there were other differences. In 1956, desegregation was moving into communities deeply southern in tradition if not in location. Further, as a young lawyer in Clinton said, "What the hell do you expect these people to do when they have 90 some odd congressmen from the South signing a piece of paper [the Southern Manifesto] that says you're a southern hero if you defy the Supreme Court?"

Resistance to the court-ordered school change materialized elsewhere. In Mansfield, a northeast Texas town, effigies of Negroes were hung about the community and crowds gathered at the school to protest the expected registration of three Negro children along with 250 white children at the Mansfield High School. National Guard troops were ordered into Sturgis and Clay, two west Kentucky farming and mining towns, to protect 13 Negro children from crowds of angry white adults gathered at the schools in each community. In Henderson, Kentucky, some 30 miles north of Sturgis and Clay, county officials, ministers and civic leaders engaged in a struggle with the white Citizens Council which attempted to maintain a white student boycott of a desegregated county school until the five Negroes attending class there were removed.

Peaceful Points

While these communities claimed the headlines of the nation's press, desegregation proceeded peaceably elsewhere, sometimes not very many miles away from a point of resistance.

Not far away from Milford, for example, Newcastle, Delaware, desegregated without incident and last school year 106 Negro children were attending school with 2,190 white classmates. While trouble brewed in Greenbrier County, neighboring Pocahontas County desegregated without incident and last year 77 Negro children were attending class with 2,788 white children.

The same held true in Kentucky. Opposition to desegregation in Sturgis and Clay ignited opposition sentiment in Henderson County and its seat of government, the City of Henderson. Student boycotts resulted. But desegregation remained in effect as five Negro children attended the county's Weaverton school and seven Negro first-graders attended the city's elementary schools.

There was no proximation of this in the case of Mansfield, Texas, however, and with understandable reason. While desegregation did occur in some two-score counties elsewhere in Texas, Tarrant County is definitely a part of east Texas, a part of the state synonymous with the word southern to the natives of the region. Mansfield is a cotton town and all that the phrase implies.

Clinton was another case altogether. While Negro children attended Anderson County's Clinton High School under the protection of National Guardsmen, Negro children at Oak Ridge, 20 miles to the west—but still in Anderson County—attended desegregated schools without incident for the second year.

The Oak Ridge school system desegregated in September 1955 and 85 Negro junior and senior high school students attended school with 2,526 white classmates. Plans to desegregate were announced eight months prior to the act by the Atomic Energy Commission which owns and operates the nation's "atomic city" of 33,500 people.

Desegregation at Oak Ridge precipitated the organization of a local chapter of the Tennessee Federation for Constitutional Government—a states' rights organization which vigorously advocates nonviolent opposition to desegregation—and stirred up talk of a parents' picket line to protest the move. But the picket line failed to materialize and opposition to desegregation receded to the conversational level.

Why was there a disturbance at Clinton and not at Oak Ridge? After all, both are in the same county which, though Union during the Civil War, has had a heavy influx of people from the Deep South since the Tennessee Valley Authority was established—an influx sharply increased by the wartime creation of Oak Ridge. As a matter of fact, Oak Ridge, while it does have residents from every state in the nation, is composed for the most part of Tennesseans.

The soundest explanation of the difference was this: Oak Ridge is a Federal reservation, analogous in relation to the school issue to an army post. Therefore, when the AEC ordered desegregation, it was similar to the commander-in-chief of an army issuing a general order, one that had to obeyed. Dr. Donald Davidson of Vanderbilt University, president of the Tennessee Federation for Constitutional Government, described the experience, however, as "Tyranny at Oak Ridge" in a pamphlet by that name.

No Rule of Thumb

There was no rule of thumb, therefore, that could be applied to any community so that a person could say, "This town will resist. This one will not."

Take Milford. It is a town of 5,170 (16.7 per cent Negro), the center of a farming area in south Delaware. Its economy is predominantly agricultural although it also gains income from canning and light industry. The town has two schools, one a consolidated (grades 1-12) school for white children, the other a Negro elementary school. The Negro high school students were transported to class at Dover, 19 miles away. The two schools serve an area population of 14,000, which includes about 3,000 Negroes.

The first 10 days of desegregation in Delaware were so peaceful that State Attorney General H. Albert Young had good reason to feel confident as he sat at his desk in Dover, the state capital, on September 17 and wrote the first words of a brief he was to deliver before the U. S. Supreme Court. He wrote substantially as follows: "There has been a remarkably peaceful transition from segregation to partial integration in a number of the Delaware public schools since the opinion of the U. S. Supreme Court on May 17th of this year."

Within a matter of days, Young tossed the first draft of his brief into the wastebasket and was busily writing another, strongly urging the Court to make clear that all states' segregation statutes were unconstitutional and that desegregation was the law of the land.

What changed Young's mind was the sudden resistance that materialized in Milford. For on September 17, the day he was so confident about peaceful desegregation, word spread through Milford that an anti-integration meeting was to take place that night at the American Legion Hall. It did. A petition protesting desegregation was signed by 1,002 of the 1,500 people present.

There were 31 Negro high school students in the Milford community. Eleven had enrolled in the Lake View Avenue School, the formerly all-white consolidated school. The remaining 20 Negroes elected to continue in school at Dover. The white enrollment at Lake View totaled 584 students.

The people who protested desegregation were angry not only because Negro children were attending the school, but also because the school board had not announced desegregation was going to take place. Indeed, the first time anyone knew the board had adopted a gradual desegregation plan (beginning in the 10th grade) was when the Rotary Club was told about it on September 6, the day before school opened.

Milford seethed with unrest. Anonymous telephone calls to the school superintendent warned of violence if the Negroes were permitted to remain at Lake View. The superintendent closed the school. Then another protest meeting was held. Schools remained closed. The state board of education warned the Milford board that it would be violating even the separate but equal provisions of Delaware's constitution if Negroes were kept out of Lake View. At that point the Milford board resigned.

Bryant Bowles, a young man from Washington, D.C., experienced in the desegregation resistance movements in Washington and Baltimore, arrived on the scene and organized a local chapter of the National Association for the Advancement of White People. Soon after, a new school board was formed. Its first act was to bar the Negro students from Lake View, an action that was overruled in a lower court decision but, in effect, was upheld temporarily by the state supreme court.

Under pressure of attack from the Milford clergy, civic clubs and, ultimately, the press, Bowles' influence dissipated. The town simmered down but Milford remained segregated. The Negro children returned to all-Negro schools in Dover and nearby Georgetown. The state supreme court, noting that the state board of education had instructed all local boards to draft desegregation plans to effect compliance with the May 17 ruling, declared that the Milford board had not done so, hence the Negro children had been admitted to the school illegally.

Suits seeking Federal court desegregation orders against the Milford board and boards in seven other Delaware communities were later filed by the National Association for the Advancement of Colored People.*

Point Two

Meanwhile, the small (estimated population: 2,643) resort town of White Sulphur Springs in Greenbrier County, West Virginia, jumped into the nation's spotlight as the next point of resistance.

Two and a half years later, D. D. Harrah, the Greenbrier County superintendent of schools, was still rather amazed that his community had become the scene of brief but tense touch-and-go resistance to desegregation that hit the headlines. "We felt in this county the people were ready for the move," he recalled. "The students' choral festivals were held on a desegregated basis prior to 1954. There had been no objections to that. The principals' association had also been desegregated prior to 1954. As a matter of fact, the president of the association in 1953 was the principal of our Negro high school. There had been no objection to that. Two children of white and Negro blood had been attending one of the white schools in the county without trouble. In another section of the county, where white students lived closer to a school in another county—and were transported to it in our buses—two Negro students rode with them to a Negro school in that county. There had been no objection to that, no trouble at all."

Harrah cited two other factors which he said made the board feel there would be no opposition to desegregation. On August 2, the board amicably discussed the possibility of desegregation that fall with representatives of the NAACP. This was published in the local press. On August 17 the board's decision to desegregate was announced in the county's four weekly newspapers and in the Charleston daily press which has considerable circulation in the county. "Furthermore," Harrah said, "the decision was spread throughout the county on the 'Greenbrier grapevine', a word of mouth news service which we feel has a tremendous contact with the people, and it was spread in school bulletins and in faculty meetings."

---

* On July 15, Federal Judge Paul Leahy consolidated the cases and delivered an opinion instructing the state board of education to submit to him within 60 days a desegregation plan for the eight districts. The application of the order was statewide—the first of its kind. The board said it would appeal.—Editor

The reaction to the decision seemed insignificant. Harrah said he received one or two telephone calls protesting desegregation and a few letters. One of these letters, a two-sentence message scrawled on a scrap of white paper, read: "Dear Sir: We want to notify the Greenbrier County Board of Education there will be no integration in the schools of White Sulphur. Otherwise there will be no school." It was unsigned and bore a White Sulphur Springs postmark, and was considered the work of a crank.

Greenbrier, a lush green, softly rolling region which draws its lifeblood from dairy and beef farming and from coal mines in its western area, was one of 29 counties in the state planning to desegregate that year. Most of the counties involved were rural counties, not dissimilar from Greenbrier, though perhaps somewhat less wealthy. When Greenbrier schools opened, most of the county's Negro high school students elected to continue at the all-Negro consolidated school in Lewisburg, the county seat. At White Sulphur, however, nine Negro high school students decided to accept the free choice plan of the board and entered the high school there with 441 white children.

Over at Rupert, in the coal mining section of the county, seven Negroes enrolled in the formerly all-white primary facility, six in the high school. There, trouble started. Twenty automobiles, filled with white adults—mostly men—circled the school telling the white students to stay out. Harrah went over. The men protested to him against desegregation. He told them it was the law of the land.

That afternoon, as the students were leaving, 50 white men stood by, silently watching. One said he was going to take a Negro child off a school bus. He made a move toward the bus. Another said the Negroes' presence on the buses overloaded them. Harrah suggested he call the state police to check. His suggestion was not followed. The children drove away from Rupert and so did trouble.

After five days of school Harrah was told by the editor of the White Sulphur Springs weekly paper that a group of high school students were preparing for a strike the next day. Further investigation disclosed that some of the boys admitted they were being paid to organize the strike, but they declined to identify their employer. Soon, rumors filtered through White Sulphur about trouble at the school, and on Monday, September 13, the strike was called. Students demonstrated, parading down the town's main street. Harrah said 150

students were out of class that morning. Other observers put the figure at 300. About 10 adults mingled with the striking children and
encouraged them.

When Harrah was informed of the strike, he was sitting in a specially called school board meeting, a meeting that started at 9 a.m.
and ended at 11 p.m. with the board rescinding its desegregation
order. Throughout the day the board had received reports of threats
of violence if the Negroes were permitted to remain in the formerly
all-white schools.

The most persistent report was that whites and Negroes were arm-
ing themselves and that there had been a run on ammunition in the
county's hardware stores. This report was never substantiated.

A Negro woman was reported to be carrying a loaded shotgun in
her car. This turned out to be true.

Two Negro students, who had put on uniforms for a football game
the preceding Friday night—even though they knew they were in-
eligible to play as transfers—reported nine white students chased
them home after the game. This was also true.

What to do?

The school board members decided to call upon the governor's
office for aid. They 'phoned twice, asking for assistance either in the
form of extra state troopers or National Guardsmen, but all to no
avail. "All we got was sympathy," said Harrah, "and we were past
the stage when that was any good."

Negro students were returned to the schools they attended the previous year "to prevent any type of violence or bloodshed," said Harrah. They were subsequently—and peaceably—readmitted a year and
a half later, under court order.

The clergy in White Sulphur publicly condemned the strife in a
public statement afterward. The weekly press in Greenbrier, while
publishing in full all board action leading to desegregation, did not
comment on it editorially. City fathers in the town did not speak out
on the desegregation question at any time prior to the opening of
school, and neither did any leaders of the 661 persons in the Negro
community.

Trouble in Texas

In Mansfield, Texas, two years later, it was different. There, everyone in the white community, from town officials on down, seemed to oppose desegregation of any kind.

The prospect of desegregation in Mansfield was nothing new to its 1,450 people, among whom were 300 Negroes. In July 1955 the school board received a petition requesting the admission of three Negroes to the Mansfield High School, and when this was denied, a suit to secure this goal was filed and won in Federal court.

The court fight, letters to the editor from white Citizens Council members—and editorials expressing similar views—were duly published in the weekly *Mansfield News*, the town's single newspaper. A Citizens Council meeting, held shortly after the suit was filed in October 1955, attracted 100 people who listened to a speaker tell them they would have to rely on "grits, guts and gerrymander" to defeat desegregation. There was no voice in the community that urged moderation of even the most general sort.

The school board fought desegregation to the bitter end. The board's attorney, on August 29—a day before students were supposed to register—asked the Federal district judge in Fort Worth to stay for a year the execution of the court's order to desegregate. The judge denied the plea but at the same time, in a remark of obiter dicta, told the board's attorney: "I want to say that the attitude that has been taken in this case and that is now being taken by you is one of prayerful obedience to the law and in so doing, that high school will stand as a monument to the patriotism and wisdom of the school board."

The next day, the first of 250 white children to register at the school were closely watched by a crowd of some 200 to 300 white people who stood about the school grounds, waiting for the three Negro students who were expected to enroll. Earlier that week, a six-foot effigy of a Negro had been strung up over Main Street. A couple of crosses had been burned in the Negro section of Mansfield, but the effigy, said the sheriff of Tarrant County, made him "uneasy" about the situation.

When he appeared at the school on opening day he and his deputies were heckled by the crowd. The sheriff cautioned them not to take the law into their own hands. The sheriff, in turn, was warned by a voice in the crowd that if he or his men escorted one Negro student into the school, "we're gonna have to get guns ourselves."

The sheriff said he would file charges against anyone found armed at the school.

"You'd better clean out your jail!" cried another voice from the crowd, "you're gonna have a lot of us down there!"

The sheriff replied, "We have plenty of room."

Most of the town's business establishments closed for the day—either as a sign of sympathy with the protest or at the request of the Citizens Council.

When it became apparent the Negro children would not appear, the stores reopened. One, a drug store, did a landoffice business. The store owner, a strong segregationist, said business was fine and that he had not seen a lot of his customers for some time. Most, he said, were from the county around.

The school officials did little to facilitate the admission of the Negroes to the school. The superintendent was requested by the Negro attorney representing the children to enroll them by telegram, saying it would endanger their lives to appear at the school. The request was denied.

The school principal, asked by a newsman if he was going to remove the effigy of a handless Negro hanging over the school entrance, said he was not. "I didn't put it up there," he said, "and I'm not going to take it down."

The attorney for the Negro children, who was also counsel for the NAACP in Fort Worth, attempted to contact Governor Allan Shivers to request that Texas Rangers be ordered into Mansfield. Shivers could not be reached, but the next day two Rangers (in Texas they say one Ranger can take care of 1,000 rioting people) arrived with instructions to "arrest anyone, white or colored, whose actions are such as to represent a threat to the peace of Mansfield."

Governor Shivers said also, "I hope the Supreme Court will be given an opportunity to view the effect of its desegregation decision on a typical, law-abiding Texas community."

That day, the crowd at the school was larger—between 400 and 500—and its temper hotter. Reporters and photographers were jostled and an assistant district attorney general for Tarrant County was thoroughly shaken up by a group of men who said the attorney told them he was there to collect evidence on which to prosecute the leaders of the demonstration (a statement the attorney denies ever having made). The following Tuesday, the first day of class after the Labor Day week end, an Episcopal minister from Fort Worth was escorted from the middle of the crowd by a Ranger after the minister and members of the crowd heatedly discussed the Christian merits of their demonstrations and of desegregation.

That day, however, the protesting crowds dispersed with smiles on their faces. They were informed the three Negro students had been transferred out of the district under new instructions from the Governor.

Sturgis and Clay

The west Kentucky coal and farming communities of Sturgis and Clay were close to Mansfield in tradition and resistance to desegregation if not in miles. Yet in many ways, Kentucky was the focal points of news about successful desegregation in September 1956. Louisville, in one fell swoop, desegregated without incident its schools from first to 12th grade in a movement that involved 54,821 white children and 12,720 Negro children. In the whole state, most of it rural, best estimates showed "integrated situations" in 63 of the 120 counties.

Sturgis and Clay are small rural towns, located in two former slave-holding counties. Their economy is based on farming and coal mining. Sturgis has a population of 3,000 and Clay's hovers between 1,500 and 1,900. The Union County (Sturgis) Board of Education had no official desegregation plan, but decided to admit nine Negroes to the white high school at Sturgis instead of transporting them to the Dunbar (Negro) school at Morganfield 11 miles away. The children registered without incident on August 31, but when they returned to school for the first day of class after the Labor Day week end, they were turned back by a crowd of 500 white people, mostly adults, who had surrounded the school. The Union County school superintendent arrived at the scene and told the crowd the Negroes had been admitted in accordance with board policy which was based, he said, on "the Supreme Court ruling that eliminated segregation of the races in the public schools and the Governor's [A. B. 'Happy' Chandler] proclamation that Kentucky would abide by the Supreme Court order."

The crowd dispersed. The next day the crowd came back to school

but the Negro children didn't. The Negro parents were in a conference with the school board during which they agreed to re-enter their
children in the Dunbar school for the year in return for assurance that
schools would be desegregated in the fall of 1957.

But a second conference that day blew the agreement sky high.
The state Adjutant General, sent to Sturgis by the Governor, met
with Mayor J. B. Holman and school officials to see if they felt National Guardsmen were needed to keep peace and protect the lives
of the school students. The mayor and school officials vigorously opposed such action. So did one of the general's aides, but Adjutant
General J. J. B. Williams told the officials, "Gentlemen, this is my decision. I alone will decide whether troops will be sent here."

He did and they were. Early on the morning of September 6, 200
Guardsmen of the 240th tank battalion rolled into Sturgis.

The Negro parents, one of them said later, felt "obliged" to call off
their agreement with the school board when the state ordered the
Guard in, and sent their children to school. Guardsmen, with fixed
bayonets on their rifles, escorted them into the school through the
crowd of 800 heckling, shouting white people. Seven white men were
arrested for disturbing the peace, and the first of 450 white students
at the school left class in phase one of a boycott. After a white Citizens
Council meeting in the town that night—attended by 1,000—attendance at school the next day dropped to 50 per cent.

The protest movement soon spread to Clay, 11 miles to the east in
Webster County. There, the county board of education had adopted
no formal plan for desegregation but decided to admit four Negro
students to Clay consolidated school. A crowd of 150, many of them
women, stood in front of the school and turned the Negro children
back. Thirty men hovered at the bottom of the hill, blocking the road
leading up to the school to keep the press away.

The mother of two of the Negro children, who lived in the small
town of Wheatcroft, between Sturgis and Clay, was stunned by the
action. "Where do you draw the line?" she asked. "I even have a
white mother!"

But the mayor of Clay, sixty-six-year-old Herman T. Clark, a
banker, landowner and oilman, approved of the protest. He has been
mayor for 20 years. "The Supreme Court may say that integration
is the law of the land," he said, "but as far as I'm concerned—and

98 per cent of my fellow citizens agree—the law of the state of Kentucky is the law here. When the chips are down, I'm going to stand with my own people."

The Guard was sent to Clay.

For a few days, the Negro children attended the schools at Sturgis and Clay under troop protection. On September 14, however, the state Attorney General declared it was his opinion the Negro children at Clay were illegally enrolled since the county had no official plan for desegregation. The same ruling was applied to Sturgis four days later—the day when the student boycott reached its peak.

On September 18, when the Negro children reached the school under guard, they were met at the door by the principal, who read them the Union County board order instructing them to return to the Dunbar school. Receiving the news in silence, they walked back to the car which had brought them to school. As the car drove away, an elderly woman danced a jig in the street, then chased after the slowly moving car, banging on its trunk and shouting in a high-pitched voice, "Go home niggers! We don't want you here!"

An elderly man, a friend of the woman, chuckled and said, "She's a fightin' ol' rascal, ain't she?"

Boycott at Henderson

The troubles at Sturgis and Clay spilled over into Henderson, Kentucky, 30 miles to the north. While attention of everyone in the neighborhood was being focused on the smaller towns, a student boycott had been eating away at attendance in the Weaverton school.

Five Negroes, age six to nine, had been admitted to the consolidated Henderson County school on September 4. There had been no trouble and no tangible signs of opposition to the move. Further, in the Henderson city system, operating under a 12-year gradual desegregation plan—beginning in the first grade—seven Negro children attended class with white children.

By September 24, less than 300 members of the Weaverton school's 870 student body remained in classes. A crowd of 200 white adults, gathered outside the school, attempted to "talk" others out of going to school. The leader, a door and storm window salesman and a member of the white Citizens Council, urged the crowd to restrain itself from overt action and disorder. "First thing you know," he said, gesturing to a group of reporters, "they'll be calling us a mob."

After two attempts to get the school officials to withdraw the Negro students or excuse the white children, the crowd dispersed. A Citizens Council meeting that night urged a "peaceful boycott" of the school. Meeting at the same time, members of the Henderson Ministerial Association decided that regardless of personal feelings, they should oppose the boycott. The next day, ads appeared in the local paper and association-sponsored announcements were made over the radio station urging the end of the boycott.

By September 28, the boycott was beginning to lose force, and when the state Attorney General said some of the boycott leaders were possibly leaving themselves open to prosecution for conspiracy or sedition, the movement collapsed.

Clinton and Kasper

The situation did not resolve itself so easily in Clinton, the most publicized of the communities in strife.

The white and Negro children attended class peaceably and without incident while the tanks of the National Guard cast their bulky shadows over the town. They did so—for a while after the tanks and rifle-bearing soldiers left.

But the shadow of John Kasper, the young segregationist from Washington, D.C., who organized the resistance in Clinton, hovered in the background. Free on bail pending appeal of a contempt of court decision, he roamed Anderson County at will and spoke to anyone who would listen. He was arrested on state charges of sedition. And his acquittal of this charge seemed to be the signal for a campaign of harassment and intimidation directed against the Negro students and the principal of the school, D. J. Brittain.

A group of students—about 50—formed a teenage counterpart of the Citizens Council. Negro students discovered ink spilled in their books. They claimed they were tripped and jostled in the school corridors. Brittain, gaunt and angry, sat behind the eight-ball paperweight on his desk, seemingly helpless under the pressure of anonymous telephone calls to his home and his office. Meanwhile, the Citizens Council was running a slate of candidates for mayor and three aldermanic posts to be filled in a municipal election on December 4.

Brittain said later he couldn't understand what was happening to Clinton. Sure, he said, outsiders had helped cause trouble in the September crisis. Sure, he agreed, the majority of the people of Clinton and Anderson County opposed desegregation (a fact clearly substantiated by a newspaper poll in the fall). "We had done all we could to prevent it," he said. "We had exhausted every possible legal means to prevent desegregation. But we had no Negro high school in the county. And the fact these students had to be transported to Knoxville—some 16 miles away—did not help our case. If we were law-abiding citizens, and I believed at the time most of us were, we would just have to go ahead and desegregate.

"We announced our plan in the paper," he said. "We talked about it in PTA meetings, in the faculty, and we encouraged the students to discuss it in class. The only group I can see that we missed were those people in the low income brackets, those mothers and fathers who had to work and didn't pay any attention to what was going on. I guess that was a fatal mistake."

Clinton at the Polls

The Clinton situation resolved itself, for the time being at least, on election day in December. The week before, the Negro students, now down to nine (three had dropped out), stayed away from class because of what they called acts of intimidation.

On election day, a young Baptist minister, pastor of the largest church in town, escorted the children to class. He was accompanied by two other residents of Clinton. A group of about 20 men heckled them on the way. Once the Negroes were in school, the preacher walked down the street on his way back to church. As he passed the city hall, where voters were lining up to cast their ballots, he was attacked, he said, by a group of men and one woman. His nose was bloodied and his face cut in the fight.

There was a disturbance at the school. Brittain, after hurried consultations with board members by telephone, closed it.

Brittain and board members waited for the election returns. "The future of Clinton, not just this school," said one board member later, "hung in the balance."

When the votes were counted, the Citizens Council had been roundly defeated in the election. A report of the beating of the minister, and reports of intimidation of students and Brittain were presented to the U. S. District Attorney General in Knoxville, with the result that 18 persons were charged with contempt of court for violating a Federal court order—issued two days before Labor Day week end—prohibiting interference with the peaceful desegregation of the school.

Because of its broad nature (the student body itself was enjoined, apparently the first such action in judicial history) the injunction has been the center of a legal controversy which transcends the basic segregation-desegregation issue. Questions of freedom of speech, rights to separate trials and trials by jury have been raised with the result that disposition of the cases was delayed from January 1957—when they were originally scheduled to be heard—until summer.

A "Freedom Fund for Clinton" to raise money for the defense of the group was established in Tennessee, spreading later to Georgia, South Carolina, Louisiana and other states. The then attorneys general of Georgia, Louisiana and Texas said they would offer their services. One later withdrew. Custodians of the fund said that none of the money would be used in Kasper's defense. Prior to the trial, the U. S. Department of Justice said that it was willing for the cases to be heard before a jury. Shortly before setting the trial date in May 1957, U. S. District Judge Robert L. Taylor, who had issued the injunction, granted jury trials for the 18 defendants, including Kasper.*

Since the school was reopened, only two incidents have disturbed Clinton's new calm. A Negro student got in a fight with a white boy and was expelled, and dynamite was exploded in Clinton's Negro section.

Is There a Pattern?

Thus resistance to desegregation. Does it form a hard and fast pattern? From all the reported evidence, apparently not. But each of

---

* On July 23, Kasper and six of the defendants were found guilty by an all-white jury of 10 men and two women. Their attorneys filed motions for a new trial and said if it was not granted they would appeal to higher courts. Before the trial started, one defendant died in an insane asylum, charges were dropped against another, a teenager who was in the state penitentiary for grand larceny. Shortly after the trial started, charges were dropped against another defendant for reasons of health. During the trial, judgments of acquittal were rendered for four of the defendants at the request of the government. Four of the remaining defendants were acquitted by the jury.—Editor

these incidents contains established, salient facts that may or may not be determinants in whether a community will actively resist desegregation or not.

One. Based on these incidents, it appears that the intensity and power of the resistance varies directly with the organization of segregationist sentiment in the community. The resistance movements at Clinton and Clay, Mansfield, Milford and Sturgis were all, in the end, controlled by segregationist organizations.

(It might be pointed out here that organizations can have a direct effect on a community's resistance even before desegregation. For instance, in Arlington, Virginia, a segregationist organization, alarmed at what it considered pro-integration tendencies of the school board members, worked through the Virginia legislature and got a bill enacted stripping Arlington of its distinction of being the only elective school board in the state. The board is now an appointive one.

(Said a member of the organization, an Arlington shopkeeper: "I used to live in the District. When they started to mix kids there, I moved on up to Maryland. Then I understand this fellow McKeldin [Governor Theodore McKeldin] is going to mix 'em up too. So I came here. I'm in Virginia now and we're safe as long as we've got Stanley and no screwballs on the school board. And we've fixed that.")

Two. The number of Negro children involved in the desegregation movement does not seem to matter very much. The people of Mansfield objected to only three, Clay to four and Clinton to twelve.

Three. The importance of advance warning of desegregation does have an effect, but it can be taken either way. In Milford, Clay and Sturgis, for instance, there was no advance warning and there is no doubt this fact angered many of the people. On the other hand, the people of Clinton, Mansfield and White Sulphur Springs were not caught by surprise.

Four. The position of the clergy is, so far at least, indecisive. In the communities described above, the clergy usually entered the picture after the fact. In Henderson the clergy was consistently active, and resistance ended quickly in that community. In Clinton, according to observers, the fact that a preacher was beaten contributed greatly to the defeat of the Citizens Council candidates in the election.

What would have happened if a popular preacher had not been physically involved?

Five. Based on the above cases, organized, sometimes violent resistance seems to be a delaying tactic rather than a preventive one, and sometimes it works. The Negro students at White Sulphur Springs were admitted to the schools by court order about 18 months after the disturbance in the community. The schools of Sturgis and Clay are under court order (to which they have agreed) to desegregate in the fall of 1957. And in Clinton, scene of the hottest strife, Negro children, although six of the original ones dropped out, continued to attend desegregated classes throughout the school year. Mansfield and Milford, however, remain segregated, with no present evidence of any change. It should be noted also that Federal courts have concerned themselves with all six communities.

Six. Contrary to cries that blood would flow in the streets before schools would be desegregated, there had been no real bloodshed. The only blood shed so far has been that of a Nashville newspaper photographer who was struck in the face by a man who broke from National Guard arrest in Clinton; blood from a retired white miner, winged in the arm by a bullet (fired by a Negro) when a crowd of white people harassed Negro motorists in Oliver Springs, Tennessee, in a Clinton-related incident; and blood from the nose and face of the Baptist preacher in Clinton.

Seven. Will there be resistance in Clinton, Clay, Sturgis, Milford and Mansfield when (and if) Negroes seek to enter or re-enter white schools in those communities? Interviews with school and law enforcement officials and residents indicate there will be, but not in the form of 1956. Resistance at Clinton may depend to a great extent on the outcome of the trial of the 17 people arrested for violating the injunction governing desegregation at the school. The people of Sturgis are still antagonistic toward desegregation, but it is believed they will be more inclined to go along with the change now that they know it's coming. Clay, Milford and Mansfield are different. Most of the people of these communities are still unalterably opposed to desegregation, though Clay has agreed to proceed under court order. While some were shocked at last year's performance, most were not. The outcome here will depend to a great extent on the political and police powers of the local communities and the state.

Eight. While these legal issues have been so framed as to pose Negroes against whites, in no instance have Negroes taken part in crowd demonstrations. The demonstrations have involved whites against whites—against those taking issue with the pro-segregation crowds or those whites in authority.

The possible absence of organized protest next school year of the 1956 type should not be taken as evidence of complete acceptance of desegregation.

Brittain, the principal of the Clinton High School, put it this way: "It's not that the people here actually like integration any better. It's just the fact they like violence less."

4.

Along the Border

BY ROBERT LASCH

One thing that border and South had indisputably in common was statutory school segregation. This one certain likeness, this unarguable sameness began to fade soon after the Supreme Court decision.

Almost all of the desegregation—685 districts—that has taken place under the decision has occurred in the border states of Delaware, Maryland, West Virginia, Kentucky, Missouri and Oklahoma. In Texas, which has some of the characteristics of the border area, the picture has been mixed, some desegregation occurring in the southern and western sections, very little in the east Texas counties that are socially akin to Louisiana and Mississippi.

Even so, more than 1,000 biracial school districts in the border states were still segregated by the summer of 1957—counting Texas with more than 700 districts which had taken no action.

Briefly, this was the record along the border in the first three years after the decision:

Delaware. Source of one of the cases which brought the decision of May 17, 1954, this state divided sharply in compliance. Wilmington and other districts in the northern section ended segregation promptly, without incident. Beginning with elementary pupils in 1954, proceeding to junior highs in 1955 and senior highs in 1956, Wilmington integrated 3,855 Negroes and 9,187 whites. By 1957, 14 other biracial districts out of 61 in the rest of the state had followed suit. But in rural and small-town south Delaware, resistance hardened and litigation flourished. Milford, the first testing ground of Bryant Bowles and his National Association for the Advancement of White People, offered

56

one of the earliest examples of semi-violent hostility to the Court opinion which succeeded in overturning an official decision to comply.

Maryland. Baltimore, where most of the state's Negroes live, moved promptly and smoothly into desegregation after an initial disturbance. The rural areas of the Free State proceeded more slowly. In sharp contrast to Milford, Delaware, Baltimore, then with 55,000 Negroes and 85,000 whites enrolled, met firmly and put down swiftly a threat of organized violence at some schools, and experienced no more trouble thereafter. The city had no effective districts, but permitted students of any race to attend school where they wished if space allowed. By 1956-57, some 80 schools out of 177 reported mixed enrollments. Outside Baltimore, there were 138 mixed schools with an enrollment of 1,727 Negroes and 89,000 whites, and 656 unmixed schools with 41,000 Negroes and 220,000 whites. Over half of the counties admitted Negroes to some previously all-white schools, and only two of the counties with Negro populations had failed to adopt desegregation as a formal policy, to be realized at varying speeds.

West Virginia. With a relatively small Negro population, this state desegregated its schools fairly rapidly. There were a few scattered incidents of resistance, one of them prolonged. By the third academic year following the decision, all state colleges and the schools of 20 counties had been completely desegregated, 21 counties partly so. In two eastern counties, closest to Virginia, the schools retained segregation. Three-fourths of the state's 25,000 Negroes, it was estimated, were actually attending mixed classes by 1957, and many all-Negro schools had been abolished.

Missouri. The two principal cities, St. Louis and Kansas City, accounting between them for more than two-thirds of the state's Negroes, dropped color lines promptly and without major incident. St. Louis desegregated high schools in February 1955 and its elementary schools the following September. Out of some 35,000 Negroes and 60,000 whites, more than 60 per cent were attending mixed schools within a year. Kansas City desegregated all grades in September 1955. Rural and small-town areas generally followed the example except in the cotton-growing "bootheel" of southeast Missouri, the slowest section to comply. Even there, however, 10 high schools had ended segregation by 1957, by which date only four high schools in the entire state remained segregated. At the elementary level, all but some

7,000 pupils were enrolled in integrated school systems, half of the exceptions being located in the "bootheel." All told, 202 of 244 districts with Negro enrollments, involving 60,000 of the 67,000 Negro pupils in the state, had desegregated by June 1957. The number was scheduled to reach 209 districts by September 1957.

Oklahoma. This state held off action until the Court's final decree was handed down in 1955, but then moved swiftly to comply. Local districts were encouraged to desegregate by official state financial pressure. A constitutional amendment and state legislation made it financially disadvantageous for most districts to maintain separate schools. Oklahoma City and Tulsa, as well as all of the state colleges, dropped racial distinctions, as did 195 other school districts. By 1957, 64 districts remained segregated. Most of them were in "Little Dixie," the southeastern counties closest to Arkansas and Louisiana.

Kentucky. The most "southern" of the border states, Kentucky, where about three dozen districts desegregated in 1955, waited until the fall of 1956 before taking action on any large scale. Then Louisville, in a demonstration which attracted President Eisenhower's personal commendation, ended segregation under an "option" plan permitting parents of both races to transfer their children from a mixed school if they wished. The option was sparely exercised, and more than 70 per cent of the students were soon attending mixed schools in some degree. Frankfort, the state capital, also ended segregation without incident. By 1957, 92 school districts had desegregated and 17 others had adopted plans to do so, while 68 had not acted. In some rural sections, the transition did not come smoothly. At Clay and Sturgis, violent resistance required the summoning of the National Guard to keep order, and compliance was temporarily abandoned while the issue went through a Federal court.

Texas. Generally, the pattern was one of peaceful integration in the southern and western areas where Negroes were few and Latin American minorities had been going to school with whites; a standstill in the principal cities; and active resistance in east Texas, where 90 per cent of the Negro population was concentrated. Near Fort Worth, the town of Mansfield attracted national attention when white citizens picketed the school where a Federal judge had ordered integration to begin. Dallas studied the problem at some length, and was upheld in its indisposition to act by a Federal judge who made no secret of his hostility to the Supreme Court decision. By 1957, 19 of 46 tax-supported colleges were admitting Negroes, and of 841 school districts with both white and Negro enrollment, 103 had desegregated. The percentage of Negro students actually attending class with white students, however, was low—about 1 per cent. In no case was the mixture more than one Negro for 10 white children. The limited desegregation has occurred, as one on-the-spot observer reported, without incident but also without enthusiasm.

BOUNDING THE BORDER

The border states, by definition, have a different social and economic complexion from the Middle and Deep South. Of the seven here discussed, only Texas threw in its lot with the Confederacy. The plantation system had never taken root in their societies. Generally, they were more advanced industrially than most of the southern states. Some had special economic interests, such as Texas' oil and West Virginia's coal.

Actually, the only one of these states with a strong social and sentimental link to the South in the mid-twentieth century was Kentucky. Elsewhere along the border, social, economic and historical factors over the years had gradually dimmed many remnants of southern tradition and attitudes.

Missouri, after all, had voted Republican for President as long ago as 1904, and with only one exception (1956) had voted for the winner ever since. Save for small enclaves of persistant southern heritage —the eastern counties in West Virginia, the "bootheel" in Missouri, "Little Dixie" in Oklahoma—the border states had long since outgrown the agrarian past which linked them with the South.

Missouri is dominated by the urban economies of its two cities, St. Louis the dowager and Kansas City the breezy, pushing upstart.

West Virginia is a mining and industrial complex, having little in common with Mississippi or South Carolina.

Maryland's Eastern Shore and rural counties have retained some southern feeling, and there the percentages of Negro population may run from 25 to 35 per cent, while Baltimore often is regarded as more akin to cities of the East than to Charleston or Richmond.

Oklahoma is essentially a plains state, an oil and cattle domain turned westward, which was not admitted to the Union until 1907.

Texas faces two ways: Its eastern counties have most of the Negroes and most of the southern social feeling; its Democratic politicians mostly behave like southern Democrats; its cities and vast reaches of oil and cattle lands belong to another age and another society.

Because of this background, school segregation in much of the border area prior to the Court decision was a residual accident, hanging on by a legal quirk long after community sentiment was ready in most instances to see it ended. In many border communities, especially after World War II, steady and in some cases spectacular development had taken place in the field of diminishing racial discrimination.

One thing the border states have in common is a relatively small number of Negroes. In the 1950 census, the proportion ran as follows:

Delaware	14 per cent
Maryland	17 per cent
West Virginia	6 per cent
Kentucky	7 per cent
Missouri	8 per cent
Oklahoma	7 per cent
Texas	13 per cent

From these figures it would be easy to conclude that compliance came easiest where Negro numbers were smallest. But this theory cannot be pressed too far. Though each border state as a whole shows a relatively small Negro population, each has within it communities where Negro numbers are as high as in some typically southern communities. And it was in some of those communities that desegregation was accomplished with little friction and no serious problems.

When St. Louis ended segregation in 1955, Negroes made up 35 per cent of the public school enrollment. Baltimore successfully complied in 1954-55 at a time when Negroes constituted 39 per cent of the enrollment. Wilmington, Delaware, successfully mixed a white student population of 71 per cent and a Negro population of 29 per cent. In Kentucky, the most conspicuously successful example of desegregation was carried out in Louisville, which has more than one-third of all the state's Negroes, and where the student population is 26 per cent Negro.

Voice of Officialdom

What were the common elements that accounted for the relative ease with which most of the border states obeyed the Court decision? One, certainly, was the impact of official attitudes. Almost immediately after the decision was handed down, governors, attorneys general and state boards of education declared for prompt compliance and pledged their best efforts to accomplish it peacefully. In these days the segregationists were off balance and the integrationists had things pretty much their own way. In some cases, the official attitude softened somewhat when citizen opposition began to lift its head. But generally the border state officials from the first held the position that the law had been defined by the Court and it was up to the states to go along.

Thus in Delaware Governor J. Caleb Boggs, within a week after the decision, formally established state policy as "working toward adjustment to United States constitutional requirements." Attorney General Albert Young, who later came under furious attack at Milford, enrolled as an active proponent of the Court decision. In Maryland, Governor Theodore R. McKeldin took the same stand, and quietly supported compliance at every stage in the anxious months that followed. Maryland's attorney general declined to attend a protest meeting of southern attorneys general in Georgia.

West Virginia's Governor and Attorney General promised prompt compliance, and the State Superintendent of Schools urged this course on local districts. In Missouri the Attorney General, without waiting for the Supreme Court's final decree, issued an opinion in June 1954 that the state segregation statutes had been "superseded" by the Court opinion, and were henceforth unenforceable. In Oklahoma the Governor and State Board of Education pushed steadily for compliance, particularly by adopting financial incentives that sped the closing of "inefficient" Negro schools and the transfer of their enrollments to mixed schools.

In Kentucky Governor Lawrence Wetherby greeted the decision with an announcement that "Kentucky will do whatever is necessary to comply," the Attorney General regarded the state segregation laws as dead, and all of the state's congressmen and senators announced their support of the decision.

Only in Texas was the state government officially hostile to desegregation. Governor Allan Shivers early took a position in favor of the longest possible delay in compliance, and Attorney General John Ben Shepperd filed a brief with the Supreme Court following that line. The Governor remained hostile to desegregation and in the fall of 1956 he sent Texas Rangers into Mansfield with orders to arrest anyone, white or Negro, who might threaten the peace. Mansfield school authorities at the same time were directed by the Governor to transfer out any student whose presence would tend to incite violence. No Negro was enrolled. Previously, a Federal court had ordered enrollment of Negro children who sought entry to the Mansfield school.

However, in west and south Texas, 103 school districts out of 841 in the whole state having both white and Negro pupils had desegregated without incident. Some 500,000 white and some 25,000 Negro children are estimated to be in "integrated situations."

Preparing the Way

Extensive community preparation helped to make desegregation a success in many border areas. St. Louis enlisted churches, neighborhood groups, parent-teacher associations and civic clubs in a formidably organized advance effort to explain how desegregation would work, and to condition the community to accept it. St. Louis school officials took the position that compliance was not a matter of choice. From the beginning their attitude was that the choice had been made, and that the community's only task was to carry out the law, as defined by the Court, in the most practical manner.

In Louisville, Superintendent Omer Carmichael and his colleagues spent two full years in community preparation before risking the critical act of desegregation. Discussion groups met virtually every week throughout 1954 and 1955, talking about how the transition would affect the schools. Since many of these discussions took place at a time when pro-segregationists in the South were lighting bonfires of resistance, Louisville's calm ability to talk itself through the situation appeared all the more remarkable in the eyes of observers.

The most notable example of failure to engage in such preparation was at Milford, Delaware, where the school board suddenly proclaimed desegregation without prior public discussion or even consultation with state school officials. The results were disastrous. Milford became the border states' most famous instance of hostility to desegregation.

Often the desire to acquaint the public and parents with official plans for carrying out the Supreme Court decision collided with a feeling that best results would be obtained by minimizing the dramatic aspects of the change so far as the pupils were concerned. A half dozen Texas districts actually ended segregation in secrecy, in respect to general publicity at any rate. Radio stations and newspapers withheld news of integration in order to dampen the segregationist opposition they expected if too much noise were created.

In one Baltimore school, the Mississippi-born principal achieved a remarkable success in mixing 398 Negroes and 332 whites. She attributed the result to treating the matter as casually as possible with the children. Yet she held continuous discussions with parents, to keep them informed at every stage—especially when many were fretting about the threats of violence in Delaware and at some Baltimore schools.

Local Climate

Why was it that in south Delaware the pickets and mass meetings of white segregationists halted integration, while a few miles away in south Baltimore the same forces were put to rout? The explanation must be sought in difference in general community attitudes. In Baltimore, the climate was such that police could break up crowds at the first sign of gathering trouble, school officials could go on television with strong appeals against violence, and school pickets finally could be threatened with arrest on the ground that they were violating the school attendance law.

A stern readiness to enforce the law against mob violence was early established as essential to peaceful desegregation in doubtful areas. When St. Louis integrated, police patrol cars cruised the streets around every high school, with instructions to break up all gatherings. Strikes and parades had been threatened by a few segregationists, but they never materialized.

In Fairmont, West Virginia, a group of white mothers picketed a desegregated school and sent the teachers home. Called into court, they were confronted by an angry local judge, J. Harper Meredith, whose views on school segregation are unrecorded, but whose attitude toward violence was more than clear. From the bench Judge Meredith said: "This cannot continue and I will not permit it to continue. If necessary, I'll fill the jail until their feet are sticking out of the windows." The opposition collapsed.

As the border states settled into compliance, they developed patterns of action. In small towns, a common plan was to desegregate the high schools at once, but to put off change in the elementary grades. Behind this compromise lay the fact that most Negroes were residentially segregated, and so naturally attended all-Negro elementary schools, whereas the high school tapped a larger constituency, drawing from racially diverse neighborhoods.

Larger cities tended to end segregation at all levels with one blow, or in a series of short stages. Thus Baltimore, Kansas City and Louisville desegregated elementary and high schools at the same time— Baltimore in 1954, Kansas City in 1955, Louisville in 1956. All three, by the way, emphasized the "free choice" character of their plans, giving parents a theoretical opportunity, at least, to transfer their children from mixed schools if they wished. Except where one race overwhelmed the other by numbers, the option was seldom exercised.

St. Louis carried out its plan in three quick stages spread over a year. First, in September 1954, came the teachers college and the specialized schools with city-wide enrollment, which could be desegregated with the least administrative bother. One semester later, the high schools followed. Their relatively few numbers permitted administrative problems like redistricting to be worked out in a short time. In September 1956, the elementary schools, which involved a greater redistricting task and the mixing of more children, came last.

Transition—by Phase—or by Blow

There were cases, usually accompanied by special circumstances, where a phased transition began with the elementary schools. Often the reason was a shortage of high school space. While waiting for a new high school to be built to accommodate both races, the school officials might desegregate the elementary grades just to get things started. In some communities a declaration of desegregation at the elementary level meant the least upheaval in attendance patterns, since residential concentration assured predominantly white or Negro enrollments in any case.

Hopkins County, Kentucky, adopted a one-grade-a-year plan, under which the first grade would be integrated at the start, and other grades successively thereafter. Objections to this plan were filed by the National Association for the Advancement of Colored People and upheld in U. S. district court, whereupon the county adopted a new plan spread over a four-year period.

A novel staged plan was adopted in West Virginia. Kanawha County, which includes the state capital, Charleston, integrated grades one, two and seven in 1956, and grades three, four, five and six the next year. Cabell County began with grades one, two, seven and eight in 1954, followed by grade three and the high schools in 1956, and planned to wind up with grades four, five and six in 1957. Port Arthur, the only east Texas city to move toward compliance, ordered Negroes admitted to the first grade only as of September 1957. But even this limited program generated considerable opposition, and subsequently was held in abeyance after passage of a state law withholding state aid to integrated schools which took the step without a vote of the people.

Token integration was proclaimed in some communities, such as Queen Anne's County of Maryland. In the fall of 1955 this county announced that children of any race could attend any school unless their doing so were found to be impractical, to cause overcrowding or transportation difficulties. It was clear that though Negroes were technically free to attend mixed schools, they were not expected to do so.

Numerous communities, not quite sure of their attitude, adopted the transfer application as an ameliorating factor. Thus Talbot County, Maryland, in the fall of 1956 opened the first three grades of elementary schools to application for transfer by Negroes. Only 42 of 1,270 Negroes filed application. Nine were admitted to two schools, partly on the basis of their academic standing. Half were rejected because they were high school students and the county only desegregated three grades. Anne Arundel County in Maryland, another area which had delayed compliance with the Court decision, also accepted transfers to just the first three grades in September 1956.

Voice of the Gavel—and the Crowd

Pressure from the courts was often a factor which enabled or encouraged the border areas to act. Kentucky communities, having waited for the Supreme Court's final decree in 1955, were stimulated to act the following year by a U. S. district court ruling requiring Adair County to desegregate its high schools by February 1956, and elementary schools by the following September.

In Greenbrier County, West Virginia, student picket lines and the threat of near-violence in 1954 caused the school board to retreat from its decision to desegregate. The National Association for the Advancement of Colored People went to court. U. S. District Judge Ben Moore, in a pretrial conference, persuaded the parties to agree on an integration plan, and the school board in a four-minute meeting adopted the plan. This time the decision stuck. On the strength of it, several other West Virginia districts abandoned their resistance.

There were occasions, too, when court rulings only seemed to stiffen resistance, as at Clinton in Tennessee and Mansfield in Texas. Then it was up to state authorities to handle the situation. The Federal courts, though vested with great legal authority, lacked means of dealing directly with demonstrating crowds. In two states, troops were called out to deal with the situation resulting from defiance of a Federal court order.

As patterns of compliance developed, then, so did patterns of resistance. Milford, Delaware, early set the tone. A demonstration at White Sulphur Springs in Greenbrier County, West Virginia, lasted only a day but prevented desegregation for a year and a half. The outburst at Clay and Sturgis, in Kentucky, brought troops and caused the removal of a few Negro children from schools to which they did not return until after court settlements months later. The Mansfield, Texas, school in which Negroes were ordered enrolled by Federal court remains segregated.

So it went in other border states. In each, there was an area of southern tradition and feeling which lagged behind the cities in response to the Court decision: Maryland's Eastern Shore, the easternmost counties of West Virginia, Missouri's "bootheel," East Texas, Oklahoma's "Little Dixie," bordering on east Texas and Arkansas.

Parents in Opposition

Almost uniformly in these areas it was soon discovered that the opposition to integration was coming not from students but from their parents. Usually, when a school was opened to Negroes, nothing happened for a week or two—until the parents, getting reports from the children, had had time to become collectively indignant. Then there might be demonstrations, picketing, occasionally egg-throwing, and withdrawal of children from the school.

What happened at this stage depended usually upon the mettle of the school board. In Greenbrier County, West Virginia, the demonstration in 1954 caused the board to cancel its desegregation plans. In Mercer County, West Virginia, two years later, the school board stood fast and the white boycott collapsed. In Charleston, Missouri, a cotton-growing "bootheel" town, the school board refused to be intimidated by the burning of a cross on one member's lawn, and Negroes continued to attend the high school along with whites.

In Poolesville, Montgomery County, Maryland, adults picketing the integrated school succeeded in keeping 366 white children out of school the first two days. But their demonstrations were broken up by the police, the schools stayed open, and by the end of 10 days nearly all of the white boycotters were back in class.

The white Citizens Councils which played such a prominent part in organizing resistance to the Court opinion in the Deep South were active in few border states. Only in Delaware and Texas was organized resistance of this type widespread. Maryland had its "West River Proclamation" against integration and its state "Petition Committee." But in opposition to these groups parent-teacher associations and other partisans of integration organized themselves. Missouri, Oklahoma, Kentucky and West Virginia had no concerted anti-integration activity on a statewide scale.

When It Happened

Where desegregation was accomplished, what happened? In larger cities, the typical experience was that some schools remained all-Negro and all-white, due to residential segregation, but a significant number of fringe schools, serving both white and Negro neighborhoods, became the cutting edge of integration. This was particularly true in St. Louis.

The experience of a city like Tulsa, which desegregated in 1955, was different. There, the 10 per cent Negro population was so tightly concentrated that less than 3 per cent of the Negro pupils attended mixed classes. A Tulsa editor described the situation as "the essence of segregation with technical integration." Not far away in Oklahoma City, the state capital, 1,069 Negroes, or 15 per cent of the total, were soon attending classes with 3,197 whites in 10 mixed schools. But the Board of Education tightened up its transfer procedures and will not permit a Negro student to attend a school outside his own residential area without good cause, such as a difference in curriculum.

Austin, the capital city of Texas, was something like Tulsa. It started ending segregation in 1955 under a "free choice" plan. Attendance districts placed most of the Negroes in one school area and most of the whites in another, but transfers were allowed on application approved by the principal. In practice, this meant that Negroes could be talked out of transferring to a mixed school if their principal believed them academically unsuited.

In Austin as elsewhere, white students made special efforts to be friendly and helpful to Negroes in the first stages of desegregation. One West Texas high school junior class elected its only Negro student vice president on his first day. Others were nominated for "friendliest" boy or girl almost as soon as they arrived. After the novelty had worn off, the Negroes were left pretty much to their own devices, and tended to segregate themselves in the lunch room, in social activities and the like.

In still smaller communities—the typical one-high-school town of 5,000 to 15,000 population—the problem usually was one of absorbing a relatively few Negroes who had been sent to a segregated school in some neighboring town. Thus Mexico, Missouri, a town of 12,000, began in 1954 by integrating 35 Negroes with 450 whites in its senior high school. The next year, the process was extended to junior high, 65 Negroes and 500 whites being involved. In both phases, the program was described by school officials as "very successful." Student-written editorials in the school paper openly combated such hostility as expressed itself among adults "downtown."

Where parents stayed out of the matter, white and Negro students generally found little difficulty in making the purely social adjustment to going to school together.

Sports helped bridge the gap, especially where an athletically talented Negro or two contributed touchdowns or baskets to the tribal rite of muscular rivalry. That psychological problems resulted from the differing levels of academic achievement few schoolmen denied. "Separate but equal" schools had not produced much true equality, as every state and city seemed to discover when products of the two systems were suddenly thrown together.

In one suburban elementary school in the St. Louis area, the teachers reported the second year of integration harder than the first. At the start, they said, a certain novelty in the social situation sustained interest and caused difficulties to be overlooked.

But when the school settled into the routine of teaching mixed classes, the scholastic inferiority of the Negroes became painfully obvious to everybody, with the result that the Negroes grew defensive and irritable, harder to get along with.

On the other hand, the principal of a high school in St. Louis reported that the second year of integration, when Negro numbers had risen to about half the total enrollment, proved easier and smoother than the first, when whites had outnumbered Negroes two to one. At this age level and in this neighborhood, teachers said, the tensions accompanying a novel situation in the first year had almost disappeared in the second, so that students of both races worked alongside each other more relaxed, more matter-of-fact, more unselfconscious.

Whether the new experience proved easy or hard, teachers of mixed classes faced a fresh problem which some were unprepared for —the problem of handling two basically different groups in terms of family and cultural background, intellectual interests and academic aptitude. In general, the older teachers found it hardest to adjust. The younger ones, especially those who had themselves attended teachers' college with Negroes, were less aware of special new difficulties.

A direct correlation seemed to exist between the socio-economic class of the mixed school, and the ease of transition. In upper middle class white neighborhoods which typically produced easily educable and "favorably motivated" children, the introduction of Negroes from families of a considerably lower economic and cultural level brought out sharp contrasts and a consequently strenuous teaching problem. In neighborhoods where both whites and Negroes came from working class families of similar interests and background, the racial differences were less noticeable.

Different school systems faced the new problems in different ways. In the typical small system, most of the burden simply fell on individual teachers. They had to cope as best they might with the pragmatic situation confronting them. Often they gave more attention to the slower Negroes, necessarily, and hoped that the more advanced whites would not suffer. Montgomery County, Maryland, sought to deal with the problem by means of "selective integration," under which Negroes would be screened according to achievement levels before being transferred to mixed schools. A special program of corrective teaching was urged for Negroes, to prepare them for integration.

In larger school systems, adjustments in curriculum were accelerated by desegregation. St. Louis in 1957 was putting into effect a three-track curriculum (similar to the Washington, D.C., four-track scheme), one for bright, one for average and one for slow students. The plan had been shaping up before the Court decision, but mixing of large groups of differing ability undoubtedly accentuated the need for it. Negroes and whites were to be admitted to each achievement level without distinction, but in the nature of things the Negroes at first would predominate in the average and slower groups.

Everywhere in the border areas, it was easy to prove that Negroes and whites brought to integrated school systems marked differences in academic aptitude, the Negroes generally ranking lower. What was not easy to demonstrate was that whites actually suffered in educational opportunity by being mixed with Negroes. Good teachers recognized that such intangibles could not be precisely measured, and that in any case their job was to offer the best possible training to all their students irrespective of race.

After three years, the striking fact that kept hitting observers in the face was that out of 685 school districts officially reported to have desegregated, all but seven were in the border states and Texas. Outside of the fringe area, only Tennessee and Arkansas—in a mere seven districts—had made a beginning toward compliance.

But the border states, by history, social background and political inclination, seemed committed on the whole to acceptance of desegregation and the shouldering of whatever educational problems it might bring. Whatever it was that made them border states largely exempted them from the agonies of resistance which built up farther South.

During the first three years after the Court decision, doubts and hesitations in these states gave way to growing compliance. To most observers it seemed a safe guess that within three years few more traces of segregation, save in Texas and a few atypical islands elsewhere, would remain along the border.

5.

City Limits

By Edgar L. Jones

A jingle that runs the rounds of luncheon club oratory in the South and occasionally crops up in a newspaper article goes something like this:

> Cotton's going West
> Cattle's coming East
> Negro's going North
> Yankee's coming South
> —And we're all going to town!

There's solid truth in all of it—as cotton moves into the southwest and on to California; as cow hands ride the range in Florida; as New York counts a larger Negro population than South Carolina, and as the hard nasal tone of the New England engineer or factory manager is heard in a hundred southern towns that advertise: "New Industry Welcomed."

But the last line rings with a special regional resonance. The southerner is literally going to town. Pointedly, to an extent scarcely believable a generation ago, the southern Negro is rapidly becoming an urban dweller. Through his shift from farm to city, the whole question of compliance with the Supreme Court's school segregation decisions increasingly becomes a problem for large cities to handle.

Into the Cities

In the emptying out of the Negro farm dwellings, a movement that saw the loss of nearly a third of the South's Negro rural-farm population in a single decade, 1940-50, the trend decidedly has been in two

71

directions: toward northern big cities and southern big cities. Southern white families also have been on the move from farms, swelling the populations of urbanized counties, small cities and metropolitan suburbs, but their attraction to the large cities has not represented as pronounced a sociological change as in the case of Negro families. By 1950, 74 per cent of southern non-rural Negroes were located in the 53 major southern cities classified as "standard metropolitan areas."

It has been assumed that by the end of the present decade, if the movement continues, half the total Negro population of this country will be living outside the 13 traditionally southern states. And half of those remaining in the South will be in urban and predominantly metropolitan areas. Not only will the southern Negroes be in metropolitan areas, but they also will be inside the central cities of those areas.

However, a big "if" lately has become attached to this first assumption. Tennessee discovered in the spring of 1957 that whites were moving north as fast as, and perhaps even faster than, Negroes. In March 1957, Dr. Harold A. Pedersen of the Department of Sociology and Rural Life at Mississippi State College reported that between April 1950 and July 1956 Mississippi had lost to migration 80,197 citizens, of whom 51,355 were whites and only 28,842 were Negroes. This sharply reversed a trend that most had believed as recently as 1956 was in the other direction.

White urban dwellers in the South as elsewhere have flowed outward to the suburbs. The Negro movement has been to the centers of cities. The 1950 census found that while 63 per cent of the white populations of southern metropolitan areas lived inside the central cities, 74 per cent of the nonwhites were within the city proper. Six states had almost 80 per cent or more of their metropolitan Negro populations inside the central cities rather than in the suburbs, a proportion attained only by Louisiana for the white group.

In all the southern states except Arkansas and Mississippi, Negroes made up a larger percentage of the population inside the central cities than outside. In six states—Alabama, Georgia, Louisiana, North Carolina, South Carolina and Tennessee—Negroes constituted about a third of the total populations of the central metropolitan cities and a smaller fraction of adjacent counties. The urban-suburban contrast was particularly strong in Florida, Georgia, Kentucky, Tennessee, Texas and Virginia.

Of course, there are some exceptions. Asheville, Chattanooga, Roanoke and Winston-Salem fell far below the southern rate of metropolitan growth. Mississippi was the sole southern state where the percentage of white metropolitan population inside the central city was considered significantly in excess of that of the Negro population, due to policies governing the extension of Jackson city limits through white suburbs. But the trends were clearly defined in the past decade and have become intensified in this one.

As John W. Maclachlan and Joe S. Floyd point out in their statistical study, *This Changing South* (University of Florida Press, 1956), a projection of past and present population trends would indicate that by 1970 the southern Negro would be "predominantly urban, and concentrated heavily into the region's largest metropolitan areas." Thus "the interracial pattern in the South would have taken on a fundamentally different demographic character."

BORDER CITIES

The degree to which school segregation or desegregation becomes a big city issue is already seen clearly in those border regions which lie just outside the South proper but have long had southern segregation traditions. Two-thirds of all the Negro pupils in Missouri are in two cities, St. Louis and Kansas City. About 60 per cent of all Maryland Negro school children are in the one city of Baltimore. Wilmington has more than a third of Delaware's Negro school population. Washington schools have become predominantly Negro, while white suburbs in adjacent Maryland and Virginia have mushroomed. Kentucky has 28 per cent of its Negroes concentrated in Louisville.

The impact that rapid population change has on cities is tremendous, especially when white families are caught up in the centrifugal movement toward suburbs and Negroes are drawn into the older, established central housing areas. Residential displacement brings the stresses and strains of changing neighborhoods, the relocation of businesses and an unfamiliar public for churches, social agencies and recreation centers to serve. Schools particularly are affected, often finding themselves fast becoming overcrowded with pupils whose southern rural background demonstrably does not include schooling on a par with urban youngsters.

Ernst W. Swanson and John A. Griffin in their statistical survey, *Public Education in the South Today and Tomorrow* (University of North Carolina Press, 1955) make the point that "the out-migration of southern peoples means that the quality of public education in the South, especially that available to the Negro population, has more than academic importance for the nation as a whole and for certain selected non-southern states in particular." To this it might be added that the farm-to-city shift means that the quality of southern rural education is of concern to urban school systems, both South and North.

The influx of Negro children into city schools presents problems, whether the schools are segregated or integrated. After analyzing the pertinent statistics for the southern states, Swanson and Griffin conclude, "It would appear inescapable that the relatively low educational attainment of the nonwhite population of parental and grandparental age constitutes a handicap for the school-age population, since much learning takes place in the home. When it is observed that the educational attainment of the white population of the parental and grandparental ages is more than twice that of the nonwhite, the racial handicap is clear." A collateral fact is that the white attainment in the South is below that in the North and West.

At the same time, urbanization has meant an increased demand for education, particularly among Negroes. Higher standards of living have provided more time for schooling, and openings in more highly skilled trades have required more training—so much so that from the school year 1939-40 to 1951-52, Negro secondary school enrollment in the South increased nearly 55 per cent. This increase, of significance to big city school systems, was common to all southern states and came in the face of the heavy outward migration that brought, with some exceptions, a reduction of Negro pupils in the lower grades. During the same period white secondary school enrollment declined in six southern states and was off 2.8 per cent for the region as a whole.

With its rate of metropolitan population growth more than double that of the rest of the country, sweeping both white and Negro rural residents into a new environment, the South has been undergoing cultural changes as yet unmeasured. Farm families, often with several generations under one roof, have been broken down into smaller units. Some of the traditions and disciplines of country life have been weakened. The individuality of the man of the soil has given way to the anonymity of crowded city life. Church and grange-hall affiliations have been dissolved, and new metropolitan interests developed, along with new labor and business associations, new forms of social life and new ties with the rest of the country, both as producers and consumers.

Whether or not urbanization, with its governmental disciplines and its emphasis on conformity, makes big-city dwellers more amenable to steps toward racial integration is an open question. The limited experiences to date in such cities as Baltimore, Washington, St. Louis and Louisville, when compared with such rural communities as Milford, Delaware; Clinton, Tennessee; and Clay and Sturgis, Kentucky, suggest that it does. It is too early, however, for generalizations based on predominantly border-state experiences.

Public opinion polls point, in any case, to the need to distinguish between approval of desegregation and acceptance of it.

After two years of school integration without apparent public opposition in Wilmington, Delaware, a poll showed that only 45 per cent of the city's residents approved of the Supreme Court decision. Similarly, a 1954 survey in Oklahoma found only a small minority favoring desegregation, yet mixed schools are now widespread in that state. As a third example: The findings of the National Opinion Research Center as reported in the December 1956 *Scientific American* showed that in those areas of the border South where school desegregation has already taken place, more than two-thirds of the white population continued to believe that Negroes should attend separate schools.

THE COMMON GROUNDS

If a distinction is made, then, between approval and acceptance, it is possible to point out factors in the metropolitan environment that could make it easier to carry out a school desegregation program, if public officials sought to do it. How much weight the factors would have in any city, compared with anti-integration sentiments, cannot be foretold. Savannah differs from St. Louis, Birmingham is unlike

Baltimore, and Wilmington, North Carolina, is not the same as Wilmington, Delaware. But these and other cities may have some factors in common.

One of these factors is the obvious one that big-city dwellers by and large are not close to policy-making decisions. They are likely to be busy or lethargic when it comes to joining public movements and are generally resigned to the belief that there is little use trying to "fight City Hall." They may grumble about public policies, but they don't expect their opinions to cut much ice. Too, metropolitan officials have the full force of law and order on their side. If trouble comes, as it did in the early days of desegregation in Baltimore and Washington, they do not have to appeal to the governor to send troops. They have their own police force standing by, and often one that through labor disputes has had experience handling angry demonstrations.

Thus the city school board member may be far less vulnerable to adverse public reaction than the rural board member who, after making a decision in the morning, must meet his customers, say, across the counter of his general store in the afternoon. A city board is not likely to fly in the face of overwhelming public opposition; on the other hand, it may not necessarily wait until it feels it has full public approval.

THE CITY BOARD

Presumably in the cities there should be a difference between appointed and elected school boards, since members of the latter are directly answerable to the voters. So far, no such distinction is clear. Elected school boards in St. Louis, San Antonio, Louisville, Tulsa and Little Rock have moved toward desegregation, while appointed boards in Columbus, Jackson and Birmingham have not. Conversely, appointed boards in Baltimore, Wilmington (Delaware) and Nashville have adopted desegregation policies, while elected boards in Baton Rouge, Mobile and scores of other cities have not.

Some city school boards have much more freedom of action than others. In the months immediately following the Supreme Court's decision of May 17, 1954, the superintendent of Orleans Parish (New Orleans) schools, James Redmond, said that neither the school board nor his staff had discussed plans for compliance. "The parish's [county's] school system is under the control of the state," he explained, "and we have received no instructions to prepare any plans." The Baltimore Board of School Commissioners, in contrast, was sufficiently free of state control to proceed with desegregation after the May 17 decision, even though the Maryland attorney general had said that state segregation laws were still in effect and the state board of education had declared that "no program of integration can be put into effect until the decision of the Supreme Court becomes final and an effective date is set by the Supreme Court."

In the states most determined to maintain segregation, city boards could not desegregate, even if they so desired. The Norfolk board is a case in point. Its members indicated in July 1955 a willingness to comply with the Supreme Court's decision, but subsequently Virginia enacted a law that would deprive a desegregated school system of all state financial support. "Faced with this dilemma," U. S. District Judge Walter E. Hoffman said in the case of *Beckett* v. *School Board of the City of Norfolk,* "the division superintendent and the able and intelligent members of the school board are at a loss as to how to proceed."

RACE AND JOBS

Another factor of urban life that could have bearing on school desegregation is the equal status of white and Negro workers existing in some fields of employment as color lines have broken down. It does not follow that because men work together, they are ready to have their children go to school together. But as both white and Negro families have moved from farms to manufacturing centers, their breadwinners have entered into new relationships.

The Tuskegee Institute's annual reports and the Southern Regional Council's Loth-Fleming booklet on *Integration North and South* list many changes: The upgrading of Negro employes to formerly white-only positions in the major oil refining companies in the Gulf Coast region, the merger of white and Negro carpenters in Miami and white and Negro garment workers in Atlanta, the hiring of Negro clerks and office help by white firms in St. Louis and Kansas City, and the use of Negro saleswomen in Dallas, Negro insurance agents in Jacksonville, Negro airline clerks and bus drivers in Tulsa and a Negro mathematician in an aircraft plant at Marietta, Georgia.

Public agencies have furthered the movement. The Post Office Department during 1956 made appointments or increased Negro personnel in Birmingham, Mobile, Houston, Dallas, Knoxville, Memphis, Atlanta, Columbus, Tallahassee and Baton Rouge. Atomic energy plants have provided an increasingly wide range of jobs for Negroes at Oak Ridge, Tennessee; Paducah, Kentucky, and the Savannah River project near Aiken, South Carolina. Military installations, the Federal Reserve Bank, Internal Revenue Service and Social Security offices have all to some extent blurred the lines between white and Negro jobs.

More than 140 southern cities now have Negro policemen. Many patrol only Negro areas, but Negroes directing downtown traffic are a common sight in Chattanooga; and Charlotte, North Carolina, promoted a Negro to sergeant in 1956 with authority to arrest anyone, white or Negro, in his jurisdiction. Negro firemen have also been hired, the pattern varying from an all-Negro fire station in Winston-Salem to one with six white and six Negro firemen in Tulsa.

Segregation bars likewise have been lowered at some public facilities and on some public transportation lines. At least 18 cities in seven states voluntarily conformed to the anti-segregation ruling on interstate trains and buses and in waiting rooms, while Georgia, Mississippi and Louisiana moved in the opposite direction with new laws. Segregated seating has been dropped on local buses in such southern cities as Durham and Greensboro, North Carolina; Dallas and El Paso, Texas; and Richmond, Norfolk and Portsmouth, Virginia. Negroes have been admitted, often under court orders, to golf courses in Nashville, Atlanta, Asheville, Louisville, Winston-Salem, Miami Beach, Houston, Dallas and Fort Worth; to swimming pools in Oklahoma City, San Antonio, St. Louis, Kansas City, Corpus Christi, Baltimore and Washington; to formerly white parks in Tulsa, Knoxville and Austin.

The changes have not been universal. Far from it. Negroes in Mississippi's capital city of Jackson circulated petitions in 1957, asking that members of their race be hired as policemen, firemen and city bus drivers. They got a prompt turndown. And one form of mixing does not necessarily foreshadow another. Baltimore hotels, for example, until recently resisted heavy pressure to admit Negro guests, yet city schools were integrated in 1954. Conversely, schools remain

segregated in Miami, Dallas and Houston, yet some hotels in those
cities admit Negro convention delegates. In some cities with a vener-
able record of racial amity it has become more difficult to conduct
joint civic meetings, especially where food is served, and a lapse in interracial communication is noticeable. Many believe this situation
came about after 1954.

HELP FROM THE COMMUNITY

A third factor of urban life that could make desegregation less
difficult in cities than in rural areas is the presence in many instances
of groups working for the promotion of racial harmony or improvement of the status of Negroes. Rural areas are not without ministers,
for example, who are ready to rise to a community crisis, as was
shown in Clinton, Tennessee. Conversely, ministers in some big cities
of the Deep South have spoken from their pulpits in defense of segregation. But it is in the cities that one finds an Urban League, or a
Council on Human Relations, or Protestant or Catholic social action
committees or interracial ministerial groups or such agencies as the
Greater Memphis Race Relations Committee, Nashville's Community
Relations Conference, the People's Defense League in New Orleans,
and the Oklahoma City Citizens' Action Committee.

In the June 6, 1955 memorandum from Dr. Omer Carmichael to
the Louisville Board of Education, on which the latter's desegregation decision was based, the school superintendent described efforts
to create a favorable climate for the change and said: "Ministers and
their churches, parent-teacher associations and their officers, clubs
and other organizations and their leaders, and many interested individuals are helping in carefully planned programs and in many other
ways."

Another example is St. Louis. Reviewing the first year of integration there, Superintendent of Public Instruction Philip J. Hickey emphasized the community readiness that had been built up prior to the
desegregation decision: "A significant fact . . . is that while a segregated pattern prevailed in a number of aspects of city life, the responsible opinion-forming and leadership organizations had during the
preceding 10 years become convinced of the need for changing that
pattern, and were increasingly active and articulate in implementing
that conviction . . . Immediately upon announcement of the [school

board's] decision, practically all of the leadership and opinion-forming organizations communicated with the board of education, urging
it to proceed with integration and pledging their cooperation."

The reverse situation develops when the organized aid is withheld.
Chattanooga school board members, in explaining their retreat from
early compliance, said privately that they had expected opposition,
but what took them aback was the lack of support, however reluctant,
from people whom they had considered or expected to be willing to
accept desegregation.

THE RESIDENTIAL PATTERN

A fourth and final factor of urban life that affects compliance is
the amount of residential segregation in many cities. In rural areas,
where consolidated schools draw pupils from wide areas containing
both white and Negro families, desegregation could mean considerable mixing and possible placement of white children in minority situations. In many large cities, however, schools serve immediate neighborhoods that are either white or Negro, or predominantly one or the
other, and their enrollments would not be changed substantially unless they were located in fringe areas or unless their neighborhoods
changed. For this reason, cities have proved to be exceptions to the
general impression that the higher the percentage of Negroes in a
given area, the greater the problems of desegregation.

Exceptions come quickly to mind. In New Orleans, only half a
dozen of the present white schools are without at least a few Negro
children living nearby. The same patchwork housing pattern prevails
in Jackson and other cities in Mississippi, where only the smaller communities observe strict residential segregation. In Louisville, the residential pattern was such that desegregation resulted in mixed classes
at 55 out of a total of 75 schools. And as other southern cities begin
desegregation studies, it may be found that some of them, too, have
little segregation by residential areas.

Nevertheless, residential segregation is common in many cities, and
its effect on desegregation of schools in some of them has already
been demonstrated. Baltimore's Negroes are concentrated mainly
around the heart of the city and in the northwest section. Given the
opportunity to attend the school of their choice in the fall of 1954,
97 per cent of the Negro pupils continued to attend the Negro schools

in their own neighborhoods. Mixed classes occurred mainly in schools serving fringe or changing areas. The mixing has increased as a growing Negro population has expanded into formerly all-white sections, but in the third year of desegregation only 14 per cent of the Negro pupils were in formerly all-white schools.

Negroes in Oklahoma City live for the most part on the east side. Two years of desegregation produced mixing in only 10 schools, located almost entirely in fringe areas. Less than 7 per cent of the city's white school pupils and about 15 per cent of the Negro pupils were affected. Tulsa's Negroes live in the near northeast section of the city. Only 110 of that city's 4,500 Negro pupils were enrolled at formerly all-white schools in the second year of desegregation. St. Louis and Kansas City likewise have concentrated Negro residential areas, with the result that most of the mixed classes have occurred at schools serving borderline neighborhoods.

Residential segregation exists in Newport News to the extent that U. S. District Judge Walter E. Hoffman in the *Atkins* case said that only one white school would be "vitally affected" if segregation were dropped. In the Norfolk case, previously mentioned, Judge Hoffman said, "There will undoubtedly be some mixing of the races" in secondary schools, but he quoted the testimony of the school superintendent that "the percentage of white to colored children would probably be in excess of 20 to 1 in schools now occupied by white children."

A school population study in Dade County (Miami), Florida, showed that 87 per cent of the Negro school children lived in two Negro residential districts. Just two presently white schools had a preponderance of Negroes in their districts. Charlotte's Negro population also lives in a well defined geographic area. Winston-Salem is much the same, except for several small pockets of Negro residences that might find some Negro children close to white schools, if desegregation were adopted. Raleigh likewise has its primarily Negro residential areas, with the customary overlapping at the borders. But Raleigh is an exception to the general Negro metropolitan trend in that its 26 per cent Negro population recorded in 1950 is expected to be down to 22 per cent in 1960.

In Richmond, where Negro residential areas have been expanding rapidly as young white families have taken to the suburbs, most of the schools, if desegregated, would continue to serve segregated neighborhoods. One of the city's two white high schools, however, has Negroes all around it, and one white junior high school is on the dividing line between white and Negro residences.

The residential distribution in Houston is such that school people anticipate that all presently employed Negro teachers could be used, in the event of desegregation, in predominantly Negro or all-Negro schools. Little Rock's Negroes live mainly on the east side of the city, where a new high school was built for them in 1956. Desegregation was scheduled to start at the high school level in Little Rock upon the completion in the fall of 1957 of a new west side high school. Under integration, the east side school was expected to remain practically all-Negro, and the west side school practically all-white, with possibly some mixing at the centrally located third high school.

CALLING THE ROLL

Baltimore Began It

The first city to announce a definite desegregation program was Baltimore on June 10, 1954—less than a month after the original Supreme Court decision. Washington had declared its intentions before Baltimore, but its desegregation timetable was not established until two weeks after the Baltimore program was adopted. When Baltimore began integrating, it had more than 55,000 Negro school children, a figure below Washington's but well above the total in either Kentucky or Oklahoma. Negro pupils in Baltimore represented 39 per cent of the school population, a figure which exceeded the Negro pupil percentage in Alabama (34.7 per cent), Georgia (32.3 per cent) and all other southern states except South Carolina (42.7 per cent) and Mississippi (48 per cent).

The Baltimore program was the simplest yet devised. Not having any school districting, the school board merely continued its policy of allowing children to go to the schools of their choice and dropped all racial distinctions. The free-choice policy produced a minimum of mixing in the first year. Even in the third year, with 80 schools reporting some mixed classes, only 30 of them had 10 per cent or higher Negro enrollment in what had been all-white student bodies. Thirty-four schools remained all-white, and 53 all-Negro. Except for a localized outbreak of picketing and demonstrations in the fall of 1954, Baltimore's desegregation has proceeded without incident.

Checklist

Louisville's program included the most elaborate preparations to date. With 34,000 white and 12,000 Negro pupils involved, Louisville completely redistricted its school system prior to the 1956-57 semester "without gerrymandering and without regard to race," and then, through a card file of each elementary and junior high pupil, carried out a "free choice" assignment policy that allowed parents to request transfers if their children were assigned to schools which had been serving "the other race." While some adjustments had to be made for white children assigned to predominantly Negro schools, and Negroes assigned to predominantly white schools, a large majority of parents accepted the initial assignments, and mixing in 73 per cent of Louisville's schools got off to a calm start.

Oklahoma City, with 8,812 Negro pupils representing about 15 per cent of its school population, announced a month prior to the opening of school in September 1955 that an integration policy had been adopted and that a single, new set of school attendance areas would replace the former dual districting set up.

In St. Louis, where about 32,000 Negro children represented 35 per cent of the school population, the school board announced its desegregation plans about a month after the 1954 Supreme Court decision. At both the high school level in February 1955 and in the elementary schools the following fall, the school system reflected the residential pattern, with considerable mixing taking place in those neighborhoods where Negro families rapidly were replacing suburban-bound white families. By the fall of 1956 there were 37 former white elementary schools with Negro enrollments ranging from less than 1 per cent up to 56 per cent, and 13 former Negro elementary schools where white attendance ranged from 18 per cent down to less than 1 per cent. Forty-six elementary schools remained all-white, and 27 all-Negro. Six mixed high schools had from 1 to 30 per cent Negro pupils, one high school remained all-white and two all-Negro.

Kansas City in September 1955 ended an 88-year tradition of school segregation for its 10,000 Negro children, representing 16 per cent of the school population. As in St. Louis, school statistics are no longer kept on a racial basis, so the actual number of children in mixed classes is not known. The same general pattern prevails in both cities. The closest thing to trouble in either city occurred in the spring of 1956 when some white and Negro boys in Kansas City got into a fight that caused a flareup of racial feelings at one high school and a threat of a student strike, which never materialized.

In San Antonio, Texas, desegregation began on a modest scale for some 5,000 Negro pupils in September 1955. There are 93,000 school children all told in San Antonio, with many more Latin-Americans than Negroes. In the first year about 400 Negro children entered 19 elementary, 10 junior high and seven senior high schools formerly restricted to whites. Ten white pupils enrolled at two formerly Negro schools.

Considerably fewer Negroes were involved when Austin, Texas, decided to desegregate its high schools in September 1955. Only 50 Negro high school students lived within the three white high school districts. Given the opportunity to attend the white schools, 13 made the shift in the first year, without incident, and in the second year the number rose to 24.

Two to Make Ready

The two mid-South cities scheduled to begin desegregation in the fall of 1957—Nashville and Little Rock—were both located in states where desegregation in rural areas had met with opposition, and both had proportionately large Negro populations. More than a third of Nashville's school pupils were Negro (17,200 white, 10,000 Negro), and about one-fourth of Little Rock's (13,000 white, 4,440 Negro). Both, too, had indicated shortly after the Supreme Court's final decree in mid-1955 that they intended to work toward compliance. And both thereafter were subject to Negro suits; Nashville in the fall of 1955 and Little Rock the following February.

Nashville's plan for beginning desegregation in the first grade was given court approval on the condition that a timetable for action on all remaining grades be submitted by December 31, 1957. The heart of the approved approach was a transfer policy, similar to Louisville's, that permitted a pupil to transfer out of an assigned school if previously that school had served only children of the other race or if the majority of those attending the school were of the other race. Little Rock's court-approved program, which called for desegregating all three grades of senior high schools in the first year, was similar to Baltimore's voluntary desegregation in that students were to stay in their present schools or transfer of their own volition.

Under Orders

New Orleans also was under court order to desegregate, but at no specific time. The Fifth Circuit Court of Appeals in March 1957 upheld a lower court ruling that New Orleans must end segregation, but "not overnight, or even in a year or more." Both Norfolk and Newport News, as previously mentioned, had been told by their district court to begin compliance by the fall of 1957, but state laws prevented any move.

Houston, Texas, with 82,373 white and 24,537 Negro pupils, had a suit filed against its predominantly pro-segregation school board in February 1957 after prolonged desegregation studies had produced no program. The school board president said at the time that she hoped the courts would permit delay "at least until 1959, when the present school building program is expected to be completed."

In Dallas, where 15 per cent of 119,000 pupils are Negroes, a suit was dismissed in December 1956 in order to give the board "ample time" to work out desegregation problems. The Dallas school board, which had initiated desegregation studies in July 1955, contended in reply to the suit that immediate integration would result in "chaos and confusion." In mid-1957 the Fifth Circuit Court overruled the district court and ordered desegregation to proceed but without a time limit.

Under Study

In Atlanta, where one-third of about 100,000 school pupils were Negroes, the school board set itself up as a committee of the whole in July 1955 to study desegregation problems and appointed a professional research staff to bring in a report. No report has been published. It was estimated at the time that desegregation would cost the city $3,600,000 in state aid.

The Mobile, Alabama, school board also said back in 1955, before segregationist sentiments became a solid front, that it would study desegregation and added an assurance that it would "work toward compliance with the Supreme Court decision." So did the school boards of Asheville and Charlotte, North Carolina, at about the same time. Concurrently, Winston-Salem appointed a biracial citizens' desegregation study group. And a year previously, the Greensboro, North Carolina, school board had said that it was going to make a study.*

The Knoxville, Tennessee, school board was another that announced, in the months immediately following the Supreme Court's final decree, that it was studying methods of complying with the decree, but after that the board turned down Negro requests for admission to white schools. A suit was filed early in 1957 against the school system, which had a one-sixth Negro enrollment. The Chattanooga board first announced a readiness to comply and then postponed action in the face of community opposition. Memphis has made no overt moves toward desegregation, and credits an excellent separate-but-equal system of white and Negro schools for the absence of Negro integration pressure.

Under No Circumstances

Desegregation petitions filed by Negroes during 1955 in five Mississippi cities, Jackson, Vicksburg, Natchez, Yazoo City and Clarksdale, were simply ignored, and no petitions have since been made. Governor J. P. Coleman summed up the situation there in February 1956 when he said, "Mississippi will close any white public school or college forced by the courts to accept a Negro student."

In Baton Rouge the parish school board pledged itself in August 1955 to maintain segregation, and that same month the Chatham County (Savannah), Georgia school board unanimously passed a similar resolution. The following month Birmingham's school principals were notified that racial segregation would be continued. Since then the silence of other deep southern cities on the subject of compliance has spoken louder than resolutions.

ONE OF THREE—OR MORE

Thirty-three cities in states that had statutory segregation in 1954, plus Washington, D.C., are represented among the first 100 cities with

---

* In simultaneous meetings on the night of July 23, school boards in Charlotte, Greensboro and Winston-Salem announced enrollment of 12 Negro applicants to previously all-white schools. Charlotte accepted six; Greensboro, five; and Winston-Salem, one. All transfers were authorized under the state's Pupil Assignment Act. The remainder of some 40 Negro students in the three cities who had applied for transfer were rejected, mainly on geographical grounds. —Editor

standard metropolitan areas. Schools in 13 of these cities have begun or accomplished the desegregation process. Schools in three of them are under court order to desegregate at a specified time. Two have announced voluntary desegregation. All the rest are rigidly segregated.

Together, these cities with metropolitan areas account for nearly one-third of the population of the 17 southern and border states, Washington included. Their influence is heavy in their respective states. Rural and urban-rural school districts in their areas have been, and can be, profoundly affected by what they do. Some schoolmen in Texas, for example, say that many Texas districts are watching to see which way Dallas will jump.

Thus the city limits sign is a major marker on the southern horizon. Perhaps we are not *all* going to town. But for one out of three southerners and border residents—and perhaps many more—the issue has been joined.

6.

The Deep South

BY W. D. WORKMAN, JR.

Stretching across the face of the southeastern United States is a vast crescent which swings southwestward from Virginia through the Carolinas and Georgia into Alabama, Mississippi and Louisiana, with a tentacle extending into Florida. Though some would exclude Virginia and North Carolina, this in largest part is the Deep South—the storied land of "moonlight and magnolias," about which fiction is more readily believed than fact by those who do not know the land.

This is also the land (and this IS fact) where racial mores are most firmly rooted, where racial separation is most firmly entrenched in the popular thinking of the white majority and in political practice, and where desegregation of the public schools is meeting its strongest resistance. In the Deep South, the phrase "with all deliberate speed" finds the deliberation all aimed in the opposite direction—away from desegregation.

These are what the National Association for the Advancement of Colored People calls the "recalcitrant" states. In the full three years following the May 17, 1954, decision of the U. S. Supreme Court, not one Negro child had been admitted to a public school in Alabama, Florida, Georgia, Louisiana, Mississippi, North Carolina, South Carolina or Virginia. Furthermore, even in the face of insistent Federal court pressure in several of those states, notably those on the extremities of the crescent—Virginia and Louisiana—there is as yet no official hint of capitulation or voluntary compliance with desegregation directives.*

Things in Common

What have these states in common besides a manifest determination to preserve racial separation in their public schools? For one thing, they have the highest incidence of Negro population in the nation, a factor which is measurably linked with white resistance to desegregation. From the Chesapeake Bay to the Mississippi, Negroes are distributed in numbers which sometimes account for as much as 70 to 80 per cent of the total population of a county, although there are counties in Alabama, Georgia, North Carolina and Virginia with less than 1 per cent Negro populations—in the uplands or the highlands. In terms of overall state population, Negroes make up anywhere from 22 per cent to 45 per cent. In terms of school population, the Negro percentages are still higher, reflecting in part the out-migration of adult Negroes from the South. Simple arithmetic discloses that, in hundreds upon hundreds of Deep South communities, desegregation does not involve the admission of Negroes to white schools so much as it does the assignment of white children to Negro schools. That single consideration is to a large degree responsible for the repeal, either outright or conditionally, of compulsory school attendance laws in many of the states in the region.

These eight states have other characteristics in common. They all have an identity with the former Confederacy, and in varying degree with the "states' rights" philosophy of government which contributed to and endured through the War Between the States. They have a common Anglo-Saxon heritage, save perhaps for the French influence in Louisiana. Here also are more vestigial remnants of frontier thinking than probably exist in any other single section of the country, not excepting the West. The aftermath of the Civil War restored frontier conditions which, in vast areas of the South, influenced the thinking of southerners, and have persisted into present-day attitudes in the South.

And always to be considered is the fact that here flourished the

---

* Three North Carolina communities admitted a total of 12 Negro pupils to formerly all-white schools in school board actions July 23. See footnote to Chapter Five.—Editor

institution of slavery. Where slavery was strongest during its heyday, so are segregation sensibilities most acute today. The so-called "plantation culture" was only a part of the total picture (less than one-fourth of white southerners had any slaves at all), but racial consciousness spread effectively far beyond the actual lands which lent themselves to profitable cultivation by slave labor.

Through the years, the relationship of white man to black man historically evolved from one of owner-and-slave into one of master-and-servant, and gradually, in some places almost imperceptibly, into man-to-man. Yet even where the greatest strides had been taken in that direction, the Deep South was not prepared, mentally or physically, for any overthrow, voluntary or involuntary, of its pattern of racial separation in numerous institutions, notably that of the public school system.

Regional Attitudes

The "why" of the white attitude involves value judgments which it is our purpose to avoid. However, the record is full of expressions which can be taken—or left—as representation, or explanation, of a regional state of mind. For example, writing before a national audience in the January 1956 issue of *Harper's* magazine, Thomas R. Waring, editor of the *Charleston* (S.C.) *News and Courier,* said:

Southerners believe they have valid reasons, aside from "prejudice" about the color of skin, for their insistence on sending white children to exclusively white schools. Without debating superiority of either race, they are keenly aware of cultural differences.

"Volumes could be written on racial differences from many angles," Waring went on to say, "including anthropology and sociology." He summarized "five of the differences that most immediately come to the minds of white parents in the South."

They were:

Health. "The incidence of venereal disease for instance is much greater among Negroes than among whites."

Home environment. "The master and servant, or boss and laborer, relationship between whites and Negroes is still the rule rather than the exception."

Marital habits. "On the average one southern Negro child in five is illegitimate . . . Many white persons believe that morals among their own race are lax enough as it is, without exposing their children to an even more primitive view of sex habits."

Crime. "For many years, crime in the South has been more prevalent among Negroes than among white people."

Intellectual development. "For whatever the reason may be, southern Negroes usually are below the intellectual level of their white counterparts. . . . Few southern parents are willing to sacrifice their own offspring in order to level off intellectual differences . . ."

The obverse of this representation, or explanation, might be found in an article which the late Charles S. Johnson, president of Fisk University, wrote for *The New York Times Magazine* in September 1956. He said:

The present-day Southern Negro does not share the belief of the Southern white that he is inferior as a human being, even though he may earn lower wages and have fewer years of schooling . . . What is for white Southerners most difficult to understand, in these days, is the absence of both the belief in inferiority and the simulation of this belief.

Discussing white southern organizations and legislative bodies which actively oppose desegregation, Dr. Johnson wrote: "The reasons they give for insisting on racial segregation are defined as sociological and cultural, rather than moral or ethical or even humane. No Southern white opinion, respectable or otherwise, has, in the past half century, seriously ventured a moral or ethical or humane justification of the Southern way of life."

Johnson also argued:

The Southern Negro viewpoint is more broadly national than regional. There are very few, if any, Southern Negroes who do not want full American citizenship, even though there are undoubtedly those who, if they had it, would make no better use of it than some of their white counterparts. In philosophy the Southern Negro identification is with the nation and not with the Southern region, which is, in spirit, separatist.

Whatever these points of view explain or represent in the understanding of southern attitudes, the states which are the concern of this chapter are deeply conscious of their racial makeup. It is distinctive. The 1950 census gave these figures on Negro percentages of the total population in each of the states:

Alabama .... 32.1 per cent
Florida .... 22.3 per cent
Georgia .... 30.0 per cent
Louisiana .... 32.9 per cent
Mississippi .... 45.4 per cent
North Carolina .... 25.8 per cent
South Carolina .... 38.8 per cent
Virginia .... 22.1 per cent

Long before the Supreme Court decision of 1954 this pattern had exercised an influence on the physical equipment of southern schooling, though perhaps the trend then appearing was conditioned by expectations that the courts would at most demand something more in the way of "equality" than the South had been providing.

THE DRIVE FOR EQUALIZATION

In several states, school building programs were under way in an effort to bring white and Negro schools into substantial physical equality. In others, such programs were just then in the formative stage. And in a few states, there had been little change in the traditional pattern which accented the white schools in the state educational establishment. But nowhere in the broad sweep from Louisiana to Virginia was there an attitude of readiness on the part of state governments to accept any attempt to desegregate the public schools, whether by Federal direction or otherwise.

Georgia and South Carolina had already shown they were determined to preserve segregation. Along with Georgia's school equalization program, begun in 1951, there went into the general appropriations acts statements to the effect that state aid would be automatically stopped for any school that integrated white and Negro students.

South Carolina had gone a step further by removing from its constitution a requirement that the state provide for "a liberal system of free public schools." The removal of that provision was sought by the legislature and by Governor James F. Byrnes so as to free the hands of the legislature to cope promptly with any situation which might grow out of Federal court directives aimed at desegregation. The people of the state voted two-to-one in a 1952 referendum in favor of removing the constitutional requirement, and the General Assembly ratified that action in March of 1954—waiting until time for such action was about to run out, in hopes that the Supreme Court might sustain the right of states to maintain separate schools if they saw fit.

The repeal of the constitutional requirement for free public schools had no effect on the school establishment then or later, but it did leave school matters subject to statutory rather than constitutional change. Meanwhile, South Carolina continued with its ambitious program of school equalization and expansion, financed by a 3 per cent sales tax initiated in 1951. Since 1951 the state has spent or approved for school construction the sum of $174,617,124—51.4 per cent of this for Negro schools. Initial expenditures under this program went 75 per cent or better to Negro projects. Negroes make up 42.3 per cent of South Carolina's school population.

Mississippi and other states were moving forward (and still are) with extensive school equalization programs. The 1955 Mississippi legislature authorized $120 million for school physical equalization over a period of years. By April 1957 more than $13 million worth of school construction had been authorized by the Educational Finance Commission, 80 per cent of this for Negro buildings. Florida already was ahead of most southern states in this respect with a minimum foundation program which dated back to 1947. In November 1955 *Southern School News* estimated that $2,556,500,000 had been spent or appropriated for new school construction in 16 states and the District of Columbia since 1949 (save in Florida and Louisiana, which began their programs earlier).

Teacher Salaries

A trend toward equalization of white and Negro teachers' salaries had been evident for some time and continued after the Court decision. In 1953-54 Mississippi paid its white teachers on the average $2,609 a year and its Negro teachers $1,244 a year. In 1954-55 whites received $2,760 a year and Negroes received $2,010.

In some states of the Deep South, Negro teachers actually are receiving more than white teachers—because of higher accreditation for reason of additional degrees earned or lengthier teaching experience. Here is a comparison of teacher salaries in the eight states (excepting the Mississippi figures above and those for South Carolina, which has no breakdown) for the most recent periods available:

State	White	Negro
Alabama	$3,289	$3,283
Florida	(Maximum for both: $4,150)	
Georgia	3,183	3,002
Louisiana	3,635	3,206
North Carolina	3,170	3,275
Virginia	3,280	3,340

But everywhere in the region in 1954 there was official and unofficial apprehension among white leaders over what action the Supreme Court would take in the pending school desegregation suits. In Alabama, for example, there had been discussion since 1953 of the feasibility of establishing a system of "free and private" schools which could be kept on a racially segregated basis.

DECISION DAY

When the decision came, South Carolina's Governor Byrnes, himself a former justice of the U. S. Supreme Court, was "shocked" by it. North Carolina's governor, the late William B. Umstead, was "terribly disappointed." Governor Herman E. Talmadge of Georgia said flatly that his state would not accept racially-mixed schools.

Yet even as southern political leaders registered their displeasure with the Supreme Court decision, they counseled moderation on the part of white and Negro citizens alike. South Carolinians of both races were urged by Governor Byrnes "to exercise restraint and preserve order." Virginia's Governor Thomas B. Stanley wanted the decision to be received "calmly" and Virginians to "take time to carefully and dispassionately consider the situation before coming to conclusions on steps which should be taken." Even so, there were few indications that the Deep South would move toward compliance, although there was less outright defiance of the Court decision at this juncture than was to appear visibly in the months ahead.

From Virginia came this statement from the late State Superintendent of Public Instruction Dowell J. Howard: "There will be no defiance of the Supreme Court decision as far as I am concerned. We are trying to teach school children the law of the land and we will abide by it." In North Carolina, the school board of the City of Greensboro by a vote of six to one directed a study of how to comply with the Supreme Court's directive. The board chairman said: "We must not fight or attempt to circumvent this decision."

As southern political and educational leaders took stock of the situation, however, their resistance stiffened, measurably reflecting the articulate determination voiced by most of the white public throughout the region to stave off any mixing of the races. Even in Greensboro, there was a reassessment of the school board's position and a slackening in what had seemed a movement in the direction of reasonably prompt compliance.

Alabama's state board of education clarified the situation in that state by declaring that there would be no changes in the segregated pattern of schools during the coming (1954-55) school year, "irrespective of any action by any court in any case in which a unit of the public school system of Alabama is not a party." In Florida, the quasi-public Continuing Education Council agreed to do everything legally possible to put off integration. The Virginia state board of education said that segregation would be continued during the ensuing school year.

Biracial Approach?

Meanwhile, officials of the National Association for the Advancement of Colored People and Negro spokesmen acclaimed the Supreme Court decision and sought to fit themselves into the machinery which they hoped would implement the decision. They met a virtually solid front of white opposition, broken only here and there by the admission of Negro leaders to planning or study groups. In North Carolina, for example, the 19-member committee created by Governor Umstead to study the school segregation situation included three Negroes. (This was the Pearsall Committee, headed by former House Speaker Thomas J. Pearsall, of Rocky Mount.)

Four Negro leaders of Virginia met with Governor Stanley the week following the Supreme Court decision and asked that Virginia take the lead in moving the South toward integrated schools. The Governor had stated on May 17 that the views of leaders of both races would be sought in studying possible courses of action. In August, however, Governor Stanley named a bi-partisan commission of legislators (who are all white in Virginia) to study the problem and make recommendations to him and to the next General Assembly.

In Mississippi, Governor Hugh White called a sizable biracial meeting on July 30, with some 90 Negroes in attendance, to determine the attitude toward a suggested voluntary program of "segregation by choice." Hopes for Negro acquiescence in such a plan were doused when only one of the Negroes spoke out for the voluntary plan. One other suggested that emphasis be placed more on equalizing facilities than on any early efforts toward integration, but the vast majority of the Negroes seemed to favor the "strict observance of the Supreme Court's integration order," as it was put by Dr. T. R. M. Howard, president of the Mississippi Regional Council of Negro Leadership. The failure of the biracial group to reach a meeting of minds on voluntary segregation brought adjournment of the meeting, and Governor White called together the Legal Educational Advisory Committee created by the 1954 legislature prior to the Supreme Court's decision. That committee urged the governor to call a special legislative session for consideration of a "last resort" amendment to the constitution, one which would permit the abolishment of the public school system.

In South Carolina, where the constitutional requirement for a public school system already had been repealed, neither Governor Byrnes nor the re-activated Gressette Committee (a 15-man segregation study group created in 1951) considered it necessary to call a special legislative session. The governor, however, with the concurrence of the state's Educational Finance Commission, did call a temporary halt to the allocation of school construction funds until the entire situation could be reviewed. Shortly thereafter, the allocation of funds was resumed, and the building program was continued virtually without interruption.

Meanwhile, there was no effort on the state level to bring any NAACP leaders into consultation concerning South Carolina's future course with respect to public schools in the state. Some NAACP officials did appear before the Gressette Committee, and there were discussions on the local level in some communities about the state. However, there was no response to a suggestion from State NAACP President James M. Hinton that the leaders of both races "sit down and work out plans." One contributing factor to this situation was the unrelieved hostility shown by NAACP spokesmen to the school equalization program launched in 1951, and (earlier) to the establishment of a separate law school for Negroes at South Carolina State College, at Orangeburg.

In Florida, the NAACP announced shortly after the Supreme Court's decision that a test case would be initiated to force admission of Negro students to white schools in the coming school year, but two days after that announcement came another statement saying that no drastic action was planned and that the organization would strive for "social transition without social disorganization."

Perhaps the most prophetic action taken anywhere in the Deep South on the heels of the desegregation decision occurred in Louisiana, the only southern state to have a legislature in session at the time of the decision. The first reaction of the Louisiana legislature was to adopt a resolution censuring the Supreme Court for its "usurpation of power."

PATTERN OF OPPOSITION

Thereafter came a flurry of legislation by which the Louisiana legislature sought to erect other barriers against school desegregation. Later on, as other Deep South legislatures met, they too drafted statutes and constitutional amendments designed to safeguard racial segregation in their respective states. There were differences in approach throughout the region, but in general the evolving pattern was based largely on these premises:

1. That state funds be withheld from schools which accepted students of both races, whether by court order or otherwise.

2. That local school boards and administrators be given virtually plenary power over the assignment and transfer of students.

3. That the "police powers" of the state could be invoked for the public interest in enforcing racial separation on grounds of protecting the health, morals, peace and good order of the individual communities.

On an even more fundamental note, an increasing number of Deep South states began laying the ground work for possible abandonment of the public school system and the substitution in its place of a system whereby tuition could be paid individual students from state funds. Nowhere was this actually done, but in state after state the way was prepared for such a "last resort."

In one state (South Carolina) the resistance to any integration took the form of double-edged legislation aimed at turning any attack on white schools into an automatic thrust at Negro schools. This was done by statutes requiring that state aid be shut off not only from the white school to which a student might be ordered admitted, but from the Negro school from which the pupil might be transferred. Similarly, if any of the state's white colleges were closed to forestall integration, the state-supported Negro college also would be closed.

At the Polls

South Carolina's manifest determination to close its public schools rather than to open them for racial mixing is not peculiar to that state, but reflects a demonstrable conviction on the part of most of the states of the Deep South. Statements to that effect by public officials have drawn criticism from proponents of integration as being mere political bombast, and yet in every instance where the general public has been given opportunity to vote on the question, the strong determination to resist desegregation even to the point of closing the schools has been borne out. Here is a roll-call of states which have voted on that, or related questions directly concerned with maintaining segregation:

South Carolina. In November of 1952, by a vote of 187,345 to 91,823, South Carolinians approved the repeal of a constitutional section requiring the General Assembly to provide for a "liberal system of free public schools," thereby clearing the way for the legislature to alter or even abandon the public school system if the situation warranted.

Georgia. In November of 1954, by a vote of 210,488 to 181,148, Georgians approved a constitutional amendment permitting the operation of a "private school" system, supported by tuition grants of public funds, in the event the General Assembly saw fit to shut down the public schools.

Louisiana. In November of 1954, by a vote of 217,992 to 46,929, Louisianans endorsed a constitutional amendment to permit the state to use its police powers to maintain segregated schools.

Mississippi. In December of 1954, by a vote of 106,832 to 46,095, Mississippians voted to give the legislature authority to close the schools rather than submit to their desegregation.

Virginia. In January of 1956, by a vote of 304,154 to 146,164, Virginians approved the calling of a constitutional convention to permit the use of public funds as tuition grants to children attending private schools.

Alabama. In August of 1956, by a vote of 128,545 to 80,777, Alabamans endorsed a constitutional amendment giving the legislature authority to withdraw state aid from and, if considered necessary, dispose of any public school confronted with enforced integration of the races.

North Carolina. In September of 1956, by a vote of 471,657 to 101,767, North Carolinians approved enactment of legislation (amending the constitution) which would authorize state-paid tuition grants to children who would not attend mixed schools, and which would permit the closing of local schools, by election, if necessary to avoid "intolerable" situations.

INTERPOSITION

Florida alone of the Deep South states has thus far had no statewide referendum on segregation. But the Florida legislature, in April of 1957, followed the lead of seven other resistance states in adopting a so-called "interposition" resolution, doing so in the face of prior opposition and subsequent denunciation by Governor LeRoy Collins.

Florida already had protested the Supreme Court decision with a concurrent resolution of August 1, 1956, "denouncing the usurpation of power by the Supreme Court of the United States and demanding preservation of our inherent rights." That earlier resolution, which made out a bill of particulars against the Supreme Court for its "unwarranted and unauthorized acts of invasion of the powers reserved to the states and to the people," gained Governor Collins' signature. The resolution of April 1957, however, not only failed to get his signature (as a resolution, it did not have to get it), but drew his ire, as well.

What apparently distressed Governor Collins so much was the latter resolution's declaration that the Supreme Court decision in the school desegregation cases was null and void, and of no effect in the State of Florida. In the Governor's view, "the resolution is on its face a lie . . . a gesture of defiance."

Florida's declaration was no more defiant than those of several of the other Deep South states. Virginia, which led the movement for interposition, both in advocacy and in enactment of legislation proclaiming the doctrine, borrowed from the language of the Kentucky-

Virginia resolutions of 1798 and said that the Supreme Court of 1954 was guilty of "a deliberate, palpable, and dangerous attempt . . . to usurp the amendatory power that lies solely within not fewer than three-fourths of the States."

Although Virginia was the scene of the first legislative action on interposition as an identifiable doctrine, and the real well-spring of the movement, an earlier reference had cropped up in South Carolina in August of 1955. There, a statewide group of white citizens who came to be known as "The Committee of 52" issued a declaration of principles in which they urged the General Assembly of South Carolina "to take such steps as may be necessary or desirable to interpose the sovereignty of the State of South Carolina between Federal courts and local school officials with respect to any effort of such courts to usurp state authority in the matter of public education."

Catching Fire

The idea, however, did not catch fire in the South until it was expounded editorially, beginning in November of 1955, by James Jackson Kilpatrick, editor of the *Richmond News Leader*. Kilpatrick's attention had been drawn earlier to the Kentucky-Virginia interposition resolutions of 1798 by a pamphlet prepared by an attorney of Chesterfield County, Virginia—William Old, later appointed a state judge. As the editor delved deeper into the subject, he said he became convinced that the doctrine had application in the school segregation crisis, and that touched off the editorial campaign launched and sustained by the *News Leader*.

In this excerpt from a *News Leader* editorial of November 28, 1955, Kilpatrick summed up the concept of interposition to which he subscribed and for which he solicited southern (and national) support:

The right of interposition, as enunciated by Jefferson, Madison, Calhoun, Hayne, Randolph and many others, is seen historically as the States' right to interpose their sovereignty between the Federal government and the object of its encroachments upon powers reserved to the States. This right rests in the incontrovertible theory that ours is a Union of sovereign States; that the Federal government exists only by reason of a solemn compact among the States; that each respective State is a co-equal party to this compact; that if the compact is violated by the Federal government, every State has a right to judge of the infraction; and that when an issue of contested power arises, only the States themselves, by constitutional process, may finally decide the issue.

That line of reasoning drew support from other southern editors and from large numbers of public and political leaders. Within 18 months after Kilpatrick had launched his editorial campaign, all eight states of the Deep South (as well as others elsewhere) had adopted some form of what had come to be known as "resolutions of interposition or protest."

Here, in thumb-nail fashion, are reflections of the sentiments expressed by the seven states which adopted such resolutions in 1956:

Virginia. "Whenever the Federal Government attempts the deliberate, palpable, and dangerous exercise of powers not granted it, the States who are parties to the compact have the right, and are in duty bound, to interpose for arresting the progress of the evil, and for preserving the authorities, rights and liberties appertaining to them . . ."

Alabama. "[The Supreme Court decisions] are, as a matter of right, null, void, and of no effect; and the legislature of Alabama declares to all men as a matter of right, this State is not bound to abide thereby . . ."

Georgia. "It is the duty of the State in flagrant cases such as this to interpose its powers between its people and the efforts of said Court to assert an unlawful dominion over them."

South Carolina. "The State of South Carolina as a loyal and sovereign State of the Union will exercise the powers reserved to it under the Constitution to judge for itself of the infraction and to take such other legal measures as it may deem appropriate to protect its sovereignty and the rights of its people."

Mississippi. "Said decisions are in violation of the Constitutions of the United States and the State of Mississippi, and therefore, are considered unconstitutional, invalid, and of no lawful effect within the confines of the State of Mississippi."

Louisiana. "Until the usurpation herein complained of . . . be settled by legal Constitutional amendment . . . the legislature of Louisiana does hereby solemnly declare the decision of the Supreme Court . . . and any similar decisions that might be rendered in connection with the public school system and public parks and recreational facilities, insofar as such decisions may affect or apply to the sovereign State of Louisiana, to be in violation of the Constitution of the United States, and of the State of Louisiana . . ."

North Carolina. A resolution condemned "the tyrannical usurpation of power" by the U. S. Supreme Court.

THE PRESSURES

Aside from the legislative reactions to the Supreme Court decision, two other significant developments emerged in the period following May 17, 1954—developments in mutual opposition to one another. Throughout much of the Deep South, as in other southern and border states where school segregation had been in effect, the NAACP initiated informal requests, formal petitions, and, in a number of cases, lawsuits—all part of a rejuvenated drive to break through the wall of segregation.

Simultaneously, there began springing up all over the South numerous pro-segregation organizations of white citizens, dedicated to the preservation of racial separation in the public schools. In instance after instance, there was an almost predictable pattern of action and reaction: a petition or lawsuit for school integration would be filed by Negroes, whereupon opposing citizens would promptly organize a white Citizens Council, a States' Rights League, or similar group by any of a number of names which appeared in various parts of the region.

As these diametrically-opposed forces came into play, it was inevitable that pressures would be built up on both sides of the controversy. Inexorably, some of these pressures developed in the field of economy —sometimes openly, sometimes covertly, sometimes almost unconsciously. In a number of communities, white employers and businessmen registered their disapproval of integration efforts by discharging Negroes from jobs, denying them credit, or otherwise withdrawing the economic support which previously had existed without regard to racial distinctions.

The Negroes frequently banded together in a retaliatory program aimed at returning the economic pressure by way of boycott or otherwise. The school year 1955-56 seemed to be the period of greatest pressure in the economic field. Thereafter, throughout much of the Deep South, the situation resolved itself into a gradual stand-off, with the economic pressures moderating and business relations resuming some, but not all, of the prior mutuality of benefit.

Petitioners

One early manifestation of pressures in the region was the withdrawal of names from desegregation petitions. Many a Negro whose name had been signed to such a petition subsequently asked that his name be taken from the list. Some said they had misunderstood the purpose of the petition; some said they had been misled into signing; a few declared bluntly that their names had been listed without their knowledge or consent; and a number simply withdrew their names without comment.

For instance, 16 of 29 Negro signers of a school-entry petition in Dallas County, Alabama, were reported to have lost their jobs. Five withdrew their names from the petition. A Citizens Council spokesman termed the firings "spontaneous reaction" and said the Council could not accept "credit or censure."

In Moultrie District No. 2 of South Carolina's Charleston County, 13 of 124 Negro petitioners withdrew their names from a published petition. Ten claimed that their names had been fraudulently obtained and that they had thought they were petitioning for recreational facilities.

In Bullock County, Alabama, nine out of 30 Negroes asked removal of their names from a petition, claiming they didn't know what they had signed.

Boycott, Counter-boycott

In Orangeburg, South Carolina, in the aftermath of the Negro student walkout at South Carolina State College, the local NAACP reported that the organization had raised a fund of $40,000 for loans to Negroes financially distressed by denial of normal credit or other economic wants. At the same time, according to the *Charleston News and Courier*, the Citizens Councils were reported giving aid, financial and otherwise, to hard-pressed Negroes in various communities. A two-way boycott found Negroes refusing to buy products handled by Citizens Council members and segregationists refusing to buy agricultural products or services from Negroes believed sympathetic to the NAACP.

At Memphis, the NAACP and other organizations, including some northern labor unions, deposited $268,319 in the Tri-State Bank for loans to victims of economic harassment. At one time, after the Emmett Till case in Mississippi, the bank had $321,000 on deposit for loans to Mississippi Negro individuals and organizations. Meanwhile, segregationists frequently boycotted the products of firms known or alleged to have donated to the NAACP, or to have hired "too many Negroes." These boycotters asserted that they had inflicted losses of several millions of dollars on an auto maker, a brewery and a tobacco manufacturer. In some areas Negroes retaliated by boycotting white distributors of soft drinks, bread and other commodities.

DRIVE ON THE NAACP

All these developments swirled around the NAACP, which throughout all of the controversy remained the moving force behind desegregation efforts. State after state in the Deep South began to throw legislative, administrative and judicial obstacles in the way of NAACP activity, sometimes directly, sometimes indirectly. In many instances, where the issue was clear-cut, the NAACP moved into state or Federal court in an effort to safeguard its continuing identity and activity.

An interesting portrayal of the factors involved in such situations arose in South Carolina. The legislature of that state, during the 1956 session, enacted a law which flatly prohibited the employment of NAACP members by any agency of the state or its political subdivisions, including school districts. When a lawsuit was brought in Federal court to test the constitutionality of the act, it drew these divergent views from two of the three judges on the special court convened to hear the case:

Circuit Judge John J. Parker, of Charlotte—

The [NAACP] organization is engaged in activities for advancing the interests of colored people and this has involved its engaging in matters of public controversy such as the segregation cases, the results of which have been very unpopular in some sections. This, however, is no reason why it may be proscribed by law or its members denied the right of public employment. The right to join organizations which seek by lawful means to support and further what their members regard as the public interest or in the interest of a particular part of the public, is protected by the constitutional guarantees of free speech and freedom of assembly; and such right is one of the bulwarks of liberty and social progress. The fact that organizations may render themselves unpopular with the majority in a community is no reason why the majority may use its power to enact legislation denying to their members the fundamental rights of constitutional liberty.

District Judge George Bell Timmerman, of Columbia—

The statute is designed to protect young minds from the poisonous effects of NAACP propaganda. It does not, as is surmised, outlaw membership in the

NAACP. It doesn't even attempt to do so. It only prevents its members from carrying out their programs where it is deemed to be against the public interest to have them do so . . .

While the purpose of this case, in a sense, is camouflaged, it is not too well hidden. It is to secure this court's approval of the exercise of a veto over local matters . . . The Bible has been ruled out of the public schools. The fight here is to rule NAACP's theories of knowledge into them. If that is done, the government or its judges would thereby become invaders of the homes of citizens, superseding the authority and interest of parents in the rearing and training of their children. Knowing the inherent danger in such a vicious procedure, I unhesitatingly register my opposition to it: and may God protect the children of America if the courts will not and their parents cannot do so.

The particular lawsuit under discussion here seems to have been left hanging—at almost the precise moment it was appealed to the U. S. Supreme Court—by the repeal of the statute under attack. The anti-NAACP act was replaced by another which does not forbid employment of members of the NAACP or other organizations, but which does require applicants for public employment to list the names of organizations, societies and associations to which they belong. (The new law, enacted in 1957, likewise is promised a court test by the NAACP.)

'Crucial Question'

The NAACP stated its position in an instance of North Carolina litigation concerning the registration of the association as a foreign corporation doing business in the state, and as an organization seeking to influence legislation and public opinion:

"The crucial question is whether a state may deprive a group of its citizens of the right to collectively seek the attainment of full citizenship status as guaranteed by the Constitution and the decisions of the Supreme Court."

In those instances where the NAACP in a given state or community has actually been "de-activated" by official action, other organizations of similar intent have sprung up under different names. And, in other instances, some of the disbanded or suspended chapters or branches have been "adopted" by NAACP groups elsewhere in the South and nation.

TEACHER'S ROLE

The role of the Negro teacher in the desegregation controversy of the Deep South has provoked considerable conjecture. Organizations of Negro teachers have not taken a leading or crusading part in the desegregation fight, yet time and again they have adopted resolutions calling for compliance with and implementation of the Supreme Court decision. These statements have come despite the implied and in some instances openly stated threat that any desegregation would result in job losses by Negro teachers.

In December 1954 the Virginia (Negro) Teachers Association unanimously adopted resolutions endorsing efforts to hasten integration, reaffirming support of the NAACP and commending parochial schools which had desegregated. In April of 1956 the Georgia Teachers and Education Association, representing 9,000 Negro teachers in the state, called for integration "with a spirit of fair play and good will" and termed private school legislation "a serious menace to the educational process." Soon after Governor Luther Hodges of North Carolina advanced his "voluntary segregation" plan the executive board of the North Carolina (Negro) Teachers Association adopted a resolution saying, "As citizens of the state of North Carolina we feel it should not be requested that we relinquish any one of our constitutional rights for even a minute." While two state legislative committees in Virginia had the NAACP under fire in the early spring of 1957, 800 members of a district group of the VTA adopted resolutions praising the NAACP and the Southern Regional Council and reaffirmed Negro teacher support of the Supreme Court decision.

In terms of immediate effect, these Negro teachers probably stand closer to the possibility of economic upset than any other one group. In an address at Louisville, Kentucky, in February 1955, Dr. William Mason Chisolm, founder and president of Chisolm Training Institute of Rock Hill, South Carolina, accused Negro teachers of "selling us down the river" by voting for pro-segregation political candidates for fear of losing their teaching jobs. But where these organized educational groups have been vocal, they have endorsed integration. This despite the fact that in several states of the South earning capacity of Negro teachers, when measured against the general run of Negro pay, is substantially higher.

INCIDENTAL VIOLENCE

Sprinkled through the three years following the initial Court decision were occasional cases of racial violence in the Deep South which could be linked directly to the school segregation question. Other instances of violence apparently were unconnected except for such contributions as the school cases may have made to the general heightening of racial tension.

The well-publicized slaying of the Negro youth, Emmett Till, in Mississippi, falls into that last category, for there was no school segregation involvement in that instance. On the other hand, the riotous disturbance over the attempted entry of Autherine Lucy to the University of Alabama was a direct outgrowth of school desegregation directives from the Federal courts. Other Alabama violence, such as that stemming from the bus boycott in Montgomery and bombings in Birmingham, may have had an incidental connection with school desegregation, but too remote to document.

In South Carolina, the firing upon houses of NAACP leaders (coupled with firing back on at least one occasion) might be classed as episodes indirectly linked with the school desegregation crisis. And, although this too is difficult to document, so might the beating in late December 1956 of a Camden high school bandmaster who was alleged by his white assailants to have made remarks construed by them as favoring integration. (The bandmaster himself denied having made such remarks.)

Actually, there was little overt violence which could be attributed directly to the school issue. Violence which did occur over this issue was restricted largely to the mid-South and border states which had come face to face with the reality, rather than the prospect, of school desegregation.

White groups in the Deep South working for school desegregation were, on a formal, organized basis, few and far between. In many instances local interracial groups devoted their efforts to promoting racial harmony. In the Deep South, the nearest approach to a policy of school integration was that of the biracial Southern Regional Council of Atlanta and its affiliated state Councils on Human Relations. However, these latter could not be uniformly classed as integration agencies. Those of Florida, Louisiana, North Carolina and Virginia (there are others in the mid-South and border regions) are acknowledged by the SRC to fit into this classification. But in Alabama, Georgia, Mississippi and South Carolina the Human Relations Councils have less direct connection with the Southern Regional Council and can best be described as being more interested in better race relations generally than in school integration specifically. (The SRC is also discussed in the chapter, "The South's Own Civil War.") Another, but smaller, group was the Southern Conference Educational Fund of New Orleans.

Outside the realm of officialdom, there has been an ebb and flow of public statements—written and oral—which reflect the cross-currents of opinion. The vast majority have favored continuation of segregation to the maximum degree possible, and varying degrees of resistance to the Supreme Court's mandate. Yet there have been other statements from persons who term themselves "moderates" and from those who are frank proponents of integration. In the last named category relatively few white persons have come out with such statements, and most of the weight here has been carried by such Negro leaders as Charles S. Johnson, who had this to say further in his *New York Times Magazine* article:

"The issue today is human equality and national civil rights, and the touchstone is the racial segregation that prevents this human equality . . . The essence of our system of government and life is voluntary cooperation in a democratic process that respects the dignity and rights of individuals."

A lament of the white "moderates" of the South was put into words in June of 1956 when C. A. McKnight, editor of the *Charlotte Observer* and long a student of the racial question, wrote:

One of the tragic developments of the last six months has been the quiet exodus of Southern moderates from the public-debate forum. By a moderate, I mean the fellow whose mind is still open to facts and opinions on either side of the segregation issue, and whose emotions are under such firm control that he can discuss the issue with his neighbors and friends calmly, temperately and with some detachment. Moreover, he is a man who would not be averse to seeing limited school desegregation tried in a few selected communities, so that future public policy in his state could be based on facts, and not on fear and fancy. The Southern moderate, by that definition, is finding out that the middle ground upon which he has been accustomed to stand is fast shrinking beneath him. Strong pressure from the extremes is forcing him to shut up, or to join the resistance movement. If there is hope for the South, it lies in the moderates who know that the elevation of the American Negro to full equality must be an evolutionary, and not a revolutionary, process.

Across the South in Mississippi, another "moderate" newspaper editor, Greenville's Hodding Carter, has had much to say against extremists on both sides of the issue, but he readily admits that he does not have the answer. Writing in the *Saturday Evening Post* of December 17, 1955, Carter said:

I am not prophesying what is going to happen in other Southern regions. But integration is not going to become a reality in the black belt of Mississippi, Alabama, South Carolina, Louisiana and Georgia or in many areas in other Southern states until and unless the white people of those states change their minds—which isn't likely for a long time to come.

EIGHT STATES IN SUMMARY

A survey of this region over the three-year period following the Supreme Court decision discloses several factual developments which, more or less—and perhaps more than less—characterize the eight states:

In every state of the region there was a far stronger pattern of legislation aimed at preserving racial segregation than there was in 1954, although the new pattern generally avoided any outward appearance of being based on race; in no state had there been admitted a Negro student to a public school on the elementary or secondary levels; and throughout the region there was a core of resistance which surpassed that in existence in 1954.

7.

Segregation and Politics

By Bert Collier

"You can well understand that I have no heart in trying to run for governor against the tag of integrationist used by our highest [state] executive," said a Virginian from the platform of a college auditorium in the spring of 1957.

He was State Senator Ted Dalton of Radford, the Republican who had sent shudders through the Democratic organization in 1953 when he polled 45 per cent of the vote for governor and who was grimly regarded by his opponents of four years before as anything but dead politically.

Dalton says he is "no integrationist," but he will "fight with a whole heart to keep the public schools of Virginia open." His political dilemma simply is typical of many of those who bid for the favor of the voters. A full 18 months before the 1958 Democratic gubernatorial primary in Georgia, again for example, prospective candidates were hotly arguing the degree of pro-segregationist fervor in each other's record.

Debating an interposition resolution before the Florida Senate in April 1957, a speaker insisted that all southerners, be they "extremists" or "moderates," are opposed to mixed schools. An "extremist," he explained, is willing to defy the Supreme Court, or even condone violence. A "moderate" would achieve the same result, if he can, within the law.

Some who define "moderation" give it a different connotation. They say it means "gradual" compliance with the U. S. Supreme Court decisions. But within the strict context of politics, the basic goal of each group—to maintain segregation—is the same.

Thus, most political office-seekers in the South today come face to face with the necessity of taking a stand on school segregation. The preoccupation of southern politicians with the race question is deep-rooted. The Democratic Party, welded in post-Civil War violence, became in the South the vehicle for the expression of white supremacy. To deny it would be traitorous to party and people. And since there was no opposition in the solid South, the politician who denied his party had no place to go.

The South is changing, but political traditions are hardy. Here, the past is a particularly important key.

THE OLD SOUTH

Race was not a political issue in the Old South. There was little thought that the presence of Negroes in the land, often in overwhelming proportions, might become a matter of political concern to those who held tightly the control of power over the common affairs.

Politics in fact was a game. It was a sport and an avocation of the planter-professional class who monopolized the positions of authority and made the decisions that affected the lives of all. It was the recreation of the lesser men whose lives were lonely and drab, and whose delight was in the rolling thunder of polemic on the crossroad hustings at election time.

This is not to say that the men who made their ringing appeals for votes were insincere. The men who governed the Old South and represented the states in Congress included cultured and dedicated public servants and even the peerless Calhoun, whose doctrines of interposition and nullification are alive in the New South today, was not entirely alone in his eminence.

They were a small group. William E. Dodd in *The Cotton Kingdom* (Yale University Press, 1919) says that in 1850 between three and four thousand families controlled all the best plantations and a thousand of these accounted for half the total exports of cotton, sugar and rice from the South.

The point is that these men created a tradition of flamboyance in political expression, a tradition that was to reach full and outrageous exploitation by the demagogues who came a half-century after.

They, the demagogues, had an overriding issue, the preoccupation

and concern of every southern white man with the political threat of
the Negro.

This threat to white supremacy came out of the Civil War and
Reconstruction. There has been no war in our history which touched
so closely the lives and fortunes, so intimately every waking thought
and secret nightmare, of so many people. Rare was the southern family
which emerged without personal tragedy and loss. Common misfor-
tune is more powerful a bond than shared victory.

So the defeated watched the power pass, with the aid of bayonets,
into the hands of their former slaves. It was a bitterness they had not
imagined and it had a searing effect.

"For the thirty years that followed," said W. J. Cash in *The Mind
of the South* (Alfred A. Knopf, 1941), "the South was to live with
unparalleled completeness under the sway of a single plexus of ideas
of which the center was an ever growing concern with white superiority
and an ever growing will to mastery of the Negro."

The South, of course, eventually achieved that on its own terms in
the last decade of the Nineteenth Century. The struggle was a bitter
one that tried the ingenuity and sharpened the invective of the white
South. The editor of a South Carolina newspaper, the *Fairfield Herald,* described a Reconstruction legislature as "the rule of gibbering,
louse-eaten, devil-worshipping barbarians from the jungles of Da-
homey, and peripatetic buccanneers from Cape Cod, Memphremagog,
Hell and Boston."

Changing Concept

But the significant factor for the political future of the Negro was
that the tragic era changed the concept of the South's master class
toward the former slave class—from property to political menace.

The planter group, so long in control of the machinery of state,
found itself in political competition with, in political subjugation to,
the Negro. It was this group with training for its heritage of leadership
which found the way of circumventing the Fourteenth Amendment
and in one state after another moved back triumphantly into the
capitols and legislative halls. These leaders set in motion a force still
alive.

The forces that put the Negro in political competition with this
group also put him in economic competition with the landless whites.

They created a nucleus of angry men, say Cash and others, who found a common focus in their dissatisfaction with their condition. They brought about the revolt that took the form of adherence to the Farmers Alliance and the Populist Party, which were essentially national phenomena. In the South the movements reached a high point in the election of 1892, after the Populist Party convention adopted a platform calling for easy money and a graduated income tax. The old Democratic rulers fought the upstart Populists and the Negro Republicans with various weapons including multiple ballots and ballot boxes. There is no doubt that new suffrage requirements radically reduced voting, particularly Republican voting, and since the Negroes were the backbone of the Republican Party, the inference is obvious that the reduction was in the Negro vote.

Though figures were not kept on a racial basis, Florida proves a typical example. In 1888 there were 66,740 votes for governor, the Democrats getting 60.3 per cent. In 1892 after new suffrage requirements, there were 40,747 votes cast, the Democrats getting 78.7 per cent.

In Georgia, for another example, 221,750 voted in the 1894 race for governor. The turnout was not equalled again until 1920.

Viewing these changes in the Negro's influence at the polls, Henry Grady, Georgia's evangel of the South's rebirth whose oratory fascinated northern audiences, remarked that "the Negro as a political force has dropped out of serious consideration."

This fixation on the Negro voters, who were attracted by the Populist doctrines, did weaken some of the appeal of this party of the have-nots for white southerners. But the struggle of the underprivileged brought into being a new political personality. "Pitchfork Ben" Tillman of South Carolina was the first, and the extraordinary success of his emotional speeches started a trend that is not yet finished.

"Tillman brought nigger-baiting to levels of the more brutal sort," said Cash. "After him, virtually the whole host of the demagogues would owe their success to their capacity to carry things farther yet."

There were others who sought to outdo Tillman—Mississippi's Vardaman and Arkansas' Jeff Davis of the sacred name; Cole Blease later in South Carolina; Tom Watson and Hoke Smith in Georgia, and more. It was in the era of most of these men that the measures barring the Negro from full political participation found their way into the statute books.

Act of Contempt

The South ignored the Fourteenth Amendment and viewed the Civil Rights Act of 1875 with "utter contempt." The authors of this legislation designed to guarantee the rights of freed Negroes had considered a provision against segregated schools but had abandoned it. The act did declare all persons, regardles of race or color, should have full access to public transportation, hotels and theaters. The Supreme Court held the act unconstitutional in 1883, a decision that was greeted with outbursts of joy in many southern cities.

The relieved South set about closing the doors. The ballot box was sealed by property and understanding tests, the grandfather and the good conduct clauses. The concept of the Democratic Party as a private club was effective for years in making the white primaries, automatically barred to Negroes, the decisive exercise of choice through the hierachy from district constable and school trustee to governor.

The effect was to tie Negro voters to the Republican Party. White Democrats were not alarmed by this because Negro votes had kept the Radical Republicans in power in most southern states during Reconstruction.

The alliance was to remain in effect until the coming of new issues which resulted in a curious blurring of the traditional party lines.

Fractured South

The first of these questions was raised by the candidacy of Alfred E. Smith in 1928. The conservative Protestantism of the South expressed itself in the "Hoovercrat" revolt that broke the Solid South for the first time since Reconstruction, though Tennessee had gone for Harding in 1920.

An analysis of this vote showed that the South retained its paramount preoccupation with the Negro question. Areas with the largest Negro population remained loyal to the Democratic Party, while in those with few Negroes, the shift to Hoover was most marked.

"The vote distribution places the center of Southern Democracy in the Black Belt," said V. O. Key in *Southern Politics in the State and Nation* (Alfred A. Knopf, 1949). "The whites of the Black Belt were bound in loyalty to the Democracy by a common tradition and anxiety about the Negro. Whites elsewhere could afford the luxury of voting their convictions on religion."

It was in the second campaign of Franklin Delano Roosevelt that Negro voters began to sense that they had found a champion outside their traditional protector, the GOP. Roosevelt received a majority of the Negro vote.

It was, in effect, a repetition of conditions that existed in the Populist movement—a discovery of common ground between the Negroes of the South and the less privileged urban groups of the North, whose existence depended on the public welfare policies of the New Deal. The Negro remained an important part of the coalition that kept Roosevelt in the White House and the Negro's political power steadily increased.

Twenty years after the "Hoovercrats" there was revolt again in the South. This time the loyalists of '28 were the rebels of '48. Times had changed. The New Deal had remained in power with its insistence on civil rights. Its economic policies were opposed with the same vehemence by industry and by the white leaders of the Black Belt. Thus, the issues of 1948, as in 1928, were not race alone. The States' Rights Party won 39 electoral votes and more than a million popular votes and the fact that they did not cost Truman the election was credited by some to a curious American predilection for the under dog.

The elections since World War II have shown an increasing participation by Negro voters. Since the collapse of the white primary system in 1944, as the result of a Supreme Court ruling in the case of *Smith* v. *Allwright,* the Negro registration has mounted steadily. In 1952 the Southern Regional Council reported more than a million Negroes were on the voter lists in 11 states that had adhered to the Confederacy. Negroes have been elected to public office, more particularly to school boards. Negro votes played an important part in the sucess of Eisenhower in the South in 1956.

The number of Negro votes, however, remained a matter of speculation. Key wrote in 1949: "Quantitative estimates . . . are subject to a wide range of error, although certain generalizations about geographical variations in Negro voting can be made. The Negro votes least in Mississippi, South Carolina, Louisiana and Alabama. In Arkansas he encounters obstacles to voting yet manages to vote to a greater extent than in the first group of states. Larger proportions of Negroes vote in Tennessee, Virginia, North Carolina, Texas, Georgia and Florida.

"In all these states except Georgia, the number of Negro voters, both in primaries and general elections, has gradually increased without much commotion. Georgia's great upsurge in Negro voting in the 1946 Democratic primary aroused intense controversy."

The upsurge continues. In the first three months of 1957, 4,280 Negroes registered in Fulton County (Atlanta), Georgia, as compared with 7,801 whites. "It betrays the fact that our people are getting registration-minded," said the *Atlanta Daily World*, Negro newspaper.

Nevertheless, the gap between Negro and white voting appears to be wide. During the debate on civil rights legislation in July 1957, Sen. Paul Douglas (D-Ill.) said:

"In the seven southern states of Alabama, Arkansas, Georgia, Louisiana, Mississippi, South Carolina and Virginia—and in 95 of the 254 counties in Texas where 90 per cent of the Negroes reside—there is a potential Negro vote of 3.75 million. Of these, only 850,000 or 23 per cent are even registered to vote. The numbers who actuauly vote are far fewer than those who are registered."

An Issue Rekindled

Between the two latest Presidential elections, the Supreme Court segregation decision was handed down to affect radically the traditional political alignments. The preoccupation of southern politicians with the Negro question, which had tended to become less paramount, was suddenly restored to its former position as the burning issue of the day. It affected the careers of political leaders at all levels. It affected both political parties. It affected the pace of Negro registration. Resistance mounted and only about 200,000 Negro names were added to the rolls in four years, despite great efforts by the National Association for the Advancement of Colored People and other groups, determined that the power of the Negro groups be shown at the ballot box.

"Both elements [white southerners and Negroes] wanted to show the Democratic leaders that their vote could not be taken for granted", said Samuel Lubell, political analyst. "Both wanted to demonstrate their political bargaining power.

"It is against this picture of political change through the country that one should examine the new militancy of the Negro. The essence of the political drama now being acted out in the United States can be summed up perhaps in these terms—that both the Democratic and the Republican parties are being made over into truly national parties, which will be quite thoroughly sensitized to the nationalizing forces remaking the nation.

"With the migration of so many Negroes from the South to the North and West, the race problem has become one of the most powerful of these nationalizing forces."

Swing to Ike

A study of the 1956 vote showed Eisenhower had weakened the attachment of the Negro voters for the Democratic Party. In 86 urban areas with a high concentration of Negroes, the President increased his share of the votes from 25 per cent to 36 per cent. Southern Negro precincts which gave Eisenhower 19 per cent of their vote in 1952 gave him 47 per cent in 1956.

Two-Party South?

Do the Republican gains presage a genuine movement toward a two-party South? Some of the political observers who examined the question think so. Eisenhower made serious inroads and drew solid support in Negro areas, but the Democrats were almost invariably successful on the local and state level in their traditional strongholds. The paradox has been pointed out that the Eisenhower vote in the South may not have been a genuine vote for Republicanism—that both an angry white southerner and an angry Negro southerner could, and did, cast a protest vote for the same man—Eisenhower.

Nevertheless the balloting showed a willingness, new in the South, of both white and Negro voters to cross party lines. And it demonstrated the effort of the GOP to give voters a choice. Republicans contested 41 southern congressional seats in 1956, compared with 32 in 1952.

The opportunities for a two-party vote are growing, but no sharp differences have developed as yet on the segregation question. Serious GOP candidates are realistic about the feelings of the South.

Both national parties were conscious of the Negro's voting strength and the tensions of the white South as the result of the segregation decisions. Both tried to reconcile the conflicting points of view and solve the dilemma by compromise. Republicans at their San Francisco convention adopted a platform that "accepted" the Supreme Court's decision ending segregated schools.

"Progress must be encouraged and the work of the Court supported in every legal manner by all branches of the Federal government, to the end that the constitutional ideal of equality before the law, regardless of race, creed or color, will be steadily achieved," the GOP pronouncement said.

The Democrats presented a platform designed not to antagonize the white South or the Negro. It said: "Recent decisions of the Supreme Court . . . relating to segregation in publicly supported schools and elsewhere have brought consequences of vast importance to our nation as a whole and especially to communities directly affected.

"We reject all proposals for the use of force to interfere with the orderly determination of these matters by the courts."

One news analyst (James Marlow, of the Associated Press) said this left the interpretation to the individual voter. "It's like boxing with shadows," he said.

The Republican Party tried to capitalize on the ambivalence of the Democrats. At a strategy meeting of the Citizens for Eisenhower in Washington in May 1956, workers were told to emphasize that "a vote for any Democrat is a vote for Eastland." [Senator James O. O. Eastland of Mississippi, an outspoken segregationist who, in a Democratic Senate would become chairman of the sensitive Judiciary Committee.]

"In the context of Supreme Court decisions under a Chief Justice appointed by President Eisenhower, decisions as historic as the Emancipation Proclamation of Lincoln, we have a wonderful story to tell," said Richard Tobin, public relations counsel for the group. "It is my opinion that it has not been told sufficiently well to the average Negro voter."

The Campaign Trail

Both nominees were firmly on record in acceptance of the Supreme Court decision. On occasion, however, both tempered their firmness to the political realities. Adlai Stevenson said the Federal government must move slowly in enforcing the Court mandate, using education and persuasion rather than authority. His stand brought criticism from the liberal wing of the party, who called his pronouncement "inadequate, fragmentary and uninspired."

Flying to Miami in a whirlwind bid for Florida's support, Eisenhower told an audience at the airport, on October 29, 1956, of his 1952 stand on civil rights. "I urged then, as I urge now, the handling of this question to the greatest possible extent on a local and state basis," he said.

It was on a lower level that the in-fighting on the issue became sharp. In the preliminary battle between Stevenson and Senator Estes Kefauver for the Democratic nomination, Kefauver accused his opponent of working both sides of the segregation street.

Kefauver said Stevenson allowed his supporters to bill him as an all-out integrationist in California while his backers in Florida and elsewhere in the South pictured him as an advocate of moderation.

Introducing Stevenson to a Florida audience in Tallahassee, former Governor Millard Caldwell referred to Kefauver as an out-and-out apostle of race-mixing. This was an example of the manner in which national candidates, wearing the cloaks of the party platforms, tended to take on the brighter coloration of their advocates who felt that it was bad politics in the South to be an integrationist.

"No man, in my opinion," said Georgia's Attorney General Eugene Cook, "can be elected to even a minor office [in the South] unless he commits himself in a forthright and effective manner to support the pattern of segregation."

CONSIDER THE RATIO

Segregation most often is an issue in proportion to the concentration of Negro population. In some areas where industry has brought in a large number of white skilled workers from other parts of the country, whites and Negroes often labor side by side. On military reservations, mixed schools have been in operation even in the most confirmed segregationist states.

In politics segregation can become an emotional issue. Candidates who have made it such fared surprisingly well in several states. If they did not win, they forced abandonment of an official position of moderation.

Florida is a case in point. By several criteria it does not conform to the traditional southern pattern, swelling its population by about 10 per cent a year, largely from northern and eastern areas. The traditional control of state politics by the older rural sections is being increasingly challenged. Florida went for Hoover in 1928 and for Eisenhower in 1952 and 1956.

When the first Supreme Court decision was announced, the state adopted a policy of resigned acceptance. Attorney General Richard W. Ervin went ahead with his amicus curiae brief advancing the theory of moderation and gradualism. And senior Senator Spessard L. Holland advised his constituents to accept the decision as binding, although it might be repugnant to their views.

When the implementing decision was handed down a year later, with instructions to proceed "with all deliberate speed," the Florida House of Representatives, then in session, applauded the announcement from the speaker's rostrum. Ervin, whose brief was credited with helping shape the second decision, said: "I hope the Negroes won't be too aggressive and that the whites won't be too defiant. The thing will have to worked out eventually, but it will take time."

Skirmish Line

Florida was not the only southern state that felt relief. The consensus was that the South had won a skirmish, if not the battle itself.

In Arkansas, Governor Orval W. Faubus said: "It appears that the Court left some degree of decision in these matters to the Federal district courts. I believe this will guarantee against any sudden dislocations . . . Our reliance now must be upon good will that exists between the two races—the good will that has long made Arkansas a model for the other southern states in all matters affecting the relationships between the races."

Lieutenant Governor Ernest Vandiver of Georgia said: "I think the Supreme Court in some small measure attempted to correct an obnoxious decision."

"Frankly, I interpret the decree as favorable to Mississippi and the South," said Hugh White, then governor of Mississippi.

Newspapers, too, reflected the South's mood of satisfaction. The *Augusta Chronicle* called the decision "a distinct triumph for the southern viewpoint." The *Charlotte Observer* declared the ruling was "as moderate as the South could reasonably have expected." The *Tampa Tribune* suggested that the decision would "dissipate the thunderhead of turmoil and violence which had been gathering in southern skies since the Court held school segregation unconstitutional a year ago."

What happened, then, to change this first reaction and to stiffen resistance into a major political issue?

In Haste?

Some segregationists place the blame on the haste of the National Association for the Advancement of Colored People to implement the decisions. This belief led to efforts in eight states to curb the NAACP by various legislative means, or by administrative or court action.

Another group blamed the deliberate fanning of flames by candidates seeking political advantage. President Eisenhower took cognizance of this when a correspondent called his attention, in his press conference of July 31, 1956, to "a rather alarming outburst of violent talk on the race issue" in several southern primaries. The President replied that this was "a grave error and a disservice to the United States.

"The path of human progress is not along the path of hatreds; it is not along the path of extremes," the President said.

Into Politics

The emergence of segregation as a political issue, entirely unexpected in some instances, occurred in several states.

In Florida's 1956 primary, Governor LeRoy Collins was opposed by a candidate who chose to do battle on the segregation question. General Sumter Lowry, a retired National Guard officer, used such devices as a television film which showed Negro delegates to a church convention patronizing Miami Beach hotels and beaches, with a legend stating that "it can happen—it is happening—here."

As support developed for Lowry, Collins was forced to amend his pleas for moderation. He pledged that he would call an extra session of the legislature to enact laws assuring the continuance of segregated schools—a move for which there had been no demand prior to the election.

Collins won, the first gubernatorial candidate to do so in modern Florida without a run-off election. Lowry, however, piled up a large vote and led two experienced and well-known candidates, former Governor Fuller Warren and former House Speaker Faris Bryant. All four candidates had taken stands for segregation, the only difference being that Lowry made this the only issue.

The special session was called, as Collins promised, and received the report of a special commission which recommended a pupil assignment law and other measures.

One single voice was raised against these measures. "I believe segregation is morally wrong," said Representative John B. Orr, Jr., of Miami. "The fact that the custom is one of long standing makes it no less wrong. For us to set the example of hypocrisy and deceit— of disrespect for our laws—will surely do more harm to our children than will result from their being seated in a classroom next to one whose skin is of a different hue."

Orr defied the axiom of southern politics that no man can survive who attacks the traditional separation of the races. Orr survived. Although his Republican opponent, who hammered away on this theme in the general election a few months later, received more votes than any other candidate of his party except President Eisenhower, Orr was returned to the legislature.

Orr's stand was an exceptional one, but it was not unique. In Virginia, State Senator Stuart B. Carter told the General Assembly that he had a "conscientious belief" in integration. Delegate Robert Whitehead said Governor Thomas B. Stanley's legislative program to preserve segregation would put the entire state in a "plaster cast."

Camille F. Gravel, Jr., Louisiana's Democratic national committeeman and an associate of Governor Earl Long, declared that "purely as a moral proposition, segregation is wrong." His remark was in reply to criticism of his vote for a civil rights resolution at a meeting of the Democratic Advisory Council in San Francisco.

These were lonely voices. More in line with majority opinion was the stand in Virginia by Attorney General J. Lindsay Almond, Jr., an apparent candidate for governor.

Almond, with the backing of the dominant Democratic organization headed by U. S. Senator Harry F. Byrd, plumped for "massive resistance" at the state level, including denial of state funds to any local unit which permits school integration. The spokesman for the Republicans, State Senator Ted Dalton, said some integration might be permitted under a pupil assignment plan, but he favored keeping "white schools as white as possible."

The *Richmond News Leader* pointed out that the two stands were not so divergent—that both the party spokesmen favored segregation: "Their division lies at the critical point, some time in the future, when a local school at last faces the bitter choice: Mix the races or close the school. Mr. Dalton would mix. Mr. Byrd would close."

"Big Jim"

In Alabama, a stand for settling the segregation issue "within the framework of the law" cost Governor James E. Folsom much of his political following.

"Big Jim," who won his first term as Alabama's chief executive in 1946 with the aid of the CIO, rapidly lost face when he pointed out that the Supreme Court mandate had the effect of law which must prevail. Local labor unions, particularly in the Birmingham area where they are strong, cooled to Folsom's "moderation."

When an interposition resolution was pushed through the legislature by young Representative Charles W. McKay, Jr., Folsom called it "hogwash."

McKay set out to defeat Folsom for the sensitive post of Democratic national committeeman, and Folsom ruefully conceded that, because of his stand on the race issue, he doubted that he could be elected dogcatcher in his home town. McKay defeated him decisively, and every Folsom adherent who sought party office went down with him.

Folsom is serving his second term and cannot succeed himself. He is a strange figure in Alabama politics, winning twice with liberal support in a conservative state, yet being the product of a rural, traditional area. George L. Peterson, associate editor of the *Minneapolis Star and Tribune,* called him a man "with most of the attributes of a demagogue, but who has never baited the Negro. As a result, he has the solid Negro vote, which, however, isn't very big—probably 50,000 out of a half million."

Folsom—they called him "Kissin' Jim" after his first campaign tactic of bussing pretty girls—can be most undemagogic, as in his famous statement that "I ain't gonna force our fine colored children to go to school with white folks." And his act of inviting Negro Congressman Adam Clayton Powell to the governor's mansion for a Scotch and soda is being used against him.

'Festo

In North Carolina, two of the three congressmen who failed to sign the Southern Manifesto against the Supreme Court decision were rejected by the voters. In all three races, the segregation issue was raised, but in none was it the sole issue.

The Manifesto, officially the "Declaration of Constitutional Principles," and often described simply as "The 'Festo" in Washington, was introduced in Congress May 12, 1956, with the signatures of more than a hundred southerners. It assailed the "naked judicial power" of the Supreme Court in handing down the school mandate.

A non-signer, Congressman Charles B. Deane, veteran of five terms and a liberal who was influential with the congressional leadership, was opposed for re-election by Paul Kitchin. Kitchin did not stress the Manifesto issue, but replied when asked that he would have signed it had he been in Congress.

When it seemed apparent that Deane was losing ground, his supporters asked him to announce publicly that he was opposed to school integration. He refused. One source quoted him as replying: "I don't have to go to Congress, but I do have to live with Charlie Deane."

The outcome was a victory for Kitchin, 22,500 to 19,500. Deane carried the northern portion of his district where the Negro population is small, but was swamped in the southern precincts where racial feeling existed because of large Negro areas. Afterward he said he "would assume" the Manifesto issue was the paramount factor in his defeat. Political observers reported a breakdown in the labor-farmer coalition which usually supported him.

The defeat of Congressman Thurmond Chatham by Ralph J. Scott had little to do with the Manifesto. Scott scarcely mentioned that Chatham had failed to sign. Instead, he pounded away on the purely personal issue of Chatham's record of absenteeism.

In the third race, the Manifesto got top play. Congressman Harold

D. Cooley, chairman of the House Agriculture Committee, met head-on the challenge of W. E. Debnam, radio commentator, who assailed his failure to sign. In a bitter campaign, Cooley won, 35,000 to 20,500.

Governor Luther Hodges, whose stand on segregation was described as moderate, was attacked on this score by State Senator Tom Sawyer, one of three opponents. Sawyer accused him of "bartering the racial heritage of unborn children in North Carolina to keep the Negro vote within the Democratic Party." Little political capital was generated. Hodges' vote was overwhelming.

Soon after the primary, however, Hodges summoned the legislature to submit constitutional amendments preserving segregation.

HARDENING RESISTANCE

Arkansas presented an example of hardening official attitude because of political pressure. When the 1954 Supreme Court decision was announced, Governor Orval Faubus recommended moderation. Months later he was talking of "local problems almost impossible of solution." Seeking re-election in 1956, Faubus bought newspaper space to say that "since I have been your governor, no school board has been forced to desegregate its schools against its will."

Faubus' opponents included James D. Johnson, director of the white Citizens Councils of Arkansas. Here and in other states, the Citizens Councils made ready use of the political weapon, and found leadership among politicians. Notably in Alabama, State Senator Sam Engelhardt headed the orthodox Council movement and was the leading spokesman for the segregationists.

In Louisiana, too, the Citizens Council was headed by an office-holder, State Senator Willie Rainach, of Homer. In southern Louisiana, the leader was Leander Perez, district attorney of St. Bernard and Plaquemines parishes. He was a prominent States' Rights Democrat in 1948 and a founder of the Federation for Constitutional Government.

Asa G. "Ace" Carter, head of the North Alabama Citizens Councils, jumped into the 1957 race for police commissioner of Birmingham. Carter, who was indicted in a shooting incident at a Ku Klux Klan meeting, accused the city administration of being hesitant in enforcing municipal segregation ordinances. In the election, he ran fourth.

Several men are considered likely pro-segregation candidates for governor of Tennessee in 1958. One is Judge Raulston Schoolfield of the Chattanooga Criminal Court, who failed on the same platform in 1954. Judge Schoolfield is a strong segregationist who has been active in groups devoted to that cause.

It is no accident that such organizations became political pressure groups. The official manual of the Mississippi Citizens Councils' parent organization suggests each chapter have a Political and Education Committee, a chief duty of which is to "study candidates . . . and present their qualifications to the voters."

The basis for this study is indicated further in the manual:

"This integration scheme ties right in with the new one-world, one-creed, one-race philosophy featured by the ultra-idealists."

DIFFERENT VOICES

By any standard of classification, Georgia is a leader in resistance to integration. Here veteran Senator Walter F. George stepped down after a generation of service rather than face a bitter primary fight with his challenger, young Herman Talmadge, son of the late Eugene.

Friends advised the 77-year-old George not to risk a contest on the race issue. The Talmadges, father and son, have kept their grip on Georgia for a quarter century by appeals to the smaller counties and their preoccupation with the Negro question. Herman once urged a boycott of all television programs which featured white and Negro performers. He told his followers that "segregation is more important than all other issues at the moment."

Since his easy victory, Talmadge has become a leader of the southern congressional group working to curb the power of the Supreme Court and leave to the states the decisions on school matters. Talmadge's stand on this issue is clear: "During the last two decades, that [Supreme] Court has chipped steadily away at the reserved rights of the states. It has sought to change the very framework of our government, not by legal amendment, but through so-called judicial legislation."

Talmadge is a transition figure between the old-line demagogue and the emerging politician who dares defy the rigid lines of southern conservatism. The young senator has a direct link with the past through his father, with whom he was closely associated. He has surpassed his father, who once declared martial law to prevent the service of court papers in a suit filed against him.

"Talmadge is a much more able politician and administrator than his father, and a patient, able organizer," said Ralph McGill, in the *Atlanta Constitution*.

Senator Talmadge, say observers, realizes the significance of the new industrial age that has come to his state and he draws support from the industrialists. He is not one to boast, as did his father, that he never carried a county in which there was a streetcar.

New Voices

Throughout the South, new faces are being seen and new voices speak forthrightly on segregation. Gone are the days when a Cole Blease could whip up his South Carolina auditors by defending lynching: "When the Constitution comes between me and the virtue of the white women of the South, I say to hell with the Constitution."

The voices are different, even when the determination is to preserve segregation, if it can be done within the framework of legality.

In Mississippi, Governor J. P. Coleman steered through the legislature bills creating a State Sovereignty Commission, described by some as in effect a super-government with unlimited powers, to keep the races forever apart. Yet Coleman is a moderate by the old Bilbo standards.

"In these times, persons of responsibility must think things through before they take a position of no return," he said. "I told the people we would maintain segregation without keeping the state in a daily uproar of confusion and uncertainty. I am confident that when I go out from office separation of the races will be exactly the same as now. If we maintain the rules of racial segregation, our place in history will be secure."

Governor Frank Clement of Tennessee unhesitatingly called on state troops when disorders broke out in Clinton over admission of Negroes to a previously white high school. For that Clement became the favorite target of speakers at rallies of the Ku Klux Klans and segregationist groups, and of political figures who charged he had national ambitions which required the coddling of Negro and northern liberal votes.

"We in America face today within our country a crisis which can lead to our destruction," said Clement. "For if we cannot, as Americans, regardless of race or color, live in peace and harmony as a united people, our disunity may well destroy us. How can we be trusted with the peace of the world if we cannot keep peace among ourselves?"

Florida's Governor Collins, who dissolved a special session of the legislature that threatened to enact radical segregation laws, said no such restrictions are needed. "Good standards of morality, health and citizenship, the influence of which is not confined to color lines, do not develop in a child who grows up in a filthy, overcrowded shack under the guidance of illiterate parents," he said. "Our motive should be the doing of what is right and just."

The new political voices for the most part no longer appeal to hate. Yet in two of these states whose governors have been outspoken on the issue—Florida and Mississippi—there has been no move toward compliance with the school mandate. There is a firm resolve to continue resistance. There is sincerity in the stand, most observers agree, not merely a calculated bid for political preferment. Indeed, there is some danger and risk. The rising opposition to Folsom and Clement has been charted and Collins came under heavy fire in his own legislature.

But moderates—taking the definition that this means maintaining segregation by legal means—are winning elections and holding office. An effort to bring all southern governors into a coalition against integration failed at the Southern Governors Conference in November 1954.

Those voting against the proposal included McKeldin of Maryland, Wetherby of Kentucky, Clement of Tennessee, Cherry of Arkansas, Marland of West Virginia and Folsom of Alabama. McKeldin was particularly opposed, declaring defiance of the Supreme Court was "fantastic nonsense." When the conference met again in September 1956, the school subject was not on the official agenda and no resolutions were adopted, though several governors issued individual statements about their attitudes.

Segregation is deeply embedded in southern politics but the issue is no longer entirely one-sided. John Kasper of the Seaboard White Citizens Councils, the dominant figure in the Clinton disorders, was discredited by a Florida legislative committee when he attempted to invade that state in 1957. He was repudiated by the Tennessee Federation for Constitutional Government. In Alabama, Senator Engelhardt put a watch on Kasper to make certain he did not stir up difficulties for the Citizens Councils in that state.

There are signs of political ferment and change in the South. What they portend remains with the future. The story is still unfolding.

8.

"Be It Enacted"

By Patrick E. McCauley

"I am utterly opposed to any form of mixing of the races, now and forever. I'll be glad to come back to the legislature at any time at my own expense to keep Negroes out of white schools."

So spoke Florida's Hamilton County Representative J. W. McAlpine on June 1, 1955, after the U. S. Supreme Court announced that "all provisions of Federal, state or local law requiring or permitting . . . discrimination must yield." Not all 1,790 legislators in the southern states which have acted to counter the Court's pronouncement have been as vehement. Representative Barefoot Sanders of Dallas County, Texas, said in response to the same 1955 decision: "I can't see that any legislation here is necessary. I doubt that we could legislate validly in any way except to implement the Supreme Court's decision."

However, events then in progress, which are continuing now, indicate that a majority of legislators—in Texas, Florida and nine other states—are determined, whether by conviction or compulsion, to oppose the Supreme Court's decisions.

In this determination there seemed fulfillment of the prophecy of the late Justice Robert Jackson that the school segregation decisions would provoke "a generation of litigation." During the three years since those far-reaching decisions were announced, the stream of legislation has been almost continuous. At least 136 new measures have been enacted and ratified, all of them aimed at delaying, controlling or preventing desegregation of the schools. Here, indeed, is the stuff litigation is made of.

But the issue has not proved to be as clear-cut as Justice Jackson foresaw it. For prior to 1954, there were in 17 states and the District of Columbia 79 specific provisions requiring that separate schools be established for white and Negro children and providing for their maintenance on an equal basis. In 15 states these provisions were embedded in the state constitutions. All save Louisiana had statutory provisions for implementing the constitutional requirements.

The scope of the *Brown* decisions as they applied to these pre-1954 segregation laws was a legal question. But the centering of southern opposition to the decisions in the state legislatures changed the nature of the problem. Some seemingly clear-cut issues of law grew obscure in the hazy terrain of fundamental authority and jurisdiction. The issue when viewed from this standpoint glares forth as a political one in the broadest sense. This is not only because it involves a central function of politics, which is making the laws, but also because it raises questions in dissimilar jurisdictions to which there is no answer but a political one. The courts on the one hand seek to abide by the guiding principles of the judicial hierarchy. On the other hand, the legislators seek to preserve their prerogatives and what they conceive to be basic states' rights.

The mode of operation in the two jurisdictions is different, too. The atmosphere of the legislative hall is more susceptible to oratory than is the judicial chamber. One consequence is that in the debate over basic issues between the two jurisdictions, the legislative is apt to speak out in more fiery terms. The Georgia legislature, for example, in 1957 resolved to impeach six U. S. Supreme Court justices whom it accused of being "guilty of attempting to subvert the Constitution of the United States and of high crimes and misdemeanors in office." And Mississippi in 1956 sought to provide fines, imprisonment and civil liability for Federal officers who sought to enforce desegregation in that state. The bill was adopted, but vetoed.

Such measures may be "tomfoolery . . . pernicious . . . [and] a conglomeration of political overtures." The Georgia impeachment resolution was so labeled by its opponents in the legislature. However, they demonstrate the pervasiveness of the attitude of determined resistance, and the extent to which legislatures are apt to go.

Thus far, when it has come to education problems alone, action has been more deliberate. Still, Virginius Dabney, editor of the *Richmond*

Times-Dispatch, was prompted to observe early in 1957: "I am deeply troubled by the thought that the growing intensity in some eight or nine southern states may disrupt, and even close down entirely, the systems of public education in several of these states."

Indeed, in no less than six states the legislative groundwork has been laid for just such an eventuality. For all its finality and rather wide acceptance this step is intended as only a last stand defense against desegregation.

During the three years since the Supreme Court decisions, the legislative pattern of resistance has moved along these lines:

1. Pupil placement laws in at least eight states have been enacted to control, if not to restrain, desegregation.

2. Abolition of public schools has been authorized in six states as a last resort.

3. Financial aid to students who wish to attend segregated, private, non-sectarian schools in the event public schools are either closed or mixed has been provided in four states.

4. Curtailment of court attacks on segregation laws has been the aim of new laws in four states.

5. Miscellaneous statutes have been enacted affecting compulsory attendance, teacher tenure, transportation, and use of funds for desegregated education. Primarily these acts have been designed to adjust general education laws to the new legislation bearing directly on the segregation issue.

6. Resolutions of interposition, nullification or protest against the Supreme Court decisions have been adopted in all of the resisting states.

In the mid-South, much of this legislation has been presented and enacted in the form of studied programs. North Carolina's 1956 General Assembly adopted the Pearsall Plan, covering points two and three above. The Virginia Assembly early in 1956 adopted a portion of the Gray Plan, providing tuition grants, and then followed later in the year with the "massive resistance" program sponsored by Governor Thomas B. Stanley which went far beyond the original Gray proposals. In 1957 the Arkansas and Tennessee legislatures accepted programs of four and five bills, respectively, offered by the governors of those states. And the Texas General Assembly of 1957 also considered a program of 11 bills, most of them recommended by a governor's committee, but introduced piecemeal by several east Texas sponsors. Two laws finally were adopted.

In the five Deep South states, the segregation bills introduced have been too numerous to be considered as compact programs, save for the Louisiana 1954 enactments which followed the original *Brown* decision by about a month.

The 1956 Mississippi legislature considered a score of bills bearing directly on school segregation. The Georgia legislature had at least 16 such measures before it, and South Carolina's Assembly considered no less than 23. The Alabama Assembly in 1955 special session saw 25 school segregation bills introduced, and in 1957 was expecting the number to reach 40 during a regular session stretching into the summer.

Not all the segregated states met the decisions with legislation. No legislative action was consummated in the complying states of Missouri, Maryland, Kentucky, West Virginia and Delaware. And only Oklahoma has new laws designed to further, rather than to delay or prevent, the desegregation process.

The legislative pattern for compliance in Oklahoma has followed this course:

1. The constitution has been amended to eliminate the dual budget which prior to 1955 was a major element in the segregated school system.

2. A new school code has been adopted which, while including some segregation features, generally has permitted execution of the state board of education policy favoring desegregation through application of fiscal pressures to segregated school districts.

There is an air of anomaly about the whole situation in the resisting states. In view of Federal court rulings to the contrary, how can state legislatures continue to adopt measures with any reasonable hope of maintaining segregation? Part of the explanation lies in the determination of the legislatures to pitch the problem on the fundamental political plane. Furthermore, many legislators believe that constituents expect their representatives to take some action to shield them against the Supreme Court decisions. This is particularly evident in such states as Tennessee, Texas and Florida. One east Texan told his senator during the 1957 session, "I don't care what that Supreme Court said, east Texans don't want Negroes and white folks segregatin' around together."

Governor LeRoy Collins of Florida mirrored an executive viewpoint while condemning the interposition resolution of the 1957 legislature in his state. He said, "I am confident the legislators didn't want to do it. They were under the pressure of desperation on the part of many citizens back home, while those citizens who opposed it remained silent."

In greater part, perhaps, the explanation lies in the innate political conservatism of the South. Virginius Dabney in *Below the Potomac* (D. Appleton-Century, 1942) stated this bluntly, noting that "the South has long been the most conservative section of the country with respect to social and labor legislation, and its individual states are all backward in this regard." In any case the question is not wholly one of education, or satisfying voters, or even of race. These matters, while considered of vast importance, have merely served to crystallize the long-fragmented resistance to Federal encroachment on states' rights.

THE BLACK BELTS

This movement takes on racial overtones because it is centered, in seven states, in the Black Belts, the areas once so named because of the deep, rich black soil, but now identified as those sections with heaviest Negro population. (For purposes here, the Black Belt is limited to contiguous counties having Negro populations ranging over or near 50 per cent.) These states are Alabama, Georgia, Louisiana, Mississippi, North Carolina, South Carolina and Virginia. In each of them the Black Belts exercise disproportionate influence in the legislatures. But in all of them they have representation out of proportion to their populations.

For example, in Alabama 16 Black Belt counties with 13.5 per cent of the state's total population have 27.3 per cent of the House representation and 28.5 per cent of the Senate seats. Georgia's 37 Black Belt counties with 11.5 per cent of the population have 19 per cent of the House seats and 22.7 per cent of the Senate seats. Fourteen Louisiana Black Belt parishes (counties) have 13.8 per cent of the House representation and 18.4 per cent in the Senate, with only 8.4 per cent of the population. Mississippi's 32 Black Belt counties have

40.9 per cent of the population, 43.9 per cent of the House seats and 48.9 per cent of the Senate seats.

Virginia, North Carolina and South Carolina Black Belts are not greatly over-represented in their lower chambers. Disproportionate Senate representation exists in South Carolina, but this is a feature of bicameral legislatures. Such variations as do exist probably indicate more the dominance of rural areas generally, at the expense of urban centers, than of Black Belts over the other areas.

Consistently, however, the Black Belts send the same representatives to the legislatures over greater numbers of years than do other sections. This gives the Black Belts added influence in terms of prestige, committee and leadership appointments and in greater parliamentary experience. To some extent the same may be true also of rural constituencies generally and not only of Black Belts.

In South Carolina, average statewide senatorial service in 1957 was 7.5 years; average service for Black Belt senators was 9.7 years. The state average in the House of Representatives was 2.9 years; average for the Black Belt representatives was 4.6 years. In Virginia, average length of service for all members of the assembly was 8.2 years; for Black Belt representatives it was 12 years. In Mississippi, the seniority status of members was not as varied. Still, in the House average length of service for all representatives was 7.6 years, including those from the Black Belt who, taken separately, averaged 8 years. Average Senate service in Mississippi is difficult to compute since many counties swap senators each term due to the division of the state into senatorial districts. However, from the 11 Black Belt counties which elect a senator for every term, four members have served for 16 years, one for 12 years, five for eight years and one for four years. Of the total Senate membership of 49, the average length of service is slightly in excess of three years.

And in Georgia, which has just experienced its greatest legislative turnover in many years, average House service is 2.86 years for the whole; 3.63 years for the Black Belt.

In terms of legislative influence, this gives Black Belts the speakership of the House in Mississippi, South Carolina and Georgia. It gives the Virginia Black Belt 13 of 32 positions on the Gray Commission which designed the state's original segregation program. It gives the chairmanship of legislative segregation study committees to Black

Belt members in Louisiana, Mississippi, Virginia and South Carolina.

Thus, influence of heavily Negro-populated areas in the state legislatures is pronounced. Typical of the attitude thus prevalent is that of state Senator Sam Engelhardt of Alabama, who represents Macon County where 84 per cent of the population is Negro, the highest ratio in the nation. "As far as I am concerned," Engelhardt has said, "abolition of segregation will never be feasible in Alabama and the South. No brick will ever be removed from our segregation walls."

The determination of legislatures to preserve segregation and at the same time to strike a blow for states' rights has been inexhaustible. In searching for the best defensive ground, the school issue has first been localized, then centralized. At one moment, school districts are deemed the strongest point from which to repel the assaults, and at another moment the state capitol. If, in the process, some confusion arises, no great harm is done. For this serves to delay desegregation while the ultimate defensive barrier is being perfected.

LEGISLATIVE PATTERNS

In those states seeking to resist or control desegregation the main bulwark has been erected along the lines of one of the earliest conceived defenses. It consists in elaborating upon the inherent powers of local school boards to assign students to particular schools on the basis of educationally feasible criteria. As this idea, in its current stage of development, is tested in the courts, it assumes more the features of a controlling factor than a deterrent to integration.

Every state except Georgia has enacted a measure of this kind, and the Georgia legislators considered it in 1956. In nine states there is considerable uniformity as to methods, criteria and appeals procedures. The concept originated in the Mississippi Assembly's 1954 session prior to the *Brown* decision. Louisiana's Act 556 of the same year specified that local superintendents henceforth would designate the school each child should attend. In 1955, the North Carolina legislature adopted a similar plan in which the criteria for assignment, or placement, were spelled out in general terms and a procedure of administrative appeal was established. Later that year, the Alabama Assembly enlarged on the idea by listing the specific sociological and psychological factors upon which assignments would be made.

In 1956 and 1957, legislatures in Florida, Virginia, Tennessee and

Texas expanded the list of factors (ultimately including more than 30). And the electorate in Arkansas in a 1956 referendum approved a similar provision.

Typical of the assignment laws, except that it is permissive rather than mandatory, is the Tennessee act. This law contains the most extensive list of assignment factors, many of which are included, in much the same language, in the placement acts of the other states. It provides:

That in determining the particular public school to which pupils shall be assigned, the board of education may consider and base its decision on any one or more of the following factors: available room and teaching capacity in the various schools; the geographical location of the place of residence of the pupil as related to the various schools of the system; the availability of transportation facilities; the effect of the enrollment on the welfare and best interests of such pupil and all other pupils in said school as well as the effect on the efficiency of the operation of said school; the effect of the admission of new pupils upon established or proposed academic programs; the suitability of established curricula for particular pupils; the adequacy of the pupil's academic preparation for admission to a particular school and curriculum; the scholastic aptitude and relative intelligence or mental energy or ability of the pupil; the psychological qualifications of the pupil for the type of teaching and association involved; the effect of admission of the pupil upon the academic program of other students in a particular school or facility thereof; the effect of admission upon prevailing academic standards at a particular school; the psychological effect upon the pupil of attendance at a particular school; the effect of any disparity between the physical and mental ages of any pupil to be enrolled, especially when contrasted with the average physical and mental ages of the group with which the pupil may be placed; the sociological, psychological and like intangible social scientific factors as will prevent, as nearly as possible, a condition of socio-economic class consciousness among the pupils; the possibility or threat of friction or disorder among pupils or others; the possibility of breaches of the peace or ill will or economic retaliation within the community; the home environment of the pupil; the maintenance or severance of established social and psychological relationships with other pupils and with teachers; the choice and interests of the pupil; the sex, morals, conduct, health and personal standards of the pupil; the request or consent of parents or guardians and the reasons assigned therefor; together with any and all other factors which the board may consider pertinent.

In common with the other detailed placement acts, the Tennessee statute sets out the procedure for appeals from local school boards' decisions. First, the local school board itself must be asked to review its decision. Then the question may be taken into the state courts.

Some states' assignment acts provide for appeals to state boards of education, and Virginia's provides for appeals to the governor, in whose name the original assignment decisions are made by a special state placement board of three members. A feature unique to the Virginia act is the vesting of the assignment authority in the state board rather than the local boards where it traditionally resides.

Behind these statutes is reliance on two principles. The first is the inherent power of school boards to assign pupils to the schools under their jurisdictions. Next comes the legal principle of requiring exhaustion of "administrative remedies" before seeking relief in the courts. At the base of it all is the supposition that racial differences are sufficient to result in substantial segregation if pupils are classified along strictly educational, aptitudinal, sociological and psychological lines, without regard to race. None of the placement laws mentions race, but the Texas statute specifies that neither national origin nor language shall be considered in assigning students, an obvious reference to another minority group prevalent in that state, the Latin-Americans.

Pupil assignment in 1957 appeared as the focal point of legislative resistance to the school decisions for one paramount reason. Of the legislation thus far tested in court, only placement has been given tentative approval. Even this was not universal. The Louisiana placement act was declared "invalid" on its face in the first court test of post-1954 legislation for two reasons: it left too much to the discretion of the assigning authority, which in this case was the district superintendent; second, the district court said (in a decision upheld by the U. S. Supreme Court) the Louisiana act was adopted to implement a companion act which required separate schools for white and Negro children. In a similar case, the Virginia placement act was called "invalid on its face" because the "efficient" system of education it was designed to provide was defined in a companion act as "separate." In both the Louisiana and the Virginia cases, the courts went behind the placement acts to determine the intent for which they were adopted.

The pupil assignment concept, however, was approved in effect in a case involving the North Carolina statute which a circuit court upheld in part. The U. S. Supreme Court declined to review the decision. The lower court approved the inherent powers of local school boards to assign students on the basis of educationally feasible criteria and the necessity of exhausting administrative remedies before seeking relief in Federal courts. The court meanwhile frowned on a provision that appeals procedures be carried through the state courts.

The shortcoming of the placement concept, from the determined segregationist point of view, is that, fairly administered, it can only control and not prevent desegregation. This was recognized in many of the legislatures which have chosen the placement course. William T. Joyner, vice chairman of the North Carolina Advisory Committee on Schools which designed and recommended for adoption the North Carolina assignment bill, has said:

I think that some mixing in the schools is inevitable and must occur. I think that the result of free choice and honest assignment according to the best interest of the child will be separation so substantially complete as to be tolerable to our people . . . I do not hesitate to advance my personal opinion and it is that the admission of less than 1 per cent—for example, one-tenth of 1 per cent—of Negro children to the schools heretofore attended only by white children is a small price to pay for the ability to keep the mixing within bounds of reasonable control.

This is not likely to suffice in some of the strongly resisting states. In Virginia, the first state to implement its assignment plan to any significant degree, difficulties have arisen. In the spring of 1957 when the first 1,500 applicants, mostly recent newcomers to the state, were assigned to schools there was a question what the result was going to be. While the application forms used in administering the placement act show no race, it was suspected that the birth certificates required along with the applications would do so. However, since some out-of-state birth certificates did not indicate race, the Pupil Placement Board was frankly in a quandary. Should placement result in some mixing, the schools so affected would be cut off from state funds and closed by the governor under provision of other legislation.

This, indeed, was the intent of the Virginia legislative program which provided that if the placement failed to prevent desegregation, the last resort, school-closing measures would become operative.

CLOSING THE SCHOOLS

At this point the more drastic legislation takes on its greatest significance. In six states, at least, if efforts to deter litigation do not succeed, the last-stand defense against desegregation is closing the

public schools. Georgians in 1954 ratified a constitutional amendment
to end state support for schools receiving both white and Negro pupils.
A 1952 statute provided for education expense grants for children
who, in this event, would attend private schools. The South Carolina
constitution was amended in 1952, repealing the provision that required "a liberal system of free public schools for all children between
the ages of six and twenty-one." A Mississippi amendment was ratified in 1954 giving both the legislature and the local electorates authority to close schools. An amendment to the Alabama constitution
was approved in 1956 replacing the requirement that separate free
public schools be maintained with this statement of policy: ". . .
nothing in this Constitution shall be construed as creating or recognizing any right to education or training at public expense." A North
Carolina enactment of 1956 permits local electorates to decide
whether public education shall be continued in the event of desegregation. And a Virginia statute of 1956 provides for automatic closing
of desegregated schools until they can be reopened on a segregated
basis.

Most other legislation was designed largely to adjust general education laws to such eventualities. Alabama, Georgia, North Carolina and
Virginia have provided for state grants for private education. Compulsory attendance laws have been modified in Alabama, Arkansas,
Louisiana, Georgia and Virginia, and repealed outright in Mississippi
and South Carolina. Sale or lease of unneeded public education facilities to private, non-sectarian corporations has been approved in Alabama, Georgia, Mississippi and South Carolina. The use of public
funds for desegregated schools, which would be closed anyhow, has
been prohibited in Georgia, Louisiana, South Carolina and Virginia.
South Carolina appropriations bills for schools and parks since 1955
have specified the funds could be used only for segregated facilities.
Teacher tenure has been abolished in North Carolina and South
Carolina and modified in Alabama (by local act), Florida, Louisiana,
Mississippi and Virginia.

None of this legislation has been tested in the courts because none
of it has been implemented—yet. That it will be used, in the last resort,
there is said to be no doubt. And here will develop the showdown
between Federal judicial authority and state legislative authority. The
issues will be whether Federal courts can order state legislatures to

appropriate funds for education and whether maintenance of education is, in fact, a function states must perform.

But before these issues can be joined, another question must be resolved. It is whether states can curtail activities within their borders designed to promote litigation. This has been the end sought directly in Mississippi, South Carolina, Virginia and Tennessee by laws against barratry, champerty, and running and capping, which seek to curb solicitation of law suits and filing of suits without consent of the parties plaintiff. Like other, more general laws in Alabama, Arkansas and Louisiana, they have been aimed primarily at the National Association for the Advancement of Colored People. The Virginia statutes in this category were under attack by the NAACP in the spring and summer of 1957.

In addition to these rather uniform trends in legislation, several of the states have launched out in other directions. Louisiana, for example, is the only state thus far to adopt a program for resegregating its colleges. In widely varying ways, the legislatures of Florida, South Carolina, Mississippi and Georgia have given their governors broad powers to cope with disorders arising from racial questions. The Louisiana legislature in 1956 specified that school suits henceforth must be directed against the state rather than the local board and then withdrew state consent to be sued. Tennessee legislators sought to dull the edge of racial desegregation by authorizing segregation by sex.

Ends and Means

In many of the legislatures which adopted the new racial laws, all was not harmonious. The disagreements, however, were more often over means than ends. In Virginia, administration forces of Governor Thomas Stanley shoved through enactments which went beyond measures proposed by the legislative study committee. In the debate whether the pupil assignment plan, originally opposed by the governor, should provide for state or local administration, these views were heatedly advanced:

Senator Stuart B. Carter of Botetourt County, the only legislator who publicly admitted a "conscientious belief in integration," argued that abandoning segregation represents a "great change" but is inevitable. Therefore, he said, "the best method of making the change is to have gradual orderly integration where necessary controlled and regulated by the people in the school district."

Countered Senator A. S. Harrison, Jr., of Lawrenceville: "And who plays God to decide which superior colored child [should be integrated]?"

In Florida, when the legislature in 1956 sought to go beyond what had been proposed by the administration, Governor Collins in an unprecedented move dissolved the special session. And in Texas, two senators from districts with heavy Latin-American constituencies spelled by four others carried on a 36-hour filibuster against the pupil assignment bill. They indicated they would employ the same tactic against every one of the 11 segregation bills introduced in the 1957 session.

They Work Together

The essential uniformity of all states' major defenses against school desegregation suggests close liaison among them. For the most part, this has been another legislative responsibility and was handled largely through the study committees authorized to compile and recommend pro-segregation laws. Subsequently the committee procedure has been expanded. In Florida, South Carolina and Virginia, specific legislation has empowered committees to investigate NAACP activities. In Arkansas and Mississippi, State Sovereignty Commissions have been directed to "protect the sovereignty of the state . . . from encroachments thereon by the Federal government." In North Carolina, South Carolina, Louisiana and Alabama continuing studies of segregation matters have kept legislative bodies busy.

In Texas, Tennessee, Arkansas, North Carolina and Florida, committees appointed by the governors designed the legislative programs. Similarities in form and verbiage, however, indicate that these groups, too, maintained liaison with segregation study groups in other states. And in Alabama, a substantial part of the contact was maintained through informal channels of the white Citizens Councils with which several influential legislators are associated.

Backing the Decision

Thus, most legislation adopted as a consequence of the Supreme Court decisions has been almost wholly designed to prevent, delay or control desegregation. As we have seen, only in Oklahoma have measures been enacted to enhance the desegregation process. In West Virginia, the 1957 General Assembly adopted legislation recognizing desegregation as a *fait accompli*.

The Oklahoma integration legislation came in 1955. It was in the form, first, of a constitutional amendment combining the separate white and Negro school budgets, and, second, a new school code. The amendment was considered as a segregation issue only in that schoolmen had viewed desegregation in Oklahoma largely as a budgetary problem. Under the amendment, a four-mill levy restricted for use in Negro schools was replaced by a general levy of the same amount for all schools.

In debating the proposed amendment, the argument was raised that it would "open the floodgates to desegregation." Neither then nor later in debate on revision of the school code did the segregation issue prove a significant factor.

Among the statutory changes embodied in the new code were sections providing for maintenance of schools on military reservations in conformity with "all Federal laws and requirements." But at least one segregation section of the 1951 school code was carried over into the 1955 and 1957 laws largely intact. Others were revised to delete references to the dual budget but kept requirements for separate schools. And a new section was added in 1955 giving local school boards specific powers "to designate the schools to be attended by children of the district."

However, the revisions were sufficient to enable the state school board to implement its policy favoring desegregation by applying fiscal pressure to districts with dual school systems.

In other desegregating states, little legislative action has been taken. Missouri legislators in 1957 repealed school segregation statutes which previously had been declared unenforceable by the state attorney general, though similar repeal efforts had failed in 1955. Maryland's Assembly in 1957 refused, as it has perennially, to ratify the Fourteenth Amendment under which the school segregation cases were decided. One measure with segregationist backing got through the 1957 Assembly, providing for popular election of the Talbot County school board. It was vetoed.

And Delaware's legislature, with some inconsistency, has retained one feature of its segregated schools in budgetary matters. In its 1955 school construction bill it continued to designate Negro schools with the initial "C". However, the designation now is defined as indicating a school supported entirely by state funds. Negro schools in Delaware traditionally have been wholly state-supported.

Legislatures v. Courts

In the resisting states and in at least three complying states the primary purpose of legislation has been to minimize the results of the school segregation decisions. The issue in its broadest sense has become largely a political one, pitting Federal judicial authority against state legislative prerogative. The courts have asserted themselves through their formal decrees and opinions, the legislatures through their enactments and resolutions.

Since early in 1956, six state legislatures—in Alabama, Florida, Georgia, Louisiana, Mississippi and Virginia—have sought to dramatize the issue by resolutions of interposition or nullification. Four states—North Carolina, South Carolina, Tennessee and Texas— have employed resolutions of protest against Federal encroachment upon states' rights. Arkansas voters approved both interposition and nullification proposals. Quite uniformly the resolutions have cited conflicts of state and Federal authority and with substantial consistency have called for constitutional amendment to resolve the issue. Four of the resolutions have declared the school segregation decisions "null and void."

Cue to Congress

The same general notion expressed in the state resolutions of interposition or protest was carried through on the national level by the "Declaration of Constitutional Principles," signed by 77 congressmen and 19 senators. Generally known as the Southern Manifesto, this document labeled the school segregation decisions a "clear abuse of judicial power [which] climaxes a trend in the Federal judiciary undertaking to legislate in derogation of the authority of Congress and to encroach upon the reserved rights of the states and the people."

Pointing up the issue, the Manifesto said:

Though there has been no constitutional amendment or act of Congress changing this established legal principle [the separate but equal concept] almost a century old, the Supreme Court of the United States, with no legal basis for such action, undertook to exercise their naked judicial power and substituted their personal political and social ideas for the established law of the land.

This unwarranted exercise of power by the Court, contrary to the Constitution, is creating chaos and confusion in the states principally affected . . .

With the gravest concern for the explosive and dangerous condition created by this decision and inflamed by outside meddlers:

We reaffirm our reliance on the Constitution as the fundamental law of the land.

We decry the Supreme Court's encroachments on the rights reserved to the states and to the people, contrary to the established law, and to the Constitution.

We commend the motives of those states which have declared the intention to resist forced integration by any lawful means.

Southern congressmen subsequently have introduced a large number of bills for the purpose of implementing this statement of principle. Included have been bills (1) to reduce the appellate jurisdiction of the Supreme Court; (2) to curb the Court's authority to reverse previous decisions; (3) to specify that sole jurisdiction over school systems shall be exercised by the states.

While the chance these measures have of adoption in the Congress may be subject to debate, they do serve to underscore the determination of southern lawmakers to write the statutes affecting racial issues in the schools of their states and to resist unequivocally what they conceive to be judicial encroachments upon their prerogatives.

The Crowded Books

So, for the most part, have white southerners spoken, or seemed to speak, through their state legislators. (There are no Negroes in legislatures in any mid-South or Deep South state and less than a handful in the border states.) The absence of legislation, or a bare minimum of enabling legislation, distinguish the border state approach—and hence speak for a broader degree of acceptance of the Supreme Court decisions. The spate of laws elsewhere, with large majorities and even unanimous votes recorded in their favor, must be taken to speak for the temper of the rest of the region. There, the incessant demand from segregationists outside legislative halls as within them has been: "*Do* something!"

As this is an era of litigation, so it is a time of legislation. More state laws dealing with school segregation have been enacted in the last three years than in all the modern history of the southern region. Perhaps no other issue has brought for such long periods legislative preoccupation with the authority and rights and sensibilities of states as opposed to authority from Washington: after all, only six months passed before secessionists got the upper hand in every legislature of the old South.

What will be the sum total of this extraordinary and unprecedented activity of 1954-57 in its effect on the overriding domestic issue of the day is yet to be seen. At any rate, the record is there—and is growing—on the statute books of one-fourth of the American states.

9.

Nation's Showcase?

By Jeanne Rogers

"We affirm our intention to secure the right of every child, within his own capacity, to the full, equal and impartial use of all school facilities, and the right of all qualified teachers to teach where needed within the school system.

"And, finally, we ask the aid, cooperation and good will of all citizens and the help of the Almighty in holding to our stated purposes."

This was the Declaration of Policy—drafted on May 25, 1954—by the board of education of Washington, D.C., a community with a southern exposure which didn't wait for the Supreme Court to tell it how and when to end public school segregation. Since full-scale integration went into effect three years ago, schools in the nation's capital, on the one hand, have become research laboratories for other cities now planning integration or chambers of horror, on the other hand, for those who believe that desegregation can't work. The Washington experience has been described as the "Nation's Showcase." To which some have added a question mark—"Nation's Showcase?"

The prediction that School Superintendent Hobart M. Corning made during the first year of desegregation has come true: "The greatest of the educational growing pains are yet to come." School officials did not kid themselves that it would be easy in one year's time to knit together two divisions of a school system which represented 104,000 students, 3,700 teachers and officers and 158 buildings. "I held my breath and I'm still holding it—at the magnitude of the job," Dr. Corning said. Earlier than 1954, however, the board of education began to concern itself with the possibility that school segregation might be declared unconstitutional. Community organizations were asked to suggest "best ways" of integrating the schools.

Hard to Handle

The public was aware that a segregated school system had become increasingly hard to handle. The school board was working continually to keep school facilities equal. An increasing Negro enrollment was coupled with a declining white registration. This resulted in some white schools operating below capacity while some Negro schools were seriously overcrowded.

In Washington—a government-worker city—1950 census figures show that two out of three residents are white. But current statistics show that in the city's classrooms, seven out of 10 students are Negro. Critics contend that Washington's rapid integration caused a flight to the suburbs in nearby Maryland and Virginia of white residents. Educators, on the other hand, declare this migration began a decade ago. They point to the records. Single persons, childless couples and those whose children are grown continue to live in the city, while young white couples with small children have moved to suburbia. Negro families have remained in Washington because school facilities for children of their race are inadequate in the suburbs. Since official population figures are now in the doldrums—or the between-census period—hard statistics on migration are difficult to come by. However, in what he calls an "educated guess," Raymond Clapp, research consultant of the District Department of Public Welfare, provides these figures:

> *School-age Children (5 to 17 years)*
> 135,000 white born in city
> 55,000 living in city, 1957
> 80,000 now living elsewhere, primarily in suburbs
> Population of white declined from 63,000 in 1950 to
> 55,000 in 1957, a 13 per cent decrease
>
> 80,000 nonwhite born in city
> 90,000 living in city, 1957
> 10,000 born elsewhere have moved into city
> Population of nonwhite increased from 52,000 in 1950 to
> 90,000 in 1957, a 73 per cent increase

Presidential Preference

The day after the Supreme Court decision, the District school board decided to go ahead with integration. President Eisenhower had let it be known he would like Washington's school system, which unlike others in America has its budget controlled by Congress, to be a model for the rest of the nation.

THE DISTRICT BEGINS

Eight days later, the school board issued a five-point anti-discrimination policy to govern the schools. Pupils and teachers would be assigned to schools without regard to race. Dr. Corning next announced a timetable which set deadlines for every step of the one-year integration program. Boundaries of former white and Negro schools were redrawn without regard to race so children could study in buildings nearer home. Under the gradual integration plan, when school opened September 13, 1954, the new zones applied only to students new to Washington schools and to youngsters who had moved from one part of the city to another. In addition, 3,000 Negro students were transferred from overcrowded schools into former white schools which had empty seats.

Opening day proceeded without "one single thing untoward happening," according to Assistant Superintendent Norman J. Nelson. A week later Corning speeded up his integration calendar, giving other students a choice of remaining in the school they were attending or transferring to the school rezoned to serve their community. Soon, Washington discovered that the racial bars fell without open friction. This could be credited, in part, to a board of education and school officers who knew and said where they were going. The community and the school faculties knew what was going to happen. (Unhappily, communications were to suffer when the novelty of innovation wore off and criticism began.)

District Truants

Then, one month after school opened, about 2,500 students from three former white high schools and six junior highs staged a four-day demonstration against racially mixed classes. School officials and the police made it clear that they didn't intend to put up with such behavior. Threatened with loss of all school honors and privileges, the students returned to class. At this point, Corning and other officials realized that the students should have been prepared in advance for their move into a new relationship. More spadework, they said, should have been done in school communities.

The class-cutting episodes took place in the three high schools which received the largest numbers of transferred Negro students. One school community has a background of racial tension over recreation and housing issues. But at other former white high schools, which received fewer Negro students through normal promotion, there was no difficulty. Charles E. Bish, principal of McKinley High, one of the schools which suffered the student walkout, said: "The cultures of the two races were not as near alike as many of us thought." Bish said he wished he had talked separately to students of both races during the first days of school. Among other things, Bish said he would have counseled the young people that certain words and expressions are offensive to members of opposite races.

Following the demonstrations, Bish did tell the new Negro students that they must observe the ground rules of his school which do not permit knife-carrying, obscenity or uncleanliness. These were some of the grievances reported by the white students to a special biracial teenage committee organized to hear and work out problems. Similar committees were set up at all the city high schools which had shown signs of student tension. Soon the students realized their problems weren't as serious as they thought and many were remedied easily. At one school, for example, a Negro girl still was wearing a sweater of her last year's school. Her new colleagues said this was disloyal. It was found the girl had no other sweater. It wasn't long before she had a new one.

During the student demonstrations and afterward, school officials leaned heavily on the student councils to keep them informed about "true student feeling." Acting on its own, the citywide association of student councils (formerly an all-white organization) invited all city schools to send delegates to meetings. For the first time, Negro representatives attended the monthly sessions where problems and programs of individual schools are discussed.

The Barriers Were Down

In the first days of desegregation it became apparent that there was a lack of communication not only between the two former school divisions but between top and bottom in the separate divisions. One particular move made by some Division II (Negro) administrators created a bad first impression among Division I (white) teachers and students, for some principals sent ill-suited students to the former white schools. This prompted Margaret Just Butcher, Negro board member and Howard University faculty member, to say that some principals had "dumped" students. (Mrs. Butcher was not reappointed by District court judges when her three-year term ran out in June 1956. The nine-member school board traditionally has three Negroes.)

The "dumping" can be understood, school officials now say, when one realizes that Negro principals took great pride in their better students and competed unofficially with the white schools for scholarships and other honors. For example, at Eastern High School, Principal John Paul Collins, now retired, said that of the 350 Negro students initially transferred there, 125 had intelligence quotients below 75, ranging down to 41. Normal IQ is 100. Five classes for retarded students were established at this school. Collins, a former Marine major, had plenty of behavior problems because of the caliber of his transfer students. The principal and his faculty looked around for a way to get across the idea to the student body that all persons must be accepted for what they are.

One result was "live history" assemblies which depicted what members of various races have contributed to American life. The Veterans Day program of 1954, for instance, was the story of American wars. For the Civil War, or the War Between the States (it was given both titles), a mixed girls' chorus sang "Battle Hymn of the Republic." The climax of the program was a short talk by a disabled Negro veteran of the Korean War.

Another overt sign of student integration occurred on November 11, 1954, when a 17-year-old Negro senior led a contingent of the integrated High School Cadet Corps in ceremonies at the Tomb of the Unknown Soldier in Arlington National Cemetery.

In athletics, school officials expressed frank amazement that mixed teams had been accepted so readily by students and adult spectators alike. The Negro players received equal support from the bleachers.

When the question of school dances first arose, officials again used the student councils as sounding boards. In some schools, parent committees discussed the issue. It was decided that schools with mixed classes would not hold dances the first year. Now the schools again are scheduling their traditional senior proms. White boys bring white girls and Negro boys bring dates of their own race. There have been no problems. One high school cancelled its final ball in 1956, however, because there were too few prospective participants to pay for an orchestra.

In February 1955 school officials made the last student transfer. Some 1,200 Negro and white junior high students were graduated into high schools nearer their homes, thus dropping the last racial barrier to high school admittance.

Grade school desegregation received little publicity because of its ease. An average integrated class in an elementary school is about one-third Negro. Some schools have only a handful of white students and others have as few as two or three Negro pupils. From the start, the younger pupils took the program in stride. During the general discussion periods which begin each school day, the children took obvious pleasure in hearing "new things" from members of the opposite race. Mixed casts acted in grade school plays.

Superintendent Corning for three years has stressed that natural differences between the two former separate divisions of the school system must be ironed out. For example, the former Negro division demanded strict discipline in the classroom while the white schools encouraged students to be natural and more informal. Corning said that the "freer atmosphere" of the white schools resulted in many Negro students letting off steam in "overcompensating" behavior. Some, he said, need to be placed in special "social adjustment" classes.

Toward the end of the first year of desegregation, the integrated District Congress of Parents and Teachers sponsored a human relations workshop. Several parents said that a paramount question in their minds was: "Will educational standards be lowered because of integration?"

A white grade school principal said this is a threat "because so many Negro children come to Washington from an inferior school environment where they had, perhaps, not the same well-trained teachers." A Negro principal suggested that it is more important to American cultural progress to "sacrifice standards to a reasonable limit to obtain the advantage of having both groups share the experience of living together."

In preparing for integration, school officials combined two lists of eligibles who had applied for teaching jobs in Washington. In the summer of 1954, additional applicants for the first time took the same teacher examination from one board of examiners without regard to race. The 250 new teachers hired were appointed and assigned without regard to race. Through the first year, officer jobs were filled in the same fashion.

IT'S COMPLICATED

The District school system is perhaps unmatched in its complexity. At the beginning of officer integration, there were six systemwide jobs, all held by white officers: superintendent, business administrator, food services director, attendance director, and associate superintendents of personnel and buildings and grounds. Otherwise, there were twin sets of officers performing similar jobs in the two divisions. After integration, Corning reshuffled the jobs of his chief lieutenants. One deputy was in charge of the operation of all schools. A new post of deputy in charge of coordinated educational services was created for the former head of Negro schools. On the supervisory level, departments are run by the two incumbent officers. Attrition will take care of this double setup and eventually save $90,000.

Thus as Corning commented in the second year of the school transition: "Desegregation, the mechanical moving of people and things, virtually has been completed. But integration, the conversion of the two segments of the schools into a smooth-running single system, still requires the work of all."

District Average

School officials expressed public concern about educational standards, and they had the backing of the community. Said one veteran District educator: "We're all running around sticking our fingers in the dike—in a lot of little holes. Unless something is done, and done fast, the dike will break."

What did he mean? On the average, Washington students do not measure up to national standards in such subjects as reading, spelling, arithmetic and social studies. This fact came to light after the first citywide series of achievement tests was given shortly after the start of integration. Test results showed that on the average, Negro students made a poorer showing than white students. In addition, school officials made known these other school situations:

More than 1,800 grade school youngsters were slow learners. This was a polite way of saying that 3 per cent of the elementary student body was retarded.

In 1955 the school research department had been asked by principals to make individual case studies of more than 3,000 maladjusted pupils. The short-staffed department was inundated by the task and couldn't keep abreast of the wave of problem children.

Junior high school officials admitted they were giving desk space to elementary-level school children, primarily Negro, who couldn't keep up and shouldn't have been there. Vocational schools were turning out an increasing number of young people ill-prepared to take advantage of job opportunities available in Washington. At the same time, high schools were receiving more and more poorly trained students in need of specialized courses to enable them to get better than "minimum wage" jobs after graduation.

The educators for the past two years in record-breaking budget requests have said, in effect, the problem of raising these educational standards can be solved only in terms of enough dedicated teachers, enough school buildings, imaginative ideas and strong educational leadership at the top. There's no doubt it will cost money to bring about these reforms and to make the Washington school system one of the best in the United States, the school people contend.

Because at a time when school officials say they're swamped with the problem of education itself, the old problems of mushrooming enrollments and overcrowding continue. Hundreds of grade school classes are accommodating 36 to 48 pupils. This crowding comes at a time when the board of education is attempting to whittle class size down to a reasonable 30 pupils per teacher, a situation long since effected by other big cities. Further, many schools in southeast and northeast Washington, where new housing developments practically sit in the schoolyards, are holding classes in lunchrooms, auditoriums, libraries and basements. There are hundreds of first-graders attending half-day classes.

District in Transit

The Washington population moves like quicksilver. One school principal reported that she enrolled pupils who attended 46 different District schools the previous year. Thus it is almost a losing battle in Washington to keep schools where children are. The Washington school administration is unalterably opposed to putting wheels under its students, although bus transportation is used successfully by District parochial schools, other large city school systems and in almost all rural areas.

The Washington school population is a migratory one. Student origin studies find large numbers of youngsters coming from inferior school systems elsewhere. It is a tough job for a teacher to reach these children, some of whom barely can carry on a conversation. Take a recent example of a principal trying to get some line on a child who had moved from pillar to post—Florida, Georgia, South Carolina—before arriving in the District in the fall.

She asked: "What's your mother's name?" The child replied, "Don't know." She continued: "Who is your father?" The reply: "Ain't got none." In desperation she said: "Well, with whom do you live?" The answer: "Helen."

More than ever before, teachers are having to step in and give many youngsters experiences they missed at home. Some children have never seen a newspaper or book. They have never heard a nursery rhyme. The Washington school system must provide education for these deprived children so they can become a useful part of the community. At the same time, District educators say they must do more for the average child and again not forget the gifted child, who is found in any neighborhood.

This is the way the Washington school population stood when school opened in the fall of 1956—the third year of full-scale integration:

The school system head count, taken October 19, showed a grand total of 108,481 students—a history-making figure. Of this number, 68 per cent or 73,723 were Negroes, and 32 per cent or 34,758 were white. By February the Negro ratio was 7 out of 10.

This compares with a 64-36 per cent Negro-white division the previous year. Thus, since the fall of 1955, the number of white students had declined by 4,010, while 4,846 more Negroes had entered classrooms. Total enrollment records showed a gain of 836 pupils in the year's time.

The decrease in white students has stayed about constant since 1954-55. This is true also of the rate of increase of Negro students for the past several years. The trend began as far back as 1945, when 56 per cent of the public school population was white and 44 per cent Negro. In 1950, the school child population was racially 50-50.

Since desegregation began in Washington, the white enrollment decline in numbers presents no consistent pattern. Between 1953-54 white enrollment dipped by 3,504. Between 1954 and 1955 the drop-off was cut back to 2,625. In 1956-57 the decrease was 4,010.

Fall statistics for 1956-557 showed these other facts:

All but 25 of the city's 169 public school buildings were integrated in some degree. In some cases, a school may have had one or two white or Negro pupils making up a minority group.

Six of the 25 schools with no pupil integration were all-white. The rest were all-Negro. (All the schools are open to members of both races.)

Children enrolled in special classes totaled 3,899, or twice as many as in the previous year. These classes included those for slow learners, retarted readers and for youngsters with sight, hearing or physical handicaps. More than 3,000 of the 3,899 special students were Negroes, the records show.

Before desegregation, the city's white school division had a number of such special classes, but the Negro side of the school system had relatively few because of the lack of funds allocated for this purpose.

Congress Investigates

During the third year of integration, District schools were caught in a national spotlight. Southern newsmen and northern magazine writers came to the nation's capital and made their own evaluation of the schools.

In September 1956 a special House District subcommittee held a 10-day public hearing on current conditions and standards of Washington's integrated school system. The probe was initiated by subcommittee member Congressman John Bell Williams (D-Miss.), a pro-segregationist who became angry with the school board when it refused to supply him with school statistics on a racial basis.

A majority of the special six-member subcommittee, headed by Congressman James C. Davis (D-Ga.), were southerners. Subcommittee counsel was William E. Gerber, a Memphis attorney.

Corning, last witness of some 50 called, defended the schools. He denied emphatically that the schools are "in a mess" because of racial integration.

A product of Washington schools himself, Corning as chief officer responsible for the segregated school divisions admitted: ". . . perhaps I made a little error" in presuming that "serious differences" did not exist between the two.

For hours Corning parried Gerber's attempts to get him to say that Negro pupils were inferior to white ones in native intelligence and ability to learn. Gerber was criticized by Washington civic organizations and religious leaders for his conduct of the school investigation which they said was designed to show that integration will not work.

'Dangerous Generalizations'

During his testimony, Corning repeatedly told Gerber "there is danger in generalizations . . . a fallacy," when the latter made blanket references to the different achievement levels of white and Negro students before and after integration. Under questioning about the speed of integration in Washington, Corning mentioned that at that time community tension was high and that eight lawsuits were pending against the schools, based on alleged inequality of school facilities. "What do you care about lawsuits?" Gerber asked. "Did you get excited about the lawsuits?" he continued. "Certainly," Corning replied, stressing, however, "They had nothing to do with hurrying integration."

Gerber asked Corning how long it would be before "we have segregated schools again" because of the number of white families moving out of Washington. "I'm no prophet," Corning said.

Williams asked Corning if the low achievement level of Washington pupils was a direct result of segregation as some persons contend. Corning said "conditions of segregation did contribute to it," but it was not the sole cause. Pushed by Williams for an answer to what advantages white children have received from integration, Corning said he had "no objective data" in the field of "intangibles." Williams again pressed Corning to say there had been White House pressure to speed integration of Washington schools. "This is not true," Corning said.

The Critical

Lead-off witness of the investigation was District School Board President C. Melvin Sharpe, who declared: "Present events indicate if we had been a little more moderate [in desegregating the schools] we would have succeeded better." He added: "We have made great advances. There is no question that we have succeeded in doing a great many things that gradually will work out."

School principals during the sessions declared integration had exposed some problems, particularly low student achievement rates and difficulties of discipline. Hugh Smith, Jefferson Junior High principal, said he favored integration but believed it would take at least 10 years to work out all problems. Smith admitted integration had sent more "retarded" youngsters into his school and that as a result teachers have to work harder. He added: "Our children have got to be taught . . . we're not going to let one bad apple ruin a bushel basket."

Still other District educators admitted they were frustrated by stealing, knife-carrying, disobedience, truancy and some sex incidents among pupils. They also pointed out that many of their problems, particularly low student achievement levels, were the result of children moving into Washington from southern states.

At Roosevelt High School, where the enrollment was 45 per cent Negro the first year of the integration program, Principal Elva Wells told the committee that "belligerency" of new Negro students upset carefully laid plans for integration. In describing the use of obscene language, the misuse of school property and curtailment of social activities, she insisted that integration was becoming "more difficult." In this vein, Arthur Storey, Macfarland Junior High principal, said disciplinary problems would be reduced at high schools if the most difficult cases could be removed to special adjustment classes. His student body of 1,300, he said, was 70 per cent Negro—in what had been an all-white school. Wilmer F. Bennett, Hine Junior High principal, whose school had the same racial ratio as Storey's, testified he had set up five classes for "atypical" students with IQs below 75.

The school inquiry drew protests from the National Association for the Advancement of Colored People, the organization which charged the schools with "moving too slowly" at the start of integration.

Complimenting the investigators, however, was the Federation of Citizens Association, a white organization which three years ago unsuccessfully sought a court order to stop board of education plans for immediate school integration. This group said the school board "moved too fast."

On Four Tracks

The subcommittee requested and received a racial breakdown of assignment to the District's new four-track plan which began in 1956 for tenth-graders. The plan actually stemmed from integration, although educators point out it is not too different from the old-fashioned "stratified" high school system. Tailor-made to meet individual differences of students, its biggest break with the traditional curriculum is the basic course which is largely remedial and designed to better prepare students destined for unskilled employment. The honors course is also unusual in that it offers greater opportunity for the "bright" student. District educators believe the experiment has been successful and have recommended its initiation for all three high school years.

The breakdown provided the subcommittee showed that 315 white and 50 Negro pupils were in a college preparatory course; 645 white and 1,453 Negro pupils were in a "terminal" course, and 158 white and 1,319 Negro students were in a "basic" course for slow learners.

Congressional Report

On December 27, 1956, the subcommittee issued majority and minority findings on the school system. The majority report said the schools were integrated too rapidly with consequences highly damaging to the city. This was signed by Congressmen Davis, Williams, Woodrow Wilson Jones (D-N.C.) and Joel T. Broyhill (R-Va.), who blamed integration for four specific things: the accelerated movement of white residents to the suburbs which, members said, "threatened the economic and cultural foundations of the city;" an "appalling" rate of juvenile delinquency and a rise in sex offenses; a demoralized teaching staff and educational retrogression; and spiraling school costs.

This report also proposed legislative remedies to modify the present integration program by liberalizing school transfers and establishing special schools for children with low mental ability or records of delinquency. The schools would be required to keep records by race and machinery for the removal of school board members would be established.

Subcommittee minority members Congressmen DeWitt S. Hyde (R-Md.) and A. L. Miller (R-Neb.) refused to sign the report. They declared the draft form circulated to them by the southern majority dealt with "sordid headline items almost entirely." Hyde and Miller issued minority views which accused the subcommittee staff of asking leading questions of "selected" witnesses. A more "objective" inquiry would have uncovered "good things" in the school system, they said, adding: "The report seems to blame all of the educational deficiencies in our school system entirely on the efforts toward integration. We cannot believe that everything that is wrong with the educational system can be blamed on integration. It is quite probable that many of the unsatisfactory conditions brought to light by the investigation may have been caused by conditions that existed prior to integration and are due to factors other than integration."

Shortly after the minority view had been tacked to the report, the subcommittee's four other members issued "additional views" of their own. They called for restoration of segregation in the District's public schools. The majority members said integration "has seriously damaged the public school system" and has impaired educational opportunities for members of both races "with little prospect of remedy in the future." Therefore, the return to a "completely separate and equal" school system was asked. They had these legislative proposals: liberalization of present student transfer policies to permit children to be moved from one school to another in accordance with the needs of the child and the desires of the parents; creation of separate trade schools for pupils of low mental ability, incapable of achieving at the high school level; modification of the present school attendance laws to give school officials greater latitude in their authority to deal with individual problem cases; and keeping of school records, statistical data and other official information by sex and race.

According to the report, the District's integrated school system "is not a model" and "cannot be copied by those who seek an orderly and successful school operation."

These and other contentions in the report drew a blast from the Washington Committee for the Public Schools. This committee of 31 civic and church leaders, formed in September 1956 to counteract the school investigation, issued its own study of integration, detailing findings in direct conflict with the Davis report. "Everyone expected the stacked Davis subcommittee to try to turn the educational clock back," said Gerhard Van Arkel, chairman of the Washington committee, "but no one expected this foolhardy attempt to smash it. The majority report may conceivably impress the white Citizens Council in Mr. Davis' Georgia district, but it will be met by Washington's enlightened citizenry with a resounding yawn."

The special subcommittee went out of existence January 3, 1957. The report was stashed away in the full House District Committee whose top aides predicted "that's the last of it."

Some Comparisons

A Jesuit priest in his doctoral dissertation has compared integration in the District's public and Catholic schools. The Reverend Albert S. Foley, S.J., of Spring Hill College, Mobile, Alabama, cited the "smooth process" in the parochial schools of the Washington archdiocese. The "quiet, behind-the-scene efforts" of Archbishop Patrick A. O'Boyle made this transition possible, he wrote. "There were no student strikes or riots in the system," the sociologist said.

Father Foley noted that Catholic school desegregation in Washington was "paralleled and accompanied by the problem of the premature panic evacuation of parish neighborhoods by white parishioners whose families formed the backbone both of school and of parish life." If the "panic evacuation" continues, he went on, it could amount to a "resegregation of areas that have become desegregated in recent years." (His testimony appeared to collide with that of public school administrators who have maintained that, on the whole, the movement to the suburbs was little influenced by desegregation.)

Archbishop O'Boyle decided segregation would be abolished in the Catholic schools in 1948. He knew, however, that the archdiocese included five rural counties in southern Maryland. Therefore, the prelate refrained from issuing a diocesewide decree and concentrated on removing racial school barriers in Washington. This step formally began in 1950. Experimental integration was tried in two high schools the year before.

Summing Up

Assistant School Superintendent Carl F. Hansen recently described Washington integration as a "miracle of social adjustment"—a "man-made miracle." He asked these questions posed by opponents and proponents of integration alike:

Why did the board of education adopt a desegregation policy so soon after the action of the Supreme Court decision declaring segregation in the District unconstitutional but before the decree was issued? Was this action ill-considered and irresponsible? Or was it in the order of statesmanship—the risks cooly calculated against the practical, moral and human values to be gained?

"The insistent battering-ram of public opinion against racial discrimination in the capital city had already broken down many traditional barriers and had evoked much preparation for change within the school system itself, so that a state of mind favorable to immediate desegregation existed at the time." So wrote Hansen.

This educator professed to see Washington's integrated school system as a national showcase, even after its exposure to an unprecedented Congressional investigation.

Hansen wrote: "The big fear, that integration will impair the education of some children in the community, is rapidly yielding to the concentrated drive to effect the big solution. The prevailing spirit in the District of Columbia is positive and dynamic. It looks forward to a growing and improving school system, to a betterment of educational opportunities for all children, and is resolved to let no transient troubles prevent the realization of the ultimate goal—a better community through brotherhood."

Others as clearly profess to view the situation as a national showcase—but one crowded with painful errors.

10.

Halls of Ivy—Southern Exposure

By Joseph B. Parham

A few months after the May 1954 desegregation decision of the U. S. Supreme Court, a Nashville Negro attorney spoke at a public hearing on a proposed segregation bill in the Tennessee legislature. Tension had mounted as pro and con speakers were heard by the mixed crowd in the state senate chambers. Then the lawyer related this story, a parody on one long told in eastern Europe:

A southern politician was praising the benefits of segregation during a radio broadcast. The system, he said, was enjoyed by everybody in the South, white and Negro alike. To prove his point, the politician instructed his chauffeur, Sam, to come to the microphone and tell the audience how he, as a Negro, enjoyed segregation. The chauffeur approached the microphone with caution. "Boss," he asked the politician, "can people way up in New York and Detroit hear this thing?" The politician said yes.

The Negro chauffeur cupped his hands around the mike, leaned close to it, and yelled, "Help!"

A roar of laughter which dissolved the tension ran through the audience.

Three Years Later

Today, three years later, Negroes are not having to yell "Help!" to obtain admission to former all-white schools of higher education in most of the states of the South. But the situation is still tense in the hard core of holdouts making up the southeastern corner of the nation. There segregation has been maintained in public universities and colleges in Mississippi, South Carolina, Florida and Georgia, and, except for a turbulent three days, in Alabama.

Desegregation in higher education at all class levels in state schools and in some private and church schools has moved at a rapid pace in Arkansas, Delaware, Kentucky, Missouri, Maryland, Oklahoma and West Virginia; slower in Texas.

It has moved haltingly in Louisiana, North Carolina, Tennessee and Virginia.

And while white and Negro go to school together, racial separation outside the classroom on and near the campus has been only partly eliminated in either of the above two groups of states.

THE COLLEGE SCOREBOARD

In the District of Columbia and the 12 states of the South which have complete or partial desegregation, 109 of 149 tax-supported former white schools now accept qualified Negro students. An estimated 2,400 Negroes are attending these schools. A total of 53 public white colleges and universities in the five holdout states have no Negro students.

An accurate accounting of the number of Negroes in southern and border colleges is difficult because many administrators say no records are kept by race. Some of these schools, however, red check or otherwise identify the card files of Negro students.

This is but one instance of the fact that, while it is not talked about, a realization of the differences in races is present and distinctions, however subtle, are observed.

The first Negro to experience these distinctions was the first Negro to be admitted to a public higher institution in a state requiring segregation in the lower schools. In 1935 the breakthrough was achieved by Donald Murray when the courts ordered his admission to the University of Maryland School of Law. In 1938 the U. S. Supreme Court did not order the University of Missouri to admit Lloyd Gaines, a Negro, but it did send the case back to Missouri for further hearing after having made the important point that use of out-of-state tuition subsidies for Negro graduate and professional students was a denial of equal protection of the laws because the state had an obligation to provide equal opportunities within its jurisdiction.

The Federal question bearing on "equal protection of the laws" guaranteed in the Fourteenth Amendment was later to arise in relation to the program of the Southern Regional Education Board.

The Southern Regional Education Compact was signed in 1948. It provides for voluntary pooling of educational facilities within regional patterns. Today, it serves 16 southern states through 65 participating colleges and universities, which offer specialized courses of study collectively through one institution and thus avoid costly duplication.

Dr. John E. Ivey, director from SREB's beginning until 1957, says the National Association for the Advancement of Colored People was suspicious of the organization at first, perhaps believing it to be merely a device to perpetuate segregation by shuttling Negroes back and forth to colored schools in the South. But in 1949, the Board took a clear position on the matter.

Esther McCready, a Negro citizen of Maryland, sought to enter the University of Maryland School of Nursing in the absence of available facilities within the state. She was refused by the University on the grounds that the training she desired was available at Meharry Medical College in Nashville, Tennessee, under regional arrangements. She continued her efforts to gain admission, however, and the court of appeals sustained her. The SREB intervened in the case as a friend of the court, stating that regional arrangements were made to supplement facilities within the states. "It is not the purpose of the Board," the brief said, "that the regional compact and the contracts for services thereunder shall serve any state as a legal defense for avoiding responsibilities under the existing State and Federal laws and court decisions."

Dr. Ivey says that undoubtedly some members of the legislatures which approved support of SREB thought the plan would help to stave off mixing of the races in higher education, but all were told that it would be of no use as a device for maintaining segregation and avoiding litigation by Negro applicants to white schools.

The legal guns of the NAACP, which were to pinpoint the target of segregation itself in the arguments leading up to the May 1954 decision, were aimed at inequalities in public higher education in the late 1940's. A string of successes followed. The University of Arkansas, in frank recognition of the state's financial limitations, was opened to graduate law students. Litigation forced admission of Negroes on a graduate basis to universities in Oklahoma and Kentucky in 1949, in

Virginia, Louisiana and Texas in 1950 and in North Carolina in 1951. Ten non-state universities in the South also began admitting Negro graduate and professional students.

It took the Supreme Court decision of three years ago, however, to accelerate the process and to remove the prohibitions against Negro undergraduates.

Private and non-Catholic church schools have been reluctant to follow in step. Although 51 per cent of former all-white public institutions and 77 per cent of Catholic schools were integrated as of the beginning of the 1956-57 school term, only 29 per cent of the Protestant institutions and 25 per cent of the private schools were integrated.

Some schools have opened the doors to Negroes but have no colored students. Dr. Guy Johnson of the University of North Carolina, an authority on the subject, reports that as of the fall term of 1956, Negroes were actually enrolled in 105 of 206 tax-supported colleges, 55 of 188 Protestant schools, 35 of 45 Catholic schools and 28 of 114 private schools in the South. The list of integrated institutions is expected to be increased by about 25 in the fall of 1957.

Tuscaloosa's Time of Trouble

College desegregation has not been followed by the regional bloodletting and unrestrained violence which some predicted would take place. But it must be noted that in the only instance in which a Negro entered a white university in one of the holdout states in which opposition to integration is most intense, stark violence erupted and a woman came very close to losing her life.

This was the Autherine Lucy case.

Alabama, as well as the rest of the South and the nation, will not soon forget the name of Autherine Lucy. It stands for three days of tumultous events on the campus of the state university at Tuscaloosa, during which a mob screamed for the life of the Negro woman.

The fuse which was to result in the Tuscaloosa explosion was perhaps first lit in December 1954, when it was announced at a convention of the Alabama NAACP that a legal battle to "open up" the University to Negroes was planned.

The preceding September the first all-white college in Alabama to admit Negroes—Spring Hill in Mobile—had accepted a Negro student with a minimum of friction. However, Spring Hill is a small Catholic school and the University of Alabama is publicly-supported, the largest college in the state. Thus the fuse spluttered closer to the powder keg when Autherine Lucy and another Negro woman, Polly Ann Myers, sought admission to the University. Their room deposit was returned and they were advised that the courses they wanted were available at Alabama State College, a school for Negroes in Montgomery.

In October 1955 the U. S. Supreme Court ordered their admission, and Autherine Lucy and Mrs. Polly Ann Myers Hudson began preparations for entering the University of Alabama for the February 1956 term.

Mrs. Hudson soon thereafter was notified she had been refused admission by the board of trustees "on the ground that the evidence before the board shows her conduct and marital record have been such that she does not meet admission standards," but on Wednesday, February 1, Miss Lucy arrived to register in the expectation of beginning classes on the following Friday.

Miss Lucy was told by University authorities that she would not be given a room or allowed cafeteria privileges, and was hurried through registration ahead of others.

On February 3 she attended two classes as campus police guarded the corridors. In the first class, the row in which she sat remained vacant. In the second, a coed wished her luck. Miss Lucy, denied living facilities on the campus, then left for Birmingham.

A crowd of students estimated at about 1,200 assembled that night, sang "Dixie" and gradually dispersed.

On Saturday, February 4, Miss Lucy, minus her police escort, attended classes without incident. But as darkness fell, the first signs of serious disturbance appeared. A crowd gathered on the campus and moved to downtown Tuscaloosa where Leonard Wilson, a pre-law student with strong segregation beliefs, made a speech. Going back to the campus, demonstrators rocked a Greyhound bus, beat their fists on a Negro car and stopped another car, before proceeding to the home of Dr. O. C. Carmichael, University president.

A number of outsiders, some of whom took an active part in whipping up the crowd, were in evidence for the first time. Ed Brown, director of the University News Bureau, said high school students, Tuscaloosa townspeople and members of extreme pro-segregation groups from Birmingham mingled with college students. The Alabama

Council on Human Relations later said the demonstrations were the result of approximately two weeks of preparation and that a survey of hotel and motel registrations in February revealed an unusually large number of Mississippi residents in Tuscaloosa at the time.

By the end of Miss Lucy's first class period on Monday, February 6, a crowd of 200 to 300 had gathered outside the building. University officials said most were outsiders. More students arrived, however, and on the way to her second class, Miss Lucy and her escorts, two female school officials, were the targets for eggs, rocks and obscene epithets.

The crowd continuel to swell, with students apparently in the majority at the time. Several observers said many adults were present and that they deliberately agitated the group. Some members of the crowd peered in windows shouting: "Where is the nigger?" "Lynch her!" "Kill her!"

By noon, the crowd had grown to 1,000 and Miss Lucy, apparently fearing for her safety, refused to leave. Finally, at 1:15 p.m., she lay on the floor of a highway patrol car which drove through the mob.

Late on the night of February 6, the Board of Trustees met and excluded Miss Lucy until further notice "lest greater violence should follow." About two-thirds of the faculty members were reported to have supported the board's decision.

In the aftermath of the campus disorders, President Carmichael denied Miss Lucy's charges that University authorities had conspired to create mob action. On March 5 the University board "permanently expelled" her for "baseless accusations" of conspiracy against the college. Later Leonard Wilson was also expelled, four students suspended and 25 other students disciplined by the board for their parts in the disturbances.

No Negroes attempted to register as students for the fall 1956 term. According to Buford Boone, Pulitzer Prize-winning publisher of the *Tuscaloosa News,* about 18 men, wearing red caps and identified as members of the Ku Klux Klan, roamed the campus during registration.

Almost a year after the riots accompanying the Negro woman's attempt to go to the University, a U. S. district court ruled that the board was justified in expelling her. The ruling, however, still leaves the school required to admit qualified Negro students.

The Lucy case has been dropped and the woman, now Mrs. H. C.

Foster, said she planned to enter the University of Texas in the fall of 1957. The incident, however, had a traumatic effect on the whole region. Sympathy for Miss Lucy and criticism of campus violence subsided after her lawyer's charges against the University and after some newspaper reports that she had arrived in "a big black Cadillac" and had presented—ostentatiously, it was said—a $100 bill for her registration fee.

Other accounts (there were many) reduced the opulence of her transportation to a Pontiac, at most, and blamed the University for thrusting her ahead of other students waiting patiently to register. Whatever the case, some saw in the white reaction to the incident an impulse toward hardened resistance and an upsurge of the white Citizens Councils. Dr. Carmichael later resigned and took an assignment with a foundation—a step which he, then near retirement, said he had been contemplating for some time.

THE HIGHEST BARRIERS

Of the five states where no Negroes are now in college classrooms, South Carolina and Mississippi have not even had to face serious attempts by Negroes to enter. Medgar Evers, an employe of the NAACP, tried to get into the law school of the University of Mississippi in 1954 but was rejected by trustees on grounds he failed to comply with all entrance requirements. A new petition has not been filed. South Carolina, which has a law providing for the closing of a white college, as well as the state college for Negroes, if a Negro is ordered admitted by court decree, has had applications to Clemson's School of Textile Chemistry from two Negroes in the armed services. The applications, received in the summer of 1956, were referred to trustees and no action on them has been announced.

Georgia, too, has a law which would close a college to which a Negro is ordered admitted. But determined efforts to break the color barrier in higher education are being made in the state. Its capital, Atlanta, is the site of several influential private Negro colleges, and, for that reason, Roy V. Harris, a member of the Board of Regents of the University System, has said that "Atlanta could be the Achilles' heel in the fight to keep segregation in Georgia."

A decision in the long drawn-out Horace Ward case was handed down by a U. S. district court in Atlanta in March 1957, and was a victory for the state's segregation-minded officials. Ward filed suit in the summer of 1952 for admission to the law school of the University of Georgia. The case was dormant until the Atlanta Negro was discharged from military service and renewed his efforts in early 1956. The court dismissed the suit on the grounds that racial discrimination was not involved and that the plaintiff did not pursue his administrative remedies.

Still pending is the case of four Negroes who filed a Federal court suit in October 1955 to gain admission to the Georgia State College of Business Administration in Atlanta. The plaintiffs contend they are otherwise qualified but are barred because of race. The suit says the four are able to meet all the requirements except those necessitating applicants to the school to submit recommendations for admission from two sponsoring alumni and specified elected officials of each applicant's home county.

Stiffer Tests

The meeting of certain standards in order to qualify for higher education has long been insisted upon. But, with more and more students of both races asking to be enrolled, the admission tests have become stiffer. This increased competition for higher education and consequent raising of entrance standards will keep out three-fourths of the Negroes who want to go to integrated colleges, in the opinion of one southern educator.

Some states apparently are taking no chances of a Negro qualifying. Requirements difficult if not impossible to meet have been set up.

Applicants in Mississippi, somewhat like those in Georgia, must have recommendations from at least five alumni of the school where entrance is sought, all living in the home county of the applicant.

Admission requirements for the three universities in Florida provide that all applicants for graduate schools undergo rigid graduate record examinations and that undergraduate applicants must have been in the top 60 per cent of their high school classes and have a superior grade in standard tests given high school seniors.

Although implementing legislation was declared unconstitutional by Federal district judges in April 1957, a movement toward resegregation was actually begun in Louisiana after the legislature passed two acts in the summer of 1956.

One new law required applicants for education at tax-supported colleges to have a certificate of scholastic eligibility and good moral character signed by the applicant's high school principal and district school superintendent. The booby trap for the Negro in this law was a companion measure which had the effect of automatically ousting school officials who signed such certificates under the theory that they were contributing to integration.

As a result, while some 400 Negroes had been attending former all-white state schools, only about 100 showed up for the February 1957 term and they were armed with a Federal court order.

Confusion resulted from the laws and the court rulings. Some students, white and Negro, apparently did not think the education they were seeking was worth all the trouble of attempting to obtain the certificates. Four Negroes, Louisiana students at the time but graduates of out-of-state high schools, obtained and filed certificates through an apparent loophole in the law. Among the white students turned down because of lack of certificates were two nuns who applied at Louisiana State University and explained they had gone to high school in Rimini, Italy. The nuns were finally admitted when authorities decided the signature of the superintendent of parochial schools in their Louisiana diocese was sufficient.

Although Louisiana had been admitting graduate students for some years, and a suit for admission to LSU by an undergraduate had been won after several years of litigation, officials applied the certificate test to graduate as well as undergraduate students.

A voluminous legal file has also accumulated in Florida as a result of the efforts of Virgil Hawkins, a Daytona Beach Negro, to enter the University of Florida School of Law. During eight years of litigation, the U. S. Supreme Court twice ordered his immediate acceptance, with the 1956 ruling emphasizing the principle that the "deliberate speed" allowed for integration in primary and secondary education does not apply in graduate and professional schools.

During the same period, the Florida Supreme Court thrice held that Florida A & M, a state school for Negroes at Tallahassee, provided suitable educational opportunities and that state law prohibited integration. In 1955 this court ruled Hawkins would have to be admitted, but not until it was determined that the school was ready to accept Negro students. When the U. S. Supreme Court said

Hawkins would have to be admitted at once, the Supreme Court of Florida some four months later recognized a duty to require admission but blocked entry by a majority opinion which contended that violence would break out if he were admitted then.

Low Hurdles

The path to integration in higher education has been much smoother in seven of the states which had barred Negroes from white schools.

Maryland had been accepting Negro graduate students and a few undergraduates for years. In June 1954 all restrictions were lifted although segregation required by Maryland law in teachers' colleges was continued for another year.

Missouri has opened all of the 14 public colleges, at least 11 of which have Negro students. The University of Missouri ended segregation soon after the Supreme Court decision and racial integration was complete by late 1955.

Oklahoma's state universities and colleges, junior and senior, were open to qualified Negro students by the summer of 1955.

Delaware dropped color bars after Negro litigants won a suit questioning the right of the state university to reject Negro students and the defendants declined to appeal.

Arkansas enrolled its first Negro graduate student in 1948 and continued this policy until Negro undergraduates were accepted in the fall of 1955.

Kentucky approved applications of Negro undergraduates in mid-1954, having previously held to the pattern of accepting only graduate or professional colored students.

West Virginia had quietly accepted a few Negro undergraduates as well as graduate students for several years before the May decision, and the policy was made official as of September 1, 1954.

The Others

Somewhere in between the defiance of the tier of states running from South Carolina to Mississippi and the compliance of the states on the outer edges of the South are the states which have with reluctance moved toward desegregation in higher education.

A few undergraduate Negroes armed with a court order joined graduates on the campuses of the three branches of the University of

North Carolina in the summer and fall of 1956. The trickle of Negro students is still merely a trickle. Western Carolina College at Cullowhee has accepted a Negro applicant and A&T College (Negro) at Greensboro accepted a white applicant, but the rest of the state's colleges are closed.

Negroes had taken graduate courses at the University of Tennessee for several years. When Negro undergraduates began knocking on the doors of state colleges, Tennessee came up with its so-called "stairstep" integration plan. Under the proposal, Negro graduate students would have been admitted at the beginning of the 1955-56 term and seniors, juniors, sophomores and freshmen in successive school years, thus effecting complete desegregation by the fall of 1959. A U. S. district court approved the "stairstep" plan, but upon appeal by five Negroes seeking admission to Memphis State University, the proposal was vetoed first by the U. S. circuit court of appeals and then by the U. S. Supreme Court. Austin Peay and East Tennessee State enrolled a few Negroes in the fall of 1956. The "stairstep" plan did not apply to the University of Tennessee, which has a separate administrative board.

More than 300 Negroes had gone through University of Texas graduate schools since a U. S. Supreme Court decision in favor of Heman Marion Sweatt established criteria so exacting for providing a legal education for a Texas Negro that separate but equal facilities on graduate and professional levels were impossible to attain. Junior colleges began opening as suits were pushed and complete desegregation was effected at the University of Texas at the beginning of the 1956-57 term.

A 1950 court order opened the way for Negro graduate students in Virginia. During 1956-57, four of 10 of the state's predominantly white schools had 38 Negroes on their campuses.

PLIGHT OF THE NEGRO COLLEGE

The Crisis, official organ of the NAACP, estimated that there were 48,787 Negroes enrolled in higher education institutions during the 1955-56 academic year. This estimate does not include several large schools. Many of these students attend Negro colleges. Educators are pondering the effect of desegregation on those Negro schools which accept white applicants, and those which do not.

Small Negro colleges, already barely surviving, may go over the brink. Storer, a Negro school at Harpers Ferry, West Virginia, founded after the Civil War to teach newly-freed Negroes to read and write, was a casualty of integration in 1955.

The view of a leading educator familiar with the race situation is that small, struggling schools may be saved by integration, however, if there is a need for a college in the community.

Presidents of practically all private Negro colleges in the South met soon after the 1954 decision to welcome the ruling and to urge immediate steps of implementation. Presidents of state-supported Negro schools were present in lesser numbers.

Leading Negro educators were swift to express a belief that Negro institutions would not fade away with desegregation. Dr. Benjamin E. Mays, president of Morehouse College of Atlanta, says that all colleges, those that serve white people and those that serve only Negroes, will be needed in the future. "First-rate" institutions have good reputations and attract students even from desegregated states, he says. He believes that Negro colleges will survive because their fees must be kept in line with the relatively low economic status of the men and women they serve.

Dr. George N. Redd, dean of Fisk University at Nashville, says that Negro colleges are more concerned about fading away because of difficulty in maintaining the high educational standards necessary for accreditation than because of desegregation in higher education.

The United Negro College Fund has said that these institutions will continue to have a major responsibility to educate Negro youth for some time to come because of basic factors of economics, geography and population. In 1952, a statement from the Fund's board of directors said that a court decision against segregated education would enable the Negro colleges to increase their usefulness.

Dr. M. S. Davage, president of Houston-Tillotson College (Negro) at Austin, Texas, points out that while Negro citizens comprise 10 per cent of the United States population, they represent only 3 per cent of America's college enrollment. Colleges for Negro students, he says, will be needed in the South despite the Supreme Court ruling.

Integration in Reverse

There has been no impressive rush on the part of white students to Negro schools. The most striking examples of reverse integration are in communities in which the needs of higher education are best served only by former Negro schools. More than 1,000 whites are attending integrated classes at West Virginia State College in the Greater Charleston area. Three hundred of Lincoln University's 800 students at Jefferson City, Missouri, are white. But Morgan State at Baltimore, one of the country's larger Negro colleges, has had few white students. A number of other colleges and universities are located in Baltimore.

A comparative trickle of white students is discernible in other essentially Negro schools, both public and private. The United Negro College Fund reported in 1956 that 67 whites were attending six of the Fund's 31 privately-supported schools. These include such schools as Fisk at Nashville and Xavier in New Orleans, which have long accepted whites, as well as Bethune-Cookman in Florida and Talladega in Alabama.

Trouble over the desegregation issue has cropped up briefly in several all-Negro colleges. A strike of students apparently motivated by resentment against a legislative probe of NAACP activities at the school was virtually 100 per cent effective at South Carolina State College at Orangeburg. Seventy per cent of the faculty members signed a resolution approving the NAACP.

As an aftermath, the college board of trustees termed the endorsement resolution "unwise," ousted 16 students and did not renew teaching contracts for three faculty members. Several other teachers did not ask for renewal.

Student unrest at Alcorn A & M in Mississippi stemmed from uneasiness over the future status of the school, as well as anger over the approach to racial relations adopted by Professor Clennon King, a history teacher, in a series of articles in the *Jackson State-Times* early in 1957. King, a Negro, was sharply critical of the NAACP.

All of the 489 striking students in the enrollment of 561 were "expelled," but all but a few were later reinstated. A new president was installed by the college board and the author of the controversial articles remained on the faculty but was given leave.

The mixing of the races in faculties has come about, although not in any great degree, as an accompaniment of desegregation in the South. There are white teachers at some state and non-state colleges which were formerly all-Negro, such as Lincoln in Missouri, where eight of the 78 on the faculty are white, Kentucky State, Dillard and

Xavier in New Orleans and Philander Smith in Little Rock, but they are few and far between. (Fisk and Talladega have had integrated faculties since their founding 90 years ago.) Even more scarce are Negro teachers on former all-white campuses. The University of Louisville (municipal) was the first southern school to employ a Negro faculty member.

The Double Standard

While some schools have not appointed Negroes to faculty posts because of the still delicate race question, there is possibly another factor working against the use of more members of their race in predominantly white institutions of higher learning.

Dr. Guy Johnson says many Negroes have what Negroes sometimes privately call "colored degrees," especially from teachers colleges outside the South. Southern Negro graduate students were extended favoritism, with professors leaning over backward to give them every chance. Dr. Johnson deplores this "double standard" of grading whites and Negroes differently and says it may cause trouble for some southern colleges conscientiously trying to integrate and maintain a single academic standard.

The implication is that Negroes may blame discrimination for what was actually academic unpreparedness. Rash and reckless charges may follow. When three of the first five Negro law students at the University of North Carolina failed a quiz, one of them got quoted in the press as charging discrimination. The unpleasantness abated when the University showed that the test papers had only numbers, not names, attached.

The standards of admission tests are being raised as the competition increases, but this is merely one of the reasons given why desegregation on a large scale in higher education is unlikely. Tuition costs are going up. The generally low economic status of the Negro thus acts to deny him entry to schools which may have policies of complete desegregation.

Apprehension over what may be regarded as tougher academic competition and a fear of flunking out, it is argued further, will make some Negroes hesitant about entering former white schools.

A final factor given weight in assumptions that there will be few

Negro students on former white college campuses in the South is that once the prize of integration is obtained, it becomes less valuable. A state official in West Virginia said the novelty of desegregation had worn off after the first year (1954-55). According to a *Southern School News* survey a shift back to racial separation was noted in 1955-56 in eight of 17 institutions, and was expected to be even more pronounced in future years. University of Texas officials anticipate that Negro enrollment will decline. After six years of desegregation, the University of Texas Law School had fewer Negroes in 1956-57 than it had in the first year of mixed classes, when 12 were enrolled.

The Top Choice

To gain the prize of integration through litigation it is obvious that, from the Negro point of view, plaintiffs of excellent reputation, high intellect, exemplary character and good emotional control are most desirable. In some cases, these ideals have been met; in others, not.

For first example, it is a little less than a secret that the Georgia Bureau of Investigation has searched high and low—and without success—for any derogatory information about Horace Ward, the Negro law student who sought to enter the state university.

It is to the advantage of the NAACP, which handles the litigation in these cases, to choose carefully. But this is not always possible. Sometimes an individual, rejected, calls on the organization for help in pleading his cause and the NAACP must go along. The operation of the selection process has been described in the *Ashmore Report (The Negro and the Schools*, Chapel Hill, 1954) as preferring "mature and serious people who were pursuing graduate or professional studies in order to advance themselves professionally."

Heman Sweatt failed in Texas. Lloyd Gaines grew weary of the prolonged legal battle in Missouri and simply did not show up at a rehearing (and, apparently, has never been heard from since). One Negro who was being admitted to a university was discovered to have had an unsavory police record and a dishonorable discharge from the Army, and accepted legal advice that he withdraw. Another, attracting unfavorable attention because of emotional reaction and bad manners, withdrew upon advice of the school's dean.

Others whose names are familiar to legal history gained admittance and began or completed successful academic careers. Silas Hunt of

Texarkana, the first Negro admitted to a school in the Old South, died in a Veterans Hospital before completing his first year of graduate study at the University of Arkansas. J. Kenneth Lee of Greensboro, the first Negro law graduate of the University of North Carolina, is the attorney in a suit to enroll Negro children in a white elementary school. Ada Lois Sipuel Fisher, the first Negro to be admitted to the University of Oklahoma Law School, now is a teacher at Langston University, a desegregated school which, however, has no white students in attendance.

The filing of charges that the NAACP unlawfully solicited litigation has been considered by several southern legislatures and such an accusation was made in Texas in connection with the Sweatt case. The NAACP denied it was guilty of barratry or that it paid Sweatt or Autherine Lucy Foster to break down segregation barriers.

A former NAACP state president in Florida, questioned by a legislative committee about the origins of the Hawkins case, testified: "We don't stir up litigation. We inform them [parents and children in school suits] of their rights and encourage them to use all facilities." He said individual NAACP branches pay court costs in most instances.

ACADEMIC AGONY

As the NAACP-directed legal attacks have continued, the moral and practical dilemma has deepened for southern professors who are torn between personal beliefs and the beliefs of the universities and the communities which they serve.

Dr. Chester C. Travelstead, dean of the School of Education at the University of South Carolina, was dismissed shortly after he made a talk favoring integration. Six faculty members at the University of Alabama resigned the spring after the Lucy case, saying the affair played a major part in their decisions. Two University of Virginia professors who favored local option desegregation quit after expressing concern over the future of the schools in the state. A teacher at Mississippi State College and another at the University of Mississippi resigned in protest after a lecture invitation extended to a television quiz show winner, the Reverend Alvin Kershaw, was withdrawn when it was learned he was an NAACP member and contributor.

The University of Georgia, which saw three educators ousted by the late Governor Eugene Talmadge for alleged pro-integration views in 1940, lost a law professor, James Lenoir, for what some of his colleagues say was disgust over the handling of the Horace Ward case. Another Georgia professor says his pro-integration viewpoint is regularly punished by denial of salary increases, promotions or needed academic assistance, though he remains in residence. Dr. Guy Wells, a former president of Georgia State College for Women, was stripped of his title of president emeritus by the board of regents because of his opinions on racial relationships.

On the other side of the coin, there are southern faculty members of strong segregation persuasion and at least one, Dr. W. C. George of the University of North Carolina medical school, has taken a vigorous part in the struggle to prevent integration by heading a statewide pro-segregation organization.

The Extracurricular Line

This dilemma is sometimes faced by campus publications. The University of Georgia's *Red and Black* editors resigned after an editorial against segregation was published. The *Florida Flambeau,* published by students at Florida State University, denied editorially it overemphasized racial topics or "too strongly favored" integration after the president of the school said the paper must devote less space to the question. A Louisiana state senator urged that LSU avoid naming "radicals as editors" after the student newspaper, the *Reveille,* criticized "idiotic pieces of legislation" passed by "the advocates of segregation." A University of South Carolina student was fired from his post as page in the state senate after he wrote an article in the college paper censuring southern governors for "obstreperous and irrational voices." Two editors resigned from *The Echo,* Furman University (Baptist) student literary magazine, following seizure by school authorities of copies of an issue containing an article sympathetic to integration.

In the realm of sports, integration in athletic events has proceeded on a par with integration generally in the complying states. But in the firmly resisting states, several games have been called on account of darkness.

The University of Mississippi and Mississippi State College basketball teams withdrew from national tournaments at Owensboro, Kentucky and Evansville, Indiana, and Jackson State College for Negroes withdrew from another tournament because of a college board ruling against racially integrated sports. Junior colleges simply have formed a segregation pact.

A request by Governor Marvin Griffin that Georgia Tech be barred by the board of regents from playing Pittsburgh, a team with one Negro player, in the 1956 Sugar Bowl caused demonstrations by students. The regents decided to let Tech play but to prevent mixed race contests in Georgia and to allow future out-of-state games to be played in accordance with customs of the host state.

Since then, a Louisiana law has been passed to force a change in Sugar Bowl policy by banning whites and Negroes from competing in athletics.

Polls show that on almost every campus, there is some pro-integration and some pro-segregation sentiment.

FSU's *Flambeau* sampled the views of editorial staffs at 11 other schools in 1954 and said a majority of southern college students believe racial integration should be gradual to avoid trouble.

The *Daily Lariat,* Baylor University student paper, said a 1956 poll showed 70 per cent had no objection to college integration. Students at Texas Christian University at Fort Worth voted in April 1957: 729 for segregation, 403 for gradual integration and 291 for immediate integration.

The Florida Board of Control, checking university students in 1956, said 41.45 per cent wanted a reasonable period of preparation before desegregation; 22.39 per cent favored immediate desegregation; 21.04 per cent opposed integration under any circumstances and 14.01 per cent urged maintenance of segregation as long as possible.

Campus Life

The treatment of Negroes, even after admission, varies in different schools.

North Carolina State College, surveyed in late 1956, had what was described as a placid transition from segregated to integrated status. Although many white students showed surprise or displeasure when a Negro joined the class, nothing approaching an incident was reported.

In the spring of the same year, a check on three Negro undergraduates at the University of North Carolina showed one living in a dormitory and two commuting. No unpleasantness has cropped up. Earlier, a Negro woman graduate student at the University was given a corner room with private bath. There was no sharing of facilities as is the case with most white girl students. Two Negro girls, enrolled at Woman's College of the University of North Carolina in Greensboro, are roommates in an otherwise white dormitory.

At the University of Missouri, Negroes live in regular college residential halls. However, some cafes and other business places in town refuse to serve them.

No Negroes were in University of Tennessee dormitories prior to the 1956-57 term start. One Negro student, living in a colored residential section, said he hadn't pushed for dormitory accommodations since the University was open to him and he wasn't going to do anything to "rock the boat."

At the University of Texas, when Negro undergraduates were admitted in 1955, only 11 of 131 housing unit operators said they would accept Negroes. Three of 16 restaurant owners in the University neighborhood said Negroes could eat at their places, but two said restrictions would be imposed. Forty-five of the 47 academic organizations not maintaining houses approved Negroes. Graduate and professional Negro students were told they could attend dances and other campus functions with no discrimination. In the late spring of 1957 a Negro coed was given the leading role in a campus opera but was withdrawn after criticism.

A Negro graduate law student at the University of Oklahoma set a precedent by being the first of his race to be elected a representative of the Independent Student Association. He defeated two white candidates.

Louisiana State University's policy generally aims to keep education activities integrated and social activities segregated. Negroes are eligible for honor societies but cannot attend their banquets; can live in dormitories but cannot share rooms with whites; can eat in desegregated dining halls and attend desegregated religious services but cannot attend campus-wide dances; can be desegregated at scholastic

ceremonies but not athletic events; can march with whites in graduation ceremonies but cannot use the swimming pool.

Generally, in the group of states which are haltingly complying,
most Negro students live in dormitories or their own homes. And if
in dormitories, they are either in separate buildings or are semi-segre-
gated in the same building from whites. At one state university, however, 13 white boys and two Negroes have chipped in to rent a house
and live under a co-op arrangement near the campus.

At West Virginia State, a former Negro college which opened its
doors to whites, some out-of-state Negro students at first were resent-
ful, feeling an increase in tuition for out-of-state students was an effort to ease them out in favor of white students. This resentment has
disappeared.

Some whites, too, were jittery. One said he was "leery about enrolling" because he had "never been in a class with Negro students."
Later he said: "It's just a classroom of students. The professors didn't
see any colors and neither do I."

Whites and Negroes room together in dormitories, play on mixed
athletic teams, participate in student activities together, join the same
clubs and share lecture notes and coffee breaks without regard to race.

The casual manner in which race relations is treated at West Virginia State is illustrated by the remark of one of a group of students
being interviewed. Parodying the Fifth Amendment, the student
turned to classmates and advised: "Don't say anything that might
tend to integrate you."

11.

Man in No Man's Land

BY GLEN ROBINSON

During a lull in the storm at Clinton, Tennessee, where court-ordered desegregation stirred a national as well as a community tempest, a team of sociologists interviewed a sampling of Anderson Countians about the incident. The interviewers received some unexpected responses to their questions.

A number of those interviewed had never heard of the U. S. Supreme Court decision against school segregation. And a few of these had never heard of the Supreme Court itself.

However, nearly all of those interviewed knew their local school administrators and some of the members of their school board. But most important, the interviewers reported that many of the persons with whom they talked blamed not the courts but their local school officials for the widely unpopular desegregation of the high school.

The schools in the South, as schools elsewhere, are close to the social and emotional heartbeat of their communities. Local control of schools is ingrained in our national tradition. Whatever or whoever seriously threatens the pattern of school operation is likely to meet with community opposition.

Where the segregation-desegregation conflict is joined in the South, the man in no man's land almost invariably is the school administrator. He is caught in a crossfire of alternatives. Regardless of the direction in which he officially moves—toward integration or toward the bulwarking of segregation—he stands great chance of being castigated as a villain and relatively small chance of being acclaimed as a hero.

183

ALONE IN A FISHBOWL

The spotlight of national domestic concern is focused on southern schools. In the present situation, disruptions in schools or communities can bring an encampment of press, radio and television correspondents to the scene of conflict. Overnight almost any southern school administrator might find himself virtually alone in a fishbowl of national publicity.

On a nationwide television program, "Clinton and the Law," Clinton High School Principal D. J. Brittain said:

I can frankly say that I've suffered nothing but personal harassment and other people too. My wife and teachers and students in school, and anybody that took a stand to obey the law, not necessarily that they agreed with it . . . the first day and night my telephone rang incessantly. I guess my life was threatened ten or twelve times by anonymous telephone callers who would hang it up. I have had my phone number changed four times to keep from getting these annoying calls . . . Quite frankly, I think, I feel like many people in Europe feel. My wife and I, since the opening of school, are always careful when we go home. We study the premises. When we get in, we lock the doors and get the lights on. Any noise or any sound that occurs, we are always concerned at what it is . . . It is just a constant thing which I'm sure is part of the organization to wear myself and my wife down. It just presses you down every day lower and lower, and to me, it is an amazing thing that an American citizen, living in the United States, has to be subjected to this, while the lawless citizens, those who refuse to abide or accept the law, continue to run free. I know this is not a true picture of America, I know it is not a true picture of the majority of the people of Anderson County, but it is a picture of myself and several other citizens in Clinton who have tried to abide by the law.

Seven months after the strife began, Principal Brittain announced that he would resign his position at the end of the school year to accept a teaching fellowship at New York University.

The school board of Hoxie, Arkansas, voted on June 25, 1955, to end racial segregation in the district. Almost from the time the board announced its decision, Superintendent K. E. Vance and school board members came under heavy attack from pro-segregation forces. The attacks ranged from personal intimidation of Vance and members of his family to charges that the superintendent was responsible for shortages in school funds. In the barrage of charges and accusations that followed the board's decision, it was almost impossible to determine the truth.

Six months barely elapsed after the board announced its decision to desegregate until the harried superintendent submitted his resignation, citing in his letter to the school board the "ordeal" to which he and his family had been subjected since opposition to integration developed in Hoxie.

Although initial steps in desegregating any school system might be considered as potentially explosive, most of the school districts that have desegregated in the border states have done so with little or no racial strife. And in a few instances the desegregation of school districts has brought school officials national acclaim and recognition, at least from a substantial group of persons outside the South, and often in their immediate localities.

Superintendent Omer Carmichael is the most notable example. After the smooth execution of a carefully prepared plan for desegregating schools in Louisville, Kentucky, President Eisenhower asked Carmichael to come to the White House and give him a personal account of the plan and procedure.

The President said: "I think Mr. Carmichael must be a very wise man. I hope to get some advice from him as to exactly how he did it."

White House Press Secretary James C. Hagerty told reporters after the conference that the President asked him to say that Mr. Carmichael "exemplifies the truly American way in which to carry out the basic principles" which are involved in the question of integration.

Several national magazines interviewed Carmichael following his visit to the White House. And the Louisville superintendent appeared on at least two national television programs.

Conviction Versus Duty

Varied social forces—official, unofficial, public, private, personal— pressure southern school officials as they grapple with the segregation- desegregation issue.

Many a southern school superintendent is caught between his personal convictions regarding racial segregation in schools and the conflicting wishes of his school board, his community, his state legislature, or the Federal courts. Administrators and other educators who feel that their school systems should and could be desegregated promptly but whose boards of education or state legislatures have passed measures designed to prevent or delay desegregation face a clash between conviction and duty.

However, frustration can be just as severe when the situation is reversed. School administrators who sincerely believe that the implementation of court orders to desegregate their school systems would severely damage the public school program or result in physical violence in their communities face a similar problem.

The inner conflicts and frustrations that confront some southern school officials are illustrated by the sequence of events in Arlington County, Virginia (adjacent to the District of Columbia). In January 1956 Superintendent of Schools T. Edward Rutter presented to the Arlington County Board of Education a plan to permit integration in certain elementary schools in the fall of 1956. The board unanimously approved the plan, stating it believed that legislation would soon be "enacted to carry out the proposed Gray Plan and that in order to meet the Supreme Court's decree for 'deliberate speed' in desegregation, it will be necessary to provide schools in which children of both races may attend classes."

This announcement touched off a bitter controversy in the Virginia General Assembly. The Assembly retaliated by enacting a bill taking from Arlington citizens the privilege of electing their school board members.

The National Association for the Advancement of Colored People quickly filed suit against the Arlington school board requesting the Federal court to grant immediate desegregation of schools. The suit was unusual in that the 14 parents and 22 children named as plaintiffs included some white persons.

Federal District Judge Albert V. Bryan ordered Arlington to end segregation in its elementary schools by January 31, 1957. The decision was appealed to the U. S. Supreme Court which upheld it in March 1957 by refusing to review the case.

On the heels of the Supreme Court's refusal, Virginia's Attorney General J. Lindsay Almond, Jr., told the Arlington school officials that they were powerless under Virginia law to comply with the federal court desegregation order. He said their proper course in dealing with Negro children seeking admission to white schools was to refer the applicants to the newly created state Pupil Placement Board. But two days later Federal District Judge Walter Hoffman held that the Pupil Placement Act was unconstitutional.

The decision facing the Arlington officials was not a simple matter of choosing either to obey or to disobey *the* law, for there were conflicting laws. If the school officials did not comply with the Federal court, they could be held in contempt of court. If they did comply by integrating white and Negro pupils, they were running a chance of dealing a crippling blow to the county's educational program.

The Virginia law states that whenever the student body of any public school "shall consist of both white and colored children" all state, county and city officials who have the power to distribute or expend public funds "severally and collectively are directed and commanded to refrain immediately" from making money available to the school district for the operation of that "class" of school.

Another law makes the funds thus withheld available to the locality for use as tuition grants for children attending private schools. And still another law requires school budgets to include money for tuition grants.

For school officials who are sincerely devoted to public education to have to choose between the defiance of court orders and the possible dismantling of the public schools requires some serious soul-searching.

Some Board Members Have It Rough

Out of the approximately 9,000 school boards in the South, only 3,000 of them preside over districts enrolling both white and Negro pupils. In some cases persons who have served on such school boards have found their position either personally or professionally uncomfortable.

A superintendent of schools in Texas reports that in a meeting of city school superintendents in his state someone brought up the question of the "decline in the quality of candidates running for school board office." The superintendents agreed, he said, that some of the more capable persons in their communities preferred to run *from* school board candidacy. These persons were concerned about the schools, yes, but for professional reasons they could not afford to become involved in a fight over desegregation.

Chairman R. G. Crossno of the Anderson County, Tennessee, school board, a prominent dairyman, told a meeting of the Clinton High School faculty following the disturbances there in 1956:

I am sure there is no doubt in your mind as to my official connection with the dairy company. As president of the Norris Creamery, Inc., we too have had threats—boycott of our produce in a number of instances. We have lost accounts which we have served for ten, twelve, fifteen years as a result of my being a member of this particular school board.

In Chattanooga, school board members who had taken an initial stand in support of compliance told a *Southern School News* reporter that public criticism had reduced appointment to board membership from an accustomed honor to an onerous duty.

Many school board memberships are elective. In the last few years the jobs have been sought in some localities by avowed segregationists with the backing of white Citizens Councils and other pro-segregation groups. Thus, in some instances school board members who have taken a stand in favor of compliance with the Supreme Court decision have had to lay their jobs on the line—and most often they have lost.

Don Nugent, executive secretary of the Texas Association of School Boards, said in June 1956 that the few candidates who supported integration were unsuccessful in spring school board elections. Wherever the issue arose, pro-segregation candidates won.

In two different elections Hoxie, Arkansas, replaced some of its pro-integration board members by electing pro-segregation candidates. Milford, Delaware, and Houston, Texas, have elected similar replacements.

The Kerrville, Texas, school board voted in March 1956 to desegregate schools beginning the next September. On April 7 there was a school board election in which two of the seven board members were selected. The incumbents did not seek re-election. Five candidates sought the two vacancies. According to observers, segregation-desegregation was the lone issue in the election. The two pro-segregation candidates defeated the only avowed pro-integration candidate by a margin of 17 to 1. The pro-segregationists also defeated two candidates who took no stand on segregation by a margin of about 2 to 1. Two days after the election the school board rescinded the integration order by a 4 to 2 vote and substituted a "study" plan.

In contrast, a few avowed supporters of segregation have been unsuccessful. For example, voters recently rejected two pro-segregation candidates in Little Rock and one in North Little Rock, Arkansas. Moreover, it should be noted that some school boards in presently

segregated areas have Negro members. Atlanta, Augusta and Gainesville, Georgia, Nashville and Richmond are examples. Governor
Luther Hodges of North Carolina recently reappointed a Negro educator, Dr. Harold L. Trigg, to the state board of education.

FEELING THE WAY

The Supreme Court has charged southern school officials with the
responsibility for accomplishing a feat never before achieved in the
history of American education—that of making a basic change in
educational policy when a large number of the persons affected are
strongly opposed. Many school administrators were not prepared for
this unprecedented task. From experience they had learned to be sensitive to public opinion and to attempt to gain wide public support for
proposed changes in school policy before making the changes. But the
implementation of the Supreme Court decision in many southern
communities has called for procedures unfamiliar to most school administrators. Consequently, school officials in the South who favor
compliance are having to feel their way.

Unilateral Action by School Boards

Several school boards have moved on their own, with little or no
public discussion, to desegregate public schools.

The Fayetteville, Arkansas, Board of Education announced a week
after the May 1954 decision of the Supreme Court that it would integrate its nine Negro high school students in September with about 500
white students in the high school. The decision was accepted and
executed with almost no protest.

The situation was much different a year later in Hoxie, Arkansas,
when the board of education announced on June 25, 1955, that it
would integrate its 25 Negro students with its 1,000 white students,
beginning with the summer term on July 11. As in the case previously
mentioned, the decision of the board was unanimous, and there was
no public discussion.

However, public protest flared. A combination of local and non-
local pressures became so strong that the board of education had to
ask for a Federal court injunction to restrain pro-segregationists from
interfering with the operations of the desegregated schools.

Study Committees as Pace Setters

A number of boards of education have named study committees to assist them in formulating policy regarding the Supreme Court decision. At least 60 such committees have been reported in Kentucky, and all but one of the county boards of education in Maryland have appointed study committees. The effectiveness of these committees in paving the way for desegregation in the community varies greatly.

In Montgomery County, Maryland, which contains part of the suburbs of Washington, D.C., the school board appointed a 19-member citizens' advisory committee on desegregation. There was full and lengthy discussion throughout the county concerning ways to desegregate. The community became confused and divided over what was the most practicable way to desegregate its schools. After lengthy deliberation, the committee submitted to the board a majority report accompanied by four minority reports. The school board rejected all of these reports and finally adopted a desegregation plan quite different from any that had been proposed by the committee. This plan was put into effect against considerable community opposition.

In nearby Prince George's County, which like Montgomery County contains suburbs of Washington, the board of education appointed a 22-member study committee. To avoid a repetition of what happened in Montgomery County, the Prince George's board unanimously passed the following resolution in setting up the committee:

Be it resolved that members of the board of education, its employees, or any member of the fact finding committee on desegregation be directed that they are not to appear before citizens' groups or other interested persons or at any time to discuss the work of this committee nor how desegregation in Prince George's County will be designated until such time as the board of education is prepared to state its policy on this matter.

The Prince George's board adopted a gradual desegregation program that followed in essential details the recommendations of the study committee. Desegregation met little opposition.

HOW TO DO IT?

Once the decision to desegregate is made—either by a board or a court, or sometimes by both—the execution of the plan becomes largely the problem of the school administrator. More often than not the superintendents have greatly influenced the choice of methods.

Most of these methods used so far to desegregate schools fit into the following categories:

1. *From the top down.* The St. Louis Board of Education took a year to desegregate its public schools. It first desegregated junior colleges and special schools, then high schools and finally elementary schools. This method of beginning desegregation at the upper grade level and working to the elementary level has been used in many school districts in the border states, especially those that have comparatively small percentages of Negro students.

2. *From the bottom up.* Some Kentucky and several Maryland districts with "southern characteristics" (counties with a heavy Negro population) have begun integrating in the primary grades of elementary schools, and have worked toward the upper grades. The school board of Nashville, Tennessee, with a 41 per cent first-grade Negro enrollment, has reported to a Federal district court that it plans to begin desegregation in the first grade in September 1957.

3. *All grades at once.* The desegregation of both elementary and high schools in one swoop has been an approach used by both small and large school systems. Baltimore, Louisville, and the District of Columbia desegregated their schools in this way. Baltimore had never had school attendance areas, so it opened all school doors in the city to pupils of both races on a free-choice basis—provided that there was room at the chosen school. Louisville established attendance areas "without regard to race" but provided a flexible transfer system for transfer to another school. Washington, D. C., used a phased process in moving from a system of biracial compulsory attendance areas to a system of racially integrated compulsory attendance areas.

4. *Selective integration.* A few school districts have begun desegregating by selecting particular Negro students for transfer to formerly all-white schools where space and program would permit. This plan is being used in Montgomery County, Maryland.

The amount of administrative work involved in some of these procedures has been prodigious. In the desegregation process many superintendents and their staffs have studied the population of residential areas with the deliberation of a census-taker. They have considered school capacities, teacher loads, pupil achievement, preference of school and the like. Additional paper work has been mountainous. The Louisville system alone issued tens of thousands of cards to parents who, if they were unhappy about their child's assignment, could indicate first, second and third choice of alternative schools.

HOLDING THE DIKE

Deeper South, the decision-making responsibility of the local school official may diminish—sometimes in accordance to his liking. There, some state legislators feel that the preservation of segregation is too grave a matter to be left to the discretion of local school authorities. For example, the Georgia legislature in 1955 passed a law making it "a felony punishable by two years' imprisonment for any state, county or city school official to allow any state or local funds to be used in a mixed class."

Some anomalies occur. Arkansas' school districts are officially regarded as autonomous, yet by statewide referendum in a campaign considered a triumph for segregation, the people pressed upon local boards the power—which they already had—to assign pupils. Virginia, which among southern states contributes a near-minimum to the support of local schools, put pupil placement in the hands of a three-man state board and gave its governor power to close integrated schools.

Theoretically, however, in seven of the eight states having pupil assignment or placement laws, the power of assignment rests with the locality. Even so the school administrator may not be certain whether this power is ultimate—in the light of the constitutionality or unconstitutionality of placement laws; in the light, moreover, of purportedly countervailing state laws. For he must remember that, like his school board, he is liable in Federal court proceedings.

Superintendents in Arlington County and Charlottesville, Virginia, were informed pointedly by Federal district courts of this legal liability.

In areas of strong resistance to desegregation, most school officials are not anxious to expose themselves to judicial scrutiny, much less to advocate the desegregation of schools. Since the courts of jurisdiction did not decree integration but only enjoined racial discrimination, from the standpoint of many of these school officials, the initiative rests with persons who can claim and establish discrimination.

Six states are legislatively prepared to do away with public schools if integration is ordered. But only North Carolina and South Carolina have vested local school boards with the authority to close public schools in the event of "intolerable situations." In 1955 the legislature in South Carolina gave local school trustees the "exclusive authority to operate or not operate any public schools."

A few instances have been reported in which school boards have at least threatened to take overt steps to thwart desegregation efforts in their school districts. One of these was reported in the *Chattanooga Times* in July 1955. The *Times* quoted Alabama state Senator Sam Engelhardt, of Macon County, as telling an Alabama Senate education committee: "I got a call from the school board [of Macon County] last Friday after the petition [by Negroes to attend all-white schools] was presented. We've got 190 colored teachers in Macon County and the board tells me they'll fire every one of them that takes part in this agitation."

Most local officials in the mid-South and the Deep South have taken little if any overt action regarding the Supreme Court decision. The school superintendent of a rural county in west Tennessee stated recently, "People in our county do not seem to pay much attention to the Supreme Court's decision. We have no Citizens Councils or NAACP activities. The Negroes seem to be satisfied with the schools they have. Integration is just not a problem in our county."

In the same county, the principal of the high school for Negroes said in a private interview: "The Negro schools are on par with the white schools in our county, and I have not heard anyone even mention wanting to go to a white school. The students in my school do not seem much aware of the Supreme Court's decision. It just doesn't seem to concern them, and it seems to concern their parents even less."

This do-nothing, wait-and-see attitude has resulted in continued segregation in many school districts.

THE DEDICATED MAN

The traditional belief in free public education for all children is still strongly held by most southerners. During the early 1900's the fever of public education swept much of the South, enshrining names such as Alderman and Aycock. While on a speaking engagement in Alabama, Charles B. Aycock, North Carolina's "Educational Governor," breathed his last there as he slumped to the floor of an auditorium while exclaiming, "I have always spoken about education . . ."

Today in many parts of the region dedication to public education is being challenged by the fear of racial integration. This fear has become so great that six states have passed legislation permitting the abolition of public schools in localities that might be forced to integrate.

In most instances, school measures providing for the closing of public schools have been adopted with the understanding that there would be no statewide turnover of public schools to "private" corporations. Rather, these plans usually have been adopted in the belief that action on them would be necessary only in a few local school districts and then perhaps restricted to individual schools under court order. The school administrator cannot overlook the possibility that either an emotionally aroused public or state legislature might send the schools in his district to oblivion.

Furthermore, superintendents have added fiscal problems. A Texas city school superintendent reports that some school bond referendums in his neighboring districts in eastern and central Texas have been meeting opposition. He summarizes the difficulty in this manner: "One group of people doesn't want to spend any more money on segregated schools and the other group doesn't want to spend money on schools unless they are segregated."

The voters of Arlington County, Virginia, defeated in February 1956 a proposed $9.4 million bond issue for school construction. A few days before the referendum, Arlington had been the center of a heated controversy in the General Assembly over segregation. Thirty elementary classrooms were reported to have been placed on double shifts as a result of the defeat of the bond issue.

On the other hand, a county superintendent of schools from the vicinity of Memphis, Tennessee, remarked: "The Supreme Court decision has built school buildings for Negroes all over this section of the state."

In Mississippi a superintendent of city schools observed: "Although the Supreme Court decision is not resulting in integration in Mississippi, it has certainly stepped up interest in providing *equal but separate* school facilities for Negroes."

The area of capital outlay for school construction presents many conflicting situations. It seems impossible to ascertain the relative effects that the segregation issue and the present tight money market are having upon school bond sales in the South.

After having difficulty selling a $3 million school bond issue for Davidson County, (Nashville) Tennessee, in November 1956, County Judge Beverly Briley stated: "Financial houses simply are reluctant to purchase school bonds from southern cities and states during this crucial period because of the segregation issue."

In Virginia, some school bond issues have been bid upon or bonds sold at extraordinarily high rates; however, these school systems have not had high bond ratings. Virginia's Governor Thomas B. Stanley recently made a trip to New York in order to reassure the bond market about Virginia's situation, explaining the distinction between current operating expense and capital outlay and saying that capital outlay had first claim on the credit of governmental units.

Conversely, South Carolina—tightly segregated and engaged in a massive program of equalizing school facilities—apparently has not run into much trouble borrowing its money.

The school administrator also may find himself suddenly without funds to conduct normal school operations. Let integration come to a district in Virginia, Georgia, or South Carolina and, by law, the flow of state funds ceases.

Moreover, Virginia has a law which permits the local financing of schools on a month-to-month basis. About 20 Virginia county boards of supervisors have adopted this plan. In October 1956 both the white and the Negro local teachers associations of Hanover County complained of salary delays because of it.

Finally, the administrator may be brought face to face with the conversion of his public system to a "private" system. While no administrator has yet to come to this crossroad, educational expense grants are a very real tactic in the strategy to preserve segregation.

Four states—Virginia, Georgia, Alabama and North Carolina—have authorized these grants in varying form. The North Carolina law states:

Every child residing in this state, for whom no public school is available, or who is assigned to a public school attended by a child of another race against the wishes of his parent of guardian . . . is entitled to apply for an educational expense grant from state funds appropriated for that purpose. Such grants shall be available only for education in a private, nonsectarian school, and in the case of a child assigned to a public school attended by a child of another race.

This is something wholly new to the concept of public elementary and secondary education in this country. Yet, to many school administrators, it is a real and present concern.

THE QUESTIONS

Legislatures, state agencies and school boards themselves have raised a myriad of questions, some smaller than the foregoing, which have become of administrative concern. Perhaps they can be summarized, as follows:

Compulsory Attendance

Mississippi and South Carolina have repealed their compulsory attendance laws. Virginia, Louisiana, North Carolina, Georgia and Arkansas have provisions for suspending compulsory attendance under special conditions.

Censorship

On occasion instructional materials have been censored or banned. Three national magazines—*Time, Life* and *Look*—were removed from high school libraries of Claiborne and Bossier parishes (counties) in Louisiana. The two school boards charged that the magazines "distorted" the race issue.

In Morehouse Parish, Louisiana, the school board removed the science textbook, *Science for Better Living,* after investigating a parent's complaint that certain passages "insinuate that races breed freely with each other."

The Georgia Board of Education banned three textbooks as "anti-South." One is the songbook, *Together We Sing,* which the board removed because it said the word "darkies" in Stephen Foster's songs, "My Old Kentucky Home" and "Old Folks at Home," had been replaced by "young folks," "brothers" or other wording.

Tenure

Some legislatures have amended teacher tenure laws in such a way that teachers can be dismissed in the event of desegregation. Florida has a statute adopted in 1956 "authorizing the county board of public instruction to choose school personnel from all available personnel and certificated teachers when said board is required to or does consolidate its school program at any center and to dismiss any teachers not needed without regard to any previous contractual relationships."

In 1955 the North Carolina General Assembly passed a bill that terminated all teacher contracts and placed future contracts on a one-year basis.

How many teachers have actually lost their jobs as a result of desegregation or controversy over desegregation? At the beginning of the 1956-57 school year *Southern School News* found that about 500 teachers, most of them Negroes (there are some 75,000 Negro teachers in the 17-state area), had been either dismissed or threatened with dismissal.

Academic Freedom

The Appomattox County, Virginia, School Board refused in May 1956 to renew the contracts of two eighth-grade white women teachers, Georgia Gurney and Gertrude Kerr. Mrs. Gurney said she believed the reason the board did not renew her contract was that she voted in 1954 against a resolution favoring segregation. The *Richmond Times-Dispatch* observed, "The impression has been created that it is becoming dangerous in Virginia for teachers to express even a mild dissent from majority community opinion on the race problem."

At Mullins, South Carolina, a seventh-grade teacher and coach, Jay Clark, was suspended following remarks he made about the Autherine Lucy incident at the University of Alabama. Clark stated: "I simply asked the question if the students' attitude at Alabama was either American or Christian." After a hearing, Clark was reinstated, but he decided it was best for him to resign.

At Fort Gaines, Georgia, a Negro school principal, Harrison E. Lee, resigned and left town because of what he termed pressure from other Negroes following speeches he made asking Negroes to "forget integration." Negroes in the community submitted a petition to the school board calling for Lee's resignation in the best interest of their race. The principal claimed that he and his family had been threatened.

WHERE THEY DESEGREGATED

Compliance with the Supreme Court decision has solved some administrative problems; however, in most communities the change from a racially segregated school system to a racially integrated system has created other problems.

For example, the results of the first citywide academic achievement tests given after the District of Columbia integrated its schools shocked many persons. The achievement scores showed that the average Washington fifth-grader was working at the national fourth-grade level in arithmetic reasoning and that he was back to third-grade progress in reading comprehension. Although test results varied from school to school, in general, students in the former Division I (white) schools averaged much higher than those in the former Division II (Negro) schools.

These test results set off a barrage of charges and countercharges. Some persons said the results were factual evidence that Negro students were intellectually inferior to white students. Others said that the test results were proof positive that separate schools had never been educationally equal. Still others said that the results reflected the impoverished socio-economic and cultural backgrounds of the majority of Negro families.

Achievement test findings in other school systems began to receive wide publicity. In Dade County (Miami), Florida, Negroes on the average were found to be from one-year-nine-months to two-and-one-half years behind the national average for sixth-grade pupils, while whites surpassed the national average by several months in reading and English and trailed a few months in arithmetic and spelling. The Universtiy of Florida gave tests to high school seniors and found 96 per cent of Negro seniors scored below half of the white seniors.

The results of several other cases of mass testing of white and Negro pupils tended to show similar current lags in the median test scores of groups of Negro pupils as compared with groups of white pupils. The current existence of such differentials in test-score medians is conceded by many educators, including many Negro educators. A number of educators of both races are diligently working to develop improved remedial techniques.

The current achievement-score differentials have caused some persons to ask administrators in recently desegregated school systems: What has happened to scholastic standards after desegregation?

In officially desegregated Baltimore Superintendent John H. Fischer said: "On the basis of our experience it seems clear that by desegregating our schools we have substantially improved the educational opportunities of Negro children without reducing in any way those available to white children."

A report of desegregation in the St. Louis, Missouri, public schools prepared by the school system's instruction department, states:

> From the standpoint of organization for instructional purposes, the elementary schools have undergone no fundamental change as a result of desegregation. The systemwide policy has been to organize the program on the elementary level in such a way as to provide for range of abilities and interests in the pupil population and at the same time encourage the participation of pupils of differing abilities in common activities.

The District of Columbia apparently presents the other side of the picture. In a pamphlet published in 1957, Assistant Superintendent Carl F. Hansen listed several changes in the school program after integration; these included the following:

> 1) Curriculum reorganization already completed has resulted in an increase in homogeneous grouping at all levels, in order to reduce the range of differences in classes. This includes a four-sequence curriculum for the senior high schools under which are provided an honors curriculum for gifted students, regular college preparatory and general curriculums and a basic curriculum for the students who need additional instruction in the fundamental skills.
>
> 2) A re-emphasis upon the skills program at all levels has been officially required, along with a re-examination of promotional practices.
>
> 3) An increase of emphasis upon subject matter standards has followed, particularly in those fields and groupings where pupils can be expected to meet minimum requirements.

Extracurricular Problems

A number of school administrators who have found their communities willing to accept racial integration in classroom activities have encountered problems with racial integration in certain extracurricular and school related activities. Bonita Valien of Fisk University, in a pamphlet entitled "The St. Louis Story," states that in the desegregation of the St. Louis schools:

> The area in which there has been the greatest amount of concern, caution and

frustration has come in the strictly "social affairs," often referred to as "social mixing." Throughout the system, it is understood that there must be no activities carried on either by or through the school which will embarras any student. How to handle this is the problem of each individual school . . . One principal stated that his school was not having any social affairs, while another was having them with restriction, and still another was taking a permissive attitude, saying to the organizations: "Have them if you choose."

One of the objections most frequently voiced by persons who oppose desegregation is the effect they fear integration might have upon social activities of the school—the school sponsored parties, dances, plays, ball games, suppers, and similar activities. To realize fully the depth of this objection, one must understand the extremely important role the schools play in the social life of most southern communities, especially rural communities. As the rural school administrator well knows, the schoolhouse is often the very hub of rural community life. There, basketball games can assume a festive proportion, and the PTA-sponsored supper can be the social event of the season.

And the Negro Teacher?

A school superintendent in Kentucky recently remarked: "The problems of integrating Negro students into all-white schools are small in comparison with the problems of integrating Negro teachers into all-white schools."

Where desegregation has occurred in the larger city school systems such as St. Louis, Baltimore and Washington, Negro teachers seem to have been absorbed into the integrated schools. In many cases, however, these teachers have stayed in their former schools, which after integration have remained either all or mostly Negro.

A survey by *Southern School News* found that in desegregated schools at least 113 Negro teachers in the fall of 1956 were instructing white students. Nearly all of these teachers were in predominantly Negro schools to which white students had been either admitted or assigned.

According to the same survey, approximately 300 Negro teachers in Oklahoma had thus far been displaced as a result of desegregation. About 60 had been displaced in Kentucky, 58 in West Virginia, 20 in Missouri, and about 20 in Texas.

Nearly all the Negro teachers displaced in Kentucky, Missouri, Texas and West Virginia have been re-employed, usually in the same state. In Oklahoma, where the bulk of the displacement has occurred, a number of the displaced teachers have been unable to obtain other teaching positions in the state.

In Moberly, Missouri, 11 were dropped when the Negro school was closed at the end of the 1954-55 school year. Eight of them, with NAACP support, later filed suit in U. S. district court seeking restoration of their jobs and damages, on grounds of denial of constitutional rights. The suit was still undecided by the spring of 1957. But in the meantime seven of the 11 had been re-employed, usually at advances in salary, though they had to leave Moberly to get jobs.

In Oklahoma and Kentucky, many of the dismissals resulted from the closing of one-teacher schools and their consolidation with others. A few teachers found jobs in other desegregated school districts. Some of the displaced teachers moved to other states—Florida, California, Missouri, Texas and the Virgin Islands. And some went into different work.

In general, it appears that where the concentration of Negro population is large enough and so arranged to enable desegregated school systems to employ Negro teachers in predominantly Negro schools, Negro teachers have not been faced with termination notices. On the other hand, where the one- and two-teacher Negro school has been abolished, Negro teachers in many instances have found themselves without jobs.

It Was Planned This Way

The thing that seems to be emphasized by the variety of administrative problems resulting from the Supreme Court rulings is the diversity of ways the citizens of various communities have reacted to the far-reaching decisions. With comparatively few exceptions, so far, local school officials who have moved toward compliance have decided if, how, and when their schools would be desegregated. And, like fingerprints, these decisions and their outcomes reflect the peculiar characteristics of the individual community.

The southern school administrator may be alone in the crowd, he may have more than his share of headaches, he may bear the brunt of attacks, but this is the way the U. S. Supreme Court decreed it should be when it placed the primary responsibility upon school authorities for "elucidating, assessing and solving these problems."

EDITOR'S AFTERWORD

As classroom doors closed on 12 million southern and border state children in the third summer since the Supreme Court decision in the *Brown* case, school boards were pondering the future of segregation or looking back upon one or more years of desegregated schooling.

There are some 9,000 school districts in the 17-state area: "some," because no one can be sure of the total number, for even as these words are being read, districts are in the process of dissolution under stepped-up programs of consolidation. By most recent official count there were 9,015 districts. Of these, 3,008 had children of both races.

The last figure will astonish some non-southerners as it has surprised persons who live in the region. As a problem in racial specifics, less than 40 per cent of southern districts had both white and Negro children—or, to state it precisely, 38 per cent of the known districts were facing, or had already faced and resolved, the problem raised by the Court. And to a large degree each was doing it in its own way in the southland of many Souths.

Another figure is smaller yet. In three years, 685 districts, or 18 per cent of those having children of both races, had begun or accomplished the desegregation process.

And still to diminish: of these 685 districts, only seven were in states outside the border region—in Arkansas and Tennessee, as pointed out in the chapter "Along the Border." Eight states of the Upper and Deep South had no integration below the college level; five at no level whatever.

Yet more and more it had a local look, it appeared to be a local problem. The courts clearly said so. Some governors, notably those in North Carolina, Tennessee and Arkansas, said the same. Save for areas of clearly contiguous sentiment, such as the Black Belts, nearly every district, nearly every case, was different.

The efforts of both segregationists and integrationists to find strength in numbers articulated this difference. Virginia's "massive resistance" program was aimed at preventing the integration of any

202

child anywhere. Legislators had erected the most intricate barriers in Alabama, Louisiana, Georgia, Mississippi and South Carolina with the same absolutes in mind, while seeing them rejected in tightly-segregated Florida. (The South, which is many, is paradoxes.)

Still and all, school boards and school officers tended to look upon the problem as local—with perhaps an assist from the state capitol.

One title suggested for this book, and not wholly in jest, was: "Why We Behave Like Southerners."

Well within the maturity of all the contributors to this book, the crime of lynching had been expunged from the southern record. As the chapter "Communities in Strife" points out, little blood had been spilled in altercations directly involved with school desegregation. More than a thousand southern state legislators, and most of the South's delegations in Congress, stoutly believed it a right and a duty to adopt new legislation meant to thwart desegregation or to denounce judicial encroachment on the states.

What explained this attitude?

Perhaps at base was an observation offered by Professor A. D. Albright of the University of Kentucky. In the early stages of white southern resistance, he said, "Integration is more important to Negroes than the white man realizes, and segregation is more important to whites than the Negro realizes."

The Negro, or the Negro leadership, demonstrated the truth of this statement by scores of school entry petitions and school entry suits, from which no large body of Negroes, as a body, disassociated themselves. The courts indeed had been involved in three years of litigation, three years which—if the eight state placement acts assumed the litigious importance often assigned to them—were but a prelude.

Legislators and white pro-segregation groups as quickly underscored this truism. As the chapter "Be It Enacted . . ." emphasizes, 136 legislative measures designed to slow down or arrest any movement toward integration had been adopted since 1954. In a very real sense the states of the former Confederacy had taken up the shield and buckler of states' rights which fell, or seemed to fall, into disuse after the events of nearly a century ago.

But this over-simplifies the conflict—at least for the time being. With few exceptions, the Negro was only a political cipher. On the planes of politics and effective social attack and social defense, the struggle pitted white against white—the white vocal majority against its small vocal minority, or the white group against the indigenous Federal authority, which was white. Further, and in a response which was historical, the struggle pitted the southern white majority against all comers.

However, even in the face of this solidity the problem seemed to fragment—at least at its edges. The pending court cases deeper South, including those resolved by court-ordered and community-accepted desegregation for the fall of 1957, almost all involved urban centers—Little Rock, Nashville, New Orleans, Miami, Norfolk, Newport News and others. Here the first significant court actions were initiated, and here they progressed in the sense that they were juridically active. Even in the border areas, desegregation on any large scale began first in the cities—Baltimore, Washington, St. Louis—though this axiom broke down (again the paradox) in rural south and west Texas. Almost the very first cases, and the Supreme Court bellwethers, were all but dormant in Clarendon County, South Carolina, and Prince Edward County, Virginia, where, as the chapter on "Law of the Land" observes, judges were reluctant to fix timetables.

So the South had a sub-region which did not appear on any map. It was the rural area—an area fast disappearing as farming tended to become an industry rather than a cultural pattern, but an indentifiable area still. Here there were no racial concentrations by reason of housing. Here, in an informal sense, people were "all mixed up together" in respect to the land they worked or occupied.

The rural southern school was more than a plant for the education of rural children. It was a community center. It was literally a country club. It provided the handiest social entertainment and it made for racial cohesion even though (paradoxically once again) the rural white southerner was closer neighbor to his Negro counterpart than was any white city-dweller to the urban Negro.

Here, at any rate, the pace of desegregation regionwide was slower and more cautious. And in some conspicuous instances—Clinton, Clay and Sturgis, Mansfield and Greenbrier—it was full of tumult. Once again it could be emphasized that every case was different.

No man had the temerity to gauge the future by the past. In the areas of greatest Negro population, however, any man of objective mien could see racial relations deteriorate, while conversely he had to admit that racial relations as they had existed before 1954 were based on a concept which the Negro now seemed to believe obsolete or at least no longer comfortable. And he had to concede that each group had become ever more race-conscious.

He saw an atmosphere of hostility developing between North and South, as it had done with similar historic provocation three generations ago. But some of him professed also to see a deeper understanding of and sympathy with southern problems, born perhaps of an age of candor which owned up to extra-legal discrimination practiced outside the South.

He saw his churches once again restless and even agonized.

He saw public education re-examined, and whether it would hurt or help he could not tell.

Finally, he saw the whole region in transition and being transformed, with factory smoke on the once-still air of bayou and mountain cove, with TV masts towering above tenant cabins, with new roads lifting him out of the mud and setting him down at a drive-in theater. Not all of this had happened in three years, or in ten, but nothing like it had ever happened anywhere in so short a whistling span of time.

What would come next?

ACKNOWLEDGMENTS

What has gone before was conceived as a job of topical reporting and performed as such—in, I believe, record time. Newsmen call it a "wrap-up" and recognize its perishable qualities. The layman may have found in it a quick yet not superficial view of the southern and border region as it contemplated its schools in mid-1957.

To bring this off with dispatch and in a useful manner required close co-operation of institutions and individuals. First of all, I am grateful to the directors and officers of the Fund for the Advancement of Education who gave approval and encouragement to the project when it was first broached to them and who provided a generous underwriting. Especial thanks are due Roy E. Larsen and Ralph McGill, board members, and Philip Coombs, John K. Weiss, John Scanlon and Dorothy Mitchell of the Fund staff.

The basic editorial work, of course, is the three-year product of the correspondents of *Southern School News*. Aside from those who wrote the chapters of this book, they are William H. McDonald of the *Montgomery Advertiser,* Alabama correspondent; Thomas D. Davis of the *Arkansas Gazette,* Arkansas correspondent; William P. Frank of the *Wilmington News,* Delaware correspondent; Leo Adde of the *New Orleans Item,* Louisiana correspondent, and before him Mario Fellom, of the same newspaper; Kenneth Toler, Jackson bureau of the *Memphis Commercial Appeal,* Mississippi correspondent; Jay Jenkins, Raleigh bureau of the *Charlotte Observer,* North Carolina correspondent; Leonard Jackson of the *Oklahoma City Oklahoman-Times,* Oklahoma correspondent, and before him Mary Goddard of the same newspaper; James Elliott of the *Nashville Banner,* Tennessee correspondent; Richard Morehead, Austin bureau of the *Dallas Morning News,* Texas correspondent; Overton Jones of the *Richmond Times-Dispatch,* Virginia correspondent; and Thomas F. Stafford of the *Charleston Gazette,* West Virginia correspondent, and before him the late Frank Knight of the same newspaper. Many of these assisted by reading and criticizing various chapters.

I am indebted to all of the members of the board of directors of Southern Education Reporting Service for their approval of this project and their constant encouragement. A list of the board membership as constituted at this time appears on a facing page. Board members read and criticized various chapters and in other ways aided in the editorial and production effort. In particular Board Chairman Frank Ahlgren and former Chairman Virginius Dabney, editor of the *Richmond Times-Dispatch,* scrutinized the manuscript with knowing eyes and gave helpful suggestions.

Members of the SERS central headquarters staff labored over long weeks in the preparation and reading of the manuscript. I am indebted to my assistant Patrick E. McCauley, also a contributor, and to Natalie Rollow, a tireless and understanding secretary (and effective critic as well); to Mary Woodward, who assisted in preparation of the manuscript, and to Imogene Morgan McCauley and Marybeth Wrenne, who were in charge of research.

Many persons kindly read pertinent chapters in their roles as expert critics, and others contributed to the text in various ways. Special acknowledgment is owed Wylie H. Davis, now at the University of Illinois law school, Robert McKay of New York University and Paul Sanders of Vanderbilt University, who is editor of the valuable *Race Relations Law Reporter;* Bem Price of the *Associated Press,* Wayne Whitt of the *Nashville Tennessean,* Professor W. D. McClurkin of George Peabody College for Teachers, Reed Sarratt of the *Winston-Salem Journal and Sentinel,* and many others. Thanks are also due *The Nation's Schools* for the inclusion of certain material in the chapter, "Man in No Man's Land."

Finally, of course, I am grateful for the probationary hours—many of them late ones—granted by my wife and daughter, who always left a lamp in the window.

D.S.

ABOUT THE CONTRIBUTORS

COLLIER, BERT ("Segregation and Politics") is a native of Montgomery, Alabama, and was educated in the public schools of that city. He began newspaper work after high school and, except for interludes with Community Chests and as administrative assistant to the Georgia State Administrator of the Works Progress Administration, he has been in newspaper work all his professional life. He spent ten years on Hearst's old *Atlanta Georgian,* covering state politics and legislative matters, reporting the rise and fortunes of the elder Talmadge and Senators Russell and George. Collier is now a staff writer for the *Miami Herald,* specializing in social welfare subjects. He is a contributor to magazines and to television programs. In the summer of 1956 he traveled more than 3,500 miles through the South and wrote a 13-part series of articles on segregation-desegregation for the Chicago Daily News Service. He has won several awards for reportorial excellence, is married and has three children. He covers Florida for *Southern School News.*

JAMES, WELDON ("The South's Own Civil War") is associate editor of *The Courier-Journal* of Louisville and is Kentucky correspondent for *Southern School News.* He is the author, with Omer Carmichael, of *The Louisville Story* (Simon & Schuster, 1957). James was born in St. Charles, South Carolina and is an honor graduate of Furman University. He taught high school in Greenville, South Carolina and was a reporter on *The Greenville Piedmont.* In 1937-39 he was a war correspondent in China and Spain for the United Press and (in 1941) for the newspaper *PM* in England. He served four years in the U. S. Marine Corps (1942-46) and returned to duty in 1950-52. He is now a lieutenant colonel in the Marine Reserve. Between 1946 and 1948 he was Far Eastern editor and roving correspondent for *Collier's.* He is a contributor to magazines and a lecturer on current affairs. In 1939-40 he was a Nieman Fellow at Harvard. James is married and has three children.

JONES, EDGAR L. ("City Limits") is a graduate of Dartmouth College (1937) and the Columbia University School of Journalism (1938). He edited a weekly newspaper in Boston and did public relations work in New York prior to World War II. During the war he was successively an ambulance driver, merchant seaman, chemical warfare historian and the correspondent in the central Pacific for the *Atlantic Monthly.* After a postwar year with that publication, Jones became an editorial writer for the Baltimore *Sun,* shifting in 1953 to *The Evening Sun.* He is the Maryland correspondent of *Southern School News.*

LASCH, ROBERT ("Along the Border") grew up in Kansas City, Missouri and attended the University of Nebraska and Oxford University, England (Rhodes Scholar). He worked on the *Omaha World Herald* from 1931 to 1941. He was a Nieman fellow at Harvard in 1941-42. Later he served as editorial writer and chief editorial writer, *Chicago Sun* and *Sun-Times.* Since 1950 he has been editorial writer for the *St. Louis Post-Dispatch.* Lasch is a contributor to magazines and is the author of *Breaking the Building Blockade* (University of Chicago Press, 1946). He covers Missouri for *Southern School News*.

LEFLAR, ROBERT A. ("Law of the Land") holds the title of "Distinguished Professor" at the University of Arkansas School of Law, where he was dean from 1943 to 1954. He served as Associate Justice of the Arkansas Supreme Court from 1949 to 1951 and now directs the summer Seminar for Appellate Judges at New York University. He was co-author of "Segregation in the Public Schools—1953," 67 *Harvard Law Review* 377 (January 1954) which definitively analyzed the legal problems up to the date of the 1954 Supreme Court decision. He makes his home in Fayetteville, Arkansas.

McCAULEY, PATRICK E. ("Be It Enacted . . .") is Assistant to the Director of the Southern Education Reporting Service. A native of Alexandria, Louisiana, he attended public and parochial schools there. He served one year in the U. S. Navy during World War II. He holds a bachelor of arts degree with major in journalism from Tulane University and master of arts degree in political science from Vanderbilt University. McCauley began newspaper work in 1949 as editor of the weekly *Seacoast Echo,* Bay St. Louis, Mississippi, later serving for five years on the Huntsville (Alabama) *Times*.

PARHAM, JOSEPH B. ("Halls of Ivy—Southern Exposure") is editor of *The Macon News* and Georgia correspondent for *Southern School News*. He was born in Winder, Georgia, and received his early newspaper training on small town weekly newspapers in Georgia. Joining *The Macon News* in 1941 he served successively as reporter, sports editor, telegraph editor, managing editor and, finally, editor. He served four years in the armed forces during World War II. He is a member of the American Society of Newspaper Editors. Parham is married and has four sons.

ROBINSON, GLEN ("Man in No Man's Land") has served Southern Education Reporting Service as a consultant and was formerly Assistant to the President and instructor in school administration at George Peabody College for Teachers in Nashville. In 1957 he became Assistant Director of Research for the National Education Association in Washington, D. C. A native of Knoxville, Tennessee, Robinson holds bachelor's and master's degrees from the University of Tennessee and a Ph.D. from Peabody College. He is a former teacher of science and mathematics in Anderson County, Tennessee and he served as an infantry officer in World War II and in the Korean conflict. He lives in Bethesda, Maryland, with his wife and two children.

ROGERS, JEANNE ("Nation's Showcase?") is a native of Independence, Missouri, and a graduate of the University of Missouri. Covering the District of Columbia for *Southern School News,* she is education reporter for *The Washington Post and Times-Herald*. Her other experience includes the *Kansas City Star,* the *Washington Evening Star* and the *Washington Times-Herald*. Miss Rogers has won a number of awards in journalism, including the Newspaper Guild award in 1951 for best human interest story and the Education Writers Association award of 1952 for an outstanding single article. For her education writing she was awarded a life membership in the Parent-Teachers Association in 1956.

WESTFELDT, WALLACE ("Communities in Strife") is one of the two Tennessee correspondents of *Southern School News* and is a staff writer for *The Nashville Tennessean*. A native of New Orleans, he attended public and private schools there and received his B.A. degree at the University of the South, Sewanee, Tennessee. In 1944 he was commissioned a second lieutenant in the U. S. Marine Corps Reserve, serving 18 months overseas, ten of which were spent on the staff of Admiral Chester Nimitz. He returned to duty with the Marine Corps in 1951-52 after a brief stint with *Time* magazine in New York and graduate study at Columbia University. Later he served in the Atlanta bureau of *Time*, joining the *Tennessean* in 1953. He is married and makes his home in Nashville.

WORKMAN, W. D., Jr. ("The Deep South") is a native of Greenwood, South Carolina and represents several newspapers as capitol correspondent in Columbia. He was graduated from The Citadel, at Charleston, in 1935 and studied law for a year at George Washington University night school while working for the Navy Department by day. He entered newspapering in 1936 as a reporter for *The News and Courier* of Charleston, later becoming manager of the newspaper-owned radio station. Workman was called to active duty as an Army reserve officer in 1941, serving in England, North Africa and Hawaii, and now is a lieutenant colonel in the Army Reserve. He is a radio news analyst and commentator and South Carolina correspondent of *Southern School News*. He is married and has two children.

SHOEMAKER, DON is executive director of the Southern Education Reporting Service and editor of *Southern School News*. A native of Montreal, he was educated in the public schools of Middletown, Ohio, at the Asheville School (North Carolina) and received a B.A. degree at the University of North Carolina. After college he began his newspaper work on the *Greensboro* (North Carolina) *Record* as telegraph editor. He was later telegraph editor of the *Asheville Times,* then associate editor of *The Asheville Citizen.* He became editor in 1947, resigning in 1955 to join SERS. He was president of the Asheville Community Chest and first president of the Thomas Wolfe Memorial Association. Shoemaker is a former chairman of the North Carolina Conference of Editorial Writers and a member of the American Society of Newspaper Editors. He is a contributor to magazines, a lecturer and author. He is married and has one child.

APPENDIX

STATUS OF THE PUBLIC COLLEGES

DESEGREGATED

(In some instances desegregation is the official policy
but no Negroes have been admitted or have applied)

Agricultural and Technical College of North Carolina (Negro), Greensboro
Altus College, Altus, Oklahoma
Amarillo College, Amarillo, Texas
Arkansas Polytechnic College, Russellville
Arkansas State College, Jonesboro
Austin Peay State College, Clarksville, Tennessee
Baltimore Junior College, Baltimore, Maryland
Bluefield State College (Negro), Bluefield, West Virginia
Cameron State Agricultural College, Lawton, Oklahoma
Central Missouri State College, Warrenburg
Central State College, Edmond, Oklahoma
Cisco Junior College, Cisco, Texas
Concord College, Athens, West Virginia
Delaware State College (Negro), Dover
Del Mar College, Corpus Christi, Texas
East Central State College, Ada, Oklahoma
Eastern Oklahoma Agricultural & Mechanical College, Wilburton
El Reno Junior College, El Reno, Oklahoma
Fairmont State College, Fairmont, West Virginia
Frank Phillips College, Borger, Texas
Hardin Junior College, Wichita Falls, Texas
Henderson State Teachers College, Arkadelphia, Arkansas
Howard County Junior College, Big Spring, Texas
Lamar State College of Technology, Beaumont, Texas
Lincoln University (Negro), Jefferson City, Missouri
Louisiana State University, Baton Rouge
McNeese State College, Lake Charles, Louisiana
Marshall College, Huntington, West Virginia
Maryland State Teachers College, Frostburg
Maryland State Teachers College, Towson
Medical College of Virginia, Richmond
Memphis State University, Memphis, Tennessee
Miner Teachers College (Negro), Washington, D. C. (combined with Wilson
    Teachers College)
Montgomery Junior College, Takoma Park, Maryland
Morgan State College (Negro), Baltimore, Maryland
Murray State College, Murray, Kentucky

212

Murray State School of Agriculture, Tishomingo, Oklahoma
Muskogee Junior College, Muskogee, Oklahoma
Northeast Missouri State Teachers College, Kirksville
Northeastern State College, Tahlequah, Oklahoma
North Texas State College, Denton
Northern Oklahoma Junior College, Tonkawa
Odessa College, Odessa, Texas
Oklahoma Agricultural & Mechanical College, Stillwater
Oklahoma College for Women, Chickasha
Paducah Junior College, Paducah, Kentucky
Pan American College, Edinburg, Texas
Richmond Professional Institute, Richmond, Virginia
Rolla College of Mines and Engineering, Rolla, Missouri
San Angelo College, San Angelo, Texas
San Antonio College, San Antonio, Texas
Shepherd State College, Shepherdstown, West Virginia
Southeast Missouri State College, Cape Girardeau, Missouri
Southeastern Louisiana College, Hammond
Southeastern State College, Durant, Oklahoma
Southwest Missouri State College, Springfield
Southwestern Louisiana Institute, Lafayette
Southwestern State College, Weatherford, Oklahoma
State College of Agriculture and Engineering, Raleigh, North Carolina
Texas Southmost College, Brownsville
Texas Western College, El Paso
United States Naval Academy, Annapolis, Maryland
University of Arkansas, Fayetteville
University of Delaware, Newark
University of Kentucky, Lexington
University of Louisville, Louisville, Kentucky
University of Maryland, College Park
University of Missouri, Columbia
University of North Carolina, Chapel Hill
University of Oklahoma, Norman
University of Tennessee, Knoxville
University of Texas, Austin
University of Virginia, Charlottesville
Victoria College, Victoria, Texas
Virginia Polytechnic Institute, Blacksburg
West Liberty State College, West Liberty, West Virginia
West Virginia Institute of Technology, Montgomery
West Virginia State College (Negro), Institute
West Virginia University, Morgantown
Wharton County Junior College, Wharton, Texas
Wilson Teachers College, Washington, D. C. (combined with Miner Teachers
    College)
Woman's College, Greensboro, North Carolina

OPEN TO BOTH RACES

Agricultural & Mechanical College and Normal College (Negro), Pine Bluff,
    Arkansas

Arkansas Agricultural & Mechanical College, College Heights
Arkansas State Teachers, College, Conway
College of William and Mary, Williamsburg, Virginia
Conners State Agricultural College, Warner, Oklahoma
Coppin State Teachers College (Negro), Baltimore, Maryland
Dunbar Junior College (Negro), Little Rock, Arkansas
East Tennessee State College, Johnson City
Eastern Kentucky State College, Richmond
George Washington Carver Junior College (Negro), Rockville, Maryland
Glenville State College, Glenville, West Virginia
Hagerstown Junior College, Hagerstown, Maryland
Harris Teachers College, St. Louis, Missouri
Jefferson City Junior College, Jefferson City, Missouri
Joplin Junior College, Joplin, Missouri
Junior Agricultural College of Central Arkansas, Beebe
Junior College of Flat River, Flat River, Missouri
Junior College of Kansas City, Kansas City, Missouri
Kentucky State College (Negro), Frankfort
Langston University (Negro), Langston, Oklahoma
Little Rock Junior College, Little Rock, Arkansas
Maryland State College (Negro), Princess Anne
Maryland State Teachers College (Negro), Bowie
Middle Tennessee State College, Murfreesboro
Midwestern University, Wichita Falls, Texas
Moberly Junior College, Moberly, Missouri
Morehead State College, Morehead, Kentucky
Northeastern Oklahoma Agricultural and Mechanical College, Miami
Northwest Missouri State College, Maryville
Northwestern State College, Alva, Oklahoma
Oklahoma Military Academy, Claremore
Panhandle Agricultural and Mechanical College, Goodwell, Oklahoma
Saint Joseph Junior College, St. Joseph, Missouri
Saint Mary's Seminary Junior College, St. Mary's, Maryland
Sayre Junior College, Sayre, Oklahoma
Southern State College, Magnolia, Arkansas
Tennessee Agricultural and Industrial State University (Negro), Nashville
Tennessee Polytechnic Institute, Cookeville
Texarkana College, Texarkana, Texas
Texas Southern University (Negro), Houston
Trenton Junior College, Trenton, Missouri
University of Alabama, Tuscaloosa
Western Kentucky State College, Bowling Green

SEGREGATED

Abraham Baldwin Agricultural College, Tifton, Georgia
Alabama Agricultural and Mechanical College (Negro), Huntsville
Alabama College, Montevallo
Alabama Polytechnic Institute, Auburn
Alabama State College for Negroes, Montgomery
Albany State College (Negro), Albany, Georgia
Alcorn Agricultural and Mechanical College (Negro), Lorman, Mississippi

Alvin Junior College, Alvin, Texas
Appalachian State Teachers College, Boone, North Carolina
Arlington State College, Arlington, Texas
Armstrong College, Savannah, Georgia
Asheville-Biltmore College, Asheville, North Carolina
Blinn College, Brenham, Texas
Carver Junior College (Negro), Charlotte, North Carolina
Charlotte College, Charlotte, North Carolina
Chipola Junior College, Marianna, Florida
The Citadel, Charleston, South Carolina
Clarendon Junior College, Clarendon, Texas
Clemson Agricultural College, Clemson, South Carolina
Coahoma Junior College (Negro), Clarksdale, Mississippi
College of Charleston, Charleston, South Carolina
Copiah-Lincoln Junior College, Wesson, Mississippi
Delta State Teachers College, Cleveland, Mississippi
East Carolina College, Greenville, North Carolina
East Central Junior College, Decatur, Mississippi
East Mississippi Junior College, Scooba
East Texas State Teachers College, Commerce
Fayetteville State Teachers College (Negro), Fayetteville, North Carolina
Florence State Teachers College, Florence, Alabama
Florida Agricultural and Mechanical College (Negro), Tallahassee
Florida State University, Tallahassee
Fort Valley State College (Negro), Fort Valley, Georgia
Gainesville Junior College, Gainesville, Texas
Georgia Institute of Technology, Atlanta
Georgia Military College, Milledgeville
Georgia Southwestern College, Americus
Georgia State College for Women, Milledgeville
Georgia Teachers College, Statesboro
Gordon Military College, Barnesville, Georgia
Grambling College (Negro), Grambling, Louisiana
Henderson County Junior College, Athens, Texas
Hinds Junior College, Raymond, Mississippi
Holmes Junior College, Goodman, Mississippi
Itawamba Junior College, Fulton, Mississippi
Jackson College (Negro), Jackson, Mississippi
Jacksonville State Teachers College, Jacksonville, Alabama
Jones County Junior College, Ellisville, Mississippi
Junior College of Augusta, Augusta, Georgia
Kilgore College, Kilgore, Texas
Laredo Junior College, Laredo, Texas
Livingston State Teachers College, Livingston, Alabama
Longwood College, Farmwood, Virginia
Louisiana Polytechnic Institute, Ruston
Madison College, Harrisonburg, Virginia
Mary Washington College, Fredericksburg, Virginia
Medical College of Georgia, Augusta
Medical College of South Carolina, Charleston

Meridian Municipal Junior College, Meridian, Mississippi
Middle Georgia College, Cochran
Mississippi Southern College, Hattiesburg
Mississippi State College, State College
Mississippi State College for Women, Columbus
Mississippi Vocational College (Negro), Itta Bena
Navarro Junior College, Corsicana, Texas
North Carolina College (Negro), Durham
Northeast Louisiana State College, Monroe
Northeast Mississippi Junior College, Booneville
North Georgia College, Dahlonega
Northwestern State College of Louisiana, Natchitoches
Palm Beach Junior College, Lake Park, Florida
Panola County Junior College, Carthage, Texas
Paris Junior College, Paris, Texas
Pearl River Junior College, Poplarville, Mississippi
Pembroke State College, Pembroke, North Carolina
Perkinston Junior College, Perkinston, Mississippi
Prairie View Agricultural and Mechanical College (Negro), Prairie View,
    Texas
Ranger Junior College, Ranger, Texas
St. Petersburg Junior College, St. Petersburg, Florida
St. Philip's College (Negro), San Antonio, Texas
Sam Houston State Teachers College, Huntsville, Texas
Savannah State College (Negro), Savannah, Georgia
South Carolina State College (Negro), Orangeburg
Southern University and Agricultural and Mechanical College (Negro), Baton
    Rouge, Louisiana
South Georgia College, Douglas
Southwest Mississippi Junior College, Summit
Southwest Texas Junior College, Uvalde
Southwest Texas State Teachers College, San Marcos
State Teachers College (Negro), Elizabeth City, North Carolina
Stephen F. Austin State College, Nacogdoches, Texas
Sul Ross State College, Alpine, Texas
Sunflower Junior College, Moorhead, Mississippi
Tarleton State College, Stephenville, Texas
Temple Junior College, Temple, Texas
Texas Agricultural and Mechanical College, College Station
Texas College of Arts and Industry, Kingsville
Texas State College for Women, Denton
Texas Technological College, Lubbock
Troy State Teachers College, Troy, Alabama
University of Florida, Gainesville
University of Georgia, Athens
University of Houston, Houston, Texas
University of Mississippi, University
University of South Carolina, Columbia
Valdosta State College, Valdosta, Georgia
Virginia Military Institute, Lexington

Virginia State College (Negro), Petersburg
Washington Junior College, Pensacola, Florida
Weatherford College, Weatherford, Texas
West Georgia College, Carrollton
West Texas State College, Canyon
Wilmington College, Wilmington, North Carolina
Winston-Salem Teachers College (Negro), Winston-Salem, North Carolina
Winthrop College, Rock Hill, South Carolina

CURRENT MATERIALS

BOOKS AND PAMPHLETS

Allport, Gordon W. *The Nature of Prejudice.* Text edition. Cambridge, Mass.: Addison-Wesley Publishing Co., Inc., 1954.

Answers for Action. Atlanta: Southern Regional Council, 1954.

Ashmore, Harry S. *The Negro and the Schools.* Chapel Hill: University of North Carolina Press, 1954.

Beauchamp, Mary and others. *Building Brotherhood: What Can Elementary Schools Do?* National Conference of Christians and Jews.

Brady, Tom P. *Black Monday.* Winona, Miss.: Association of Citizens Councils, 1955.

Butcher, Margaret Just. *The Negro in American Culture.* New York: Alfred A. Knopf, 1956.

Carmichael, Omer and James, Weldon. *The Louisville Story.* New York: Simon and Schuster, 1957.

Changing Patterns in the New South. Atlanta: Southern Regional Council, 1955.

Clark, Kenneth B. *Prejudice and Your Child.* Boston: Beacon Press, 1955.

Clinton, Tenn., A Tentative Description and Analysis of the School Desegregation Crisis in. Anna Holden, Bonita Valien and Preston Valien. Nashville, Tenn.: Fisk University, Dec. 1, 1956.

Cook, Eugene. *The Ugly Truth About the NAACP.* Winona, Miss.: Association of Citizens Councils.

Davidson, Donald. *Tyranny at Oak Ridge.* Nashville: Tennessee Federation for Constitutional Government, 1956.

Davis, Robert E. *The American Negro's Dilemma.* New York Philosophical Library, 1954.

Debnam, W. E. *My Old Kentucky Home, Good Night!* Raleigh, N. C.: The Graphic Press, Inc., 1955.

Desegregation in the Baltimore City Schools. Baltimore: The Maryland Commission on Interracial Problems and Relations, The Baltimore Commission on Human Relations, 1955.

Desegregation of the St. Louis Public Schools. (A summary of measures taken by the Board of Education of the City of St. Louis to implement the Supreme Court's decision of May 17, 1954). St. Louis Public School Instruction Department, September, 1956.

Edwards, Newton. *The Courts and the Public Schools.* Revised edition. Chicago: Universtiy of Chicago Press, 1955.

Ehlers, Henry J., editor. *Crucial Issues in Education, an Anthology.* New York: Holt, 1955.

Faulkner, William and others. *The Segregation Decisions.* Atlanta: Southern Regional Council, 1956.

Fleming, Harold C. and Constable, C. *What's Happening in School Integration?* New York: Public Affairs Pamphlet No. 244, 1956.

Ginzberg, Eli. *The Negro Potential.* New York: Columbia University Press, 1956.

Grambs, Jean D. *Education in a Transition Community.* National Conference of Christians and Jews.

Griffin, John Howard and Freedman, Theodore. *What Happened in Mansfield.* Published by the Anti-Defamation League of B'nai B'rith.

Heaton, Margaret M. *Feelings Are Facts.* National Conference of Christians and Jews.

Hill, Herbert and Greenberg, Jack. *Citizen's Guide to Desegregation.* Boston: Beacon Press, 1955.

Hirsh, Selma. *Fear and Prejudice.* New York: Public Affairs Pamphlet No. 245, 1957.

Holley, Joseph Winthrop. *Education and the Segregation Issue.* New York: William Frederick Press, 1955.

It Can Be Done: Desegregation—a Progress Report. New York: National Association for the Advancement of Colored People.

A Jewish View on Segregation. Greenwood, Miss.: Association of Citizens Councils of Mississippi.

Kilpatrick, James Jackson. *The Sovereign States—Notes of a Citizen of Virginia.* Chicago: Henry Regnery Company, 1957.

Looney, Frank J. and Perez, L. H. *Re: Segregation.* New Orleans: Published by authors, 1954.

Loth, David and Fleming, Harold. *Integration North and South.* New York: The Fund for the Republic, 1956.

McKay, Robert. *"With All Deliberate Speed" A Study of School Desegregation.* New York: New York University School of Law, 1956.

Nichols, Lee. *Breakthrough on the Color Front.* New York: Random House, 1954.

Next Steps in the South. Atlanta: Southern Regional Council, 1956.

Patterns for Integration. Louisville, Ky.: Eastern Council for Moral and Spiritual Values.

Pierce, Truman M. and others. *White and Negro Schools in the South.* Englewood Cliffs, N. J.: Prentice-Hall, Inc., 1955.

Psychiatric Aspects of School Desegregation. New York: Group for Advancement of Psychiatry, 1957.

Report to the People: A summary of articles written by New England editors after their tour of Mississippi. Jackson, Miss.: Mississippi State Sovereignty Commission.

Rowan, Carl T. *Go South to Sorrow.* New York: Random House, 1957.

School Integration. Washington, D. C.: National Council of Catholic Women.

Scott, C. Winfield and Hill, Clyde M., editors. *Public Education Under Criticism.* New York: Prentice-Hall, Inc., 1954.

Segregation and the Schools. New York: Public Affairs Pamphlet No. 209, 1954.

Seidenberg, Jacob. *Negroes in the Work Group.* National Conference of Christians and Jews.

Sims, John G., Jr. *The South Must Not Turn Back.* Fort Worth, Texas: Published by the author, 1955.

Smith, Lillian E. *Now Is the Time.* New York: Dell Publishing Co., 1955.

Southern States Cooperative Program in Educational Administration, George Peabody College for Teachers, Nashville, Tenn. *The Bi-racial Picture in Southern Education and Related Problems.* Report of the Second Regional

Conference, State Boards of Education and Chief State School Officers, Atlanta, Ga., Sept. 5-7, 1954.

Spurlock, Clark. *Education and the Supreme Court.* Urbana: University of Illinois Press, 1955.

Stampp, Kenneth M. *The Peculiar Institution.* New York: Alfred A. Knopf, 1956.

Statements Adopted by Religious Groups Re Segregation in the Public Schools. Compiled by Department of Racial and Cultural Relations, National Council of the Churches of Christ in the U.S.A., New York, October 1954.

Stewart, Maxwell S. *The Negro in America.* New York: Public Affairs Pamphlet No. 95, 1955.

Suchman, Edward A. and others. *Desegregation: Some Propositions and Research Suggestions.* (A memorandum for discussion purposes.) Cornell University, August, 1954.

Swanson, Ernst W. and Griffin, John A., editors. *Public Education in the South Today and Tomorrow.* Chapel Hill: University of North Carolina Press, 1955.

Talmadge, Herman E. *You and Segregation.* Birmingham, Ala.: Vulcan Press, Inc., 1955.

The Crisis in Tennessee. Nashville: Tennessee Federation for Constitutional Government, 1957.

Valien, Bonita H. *The St. Louis Story: A Study of Desegregation.* New York: Anti-Defamation League of B'nai B'rith, 1956.

Vance, Rupert B. and Demerath, Nicholas J., editors. *The Urban South.* Chapel Hill: University of North Carolina Press, 1954.

Williams, Robin M., Jr. and Ryan, Margaret W., editors. *Schools in Transition.* Chapel Hill: University of North Carolina Press, 1954.

Warren, Robert Penn. *Segregation.* New York: Random House, 1956.

PERIODICALS

Adult Education. Published quarterly by Adult Education Association of the United States of America, Chicago, Ill.

Crisis. Published monthly Oct.-May, bi-monthly June-July, Aug.-Sept., by Crisis Publishing Co., Inc.

Defenders' News and Views. Published by Defenders of State Sovereignty and Individual Liberties, Richmond, Va.

Dixie-American: Voice of the Anglo-Saxon South. Published by The Citizens Press, Birmingham, Ala.

Education Digest. Published monthly by Education Digest, Ann Arbor, Mich.

Journal of Negro Education. Published quarterly, Howard University Press, Washington, D.C.

Negro Educational Review. Published Jan., Apr., July and Oct. by Negro Educational Review, Jacksonville, Fla.

New South. Published monthly by Southern Regional Council, Atlanta, Ga.

Phi Delta Kappan, May 1956. Entire issue on desegregation.

Southern Conservative. Published monthly by Ida M. Darden, editor, Fort Worth, Texas.

Southern Digest. Published monthly by D. E. Birdsell, editor-publisher, New Orleans, La.

Southern Patriot. Published monthly by Southern Conference Educational Fund, Inc., Nashville, Tenn.

Southerner: News of the Citizens Council. Asa E. Carter, editor. Birmingham, Ala.

Southern School News. Published monthly by Southern Education Reporting Service, Nashville, Tenn.

The Citizens' Council. Published monthly by the Citizens' Councils of America, W. J. Simmons, Jackson, Miss.

The Virginian. Published monthly, Newport News, Va.

The White Sentinel. Official Organ of the National Citizens Protective Association, John W. Hamilton, editor, St. Louis, Mo.

MAGAZINE AND NEWSPAPER ARTICLES

"The Background of Segregation," *Life,* Sept. 3-Oct. 1, 1956, five-part series.

Barrett, George. "Study in Desegregation: The Clinton (Tenn.) Story." *New York Times Magazine.* Sept. 16, 1956.

Behrens, Dorothy. "The St. Louis Story." *American Unity,* March-April, 1957.

Berger, Monroe. "The Study of Man: Desegregation, Law and Social Science," *Commentary,* May, 1957.

Bickel, Alexander M. "Integration: the Second Year in Perspective." *The New Republic,* Oct. 8, 1956.

Boyle, Sarah Patton. "Southerners Will Like Integration," *Saturday Evening Post,* Feb. 19, 1955.

Brawley, James P. "Are the Negro Colleges Good Enough?" *Church and Campus,* January-February, 1956.

Brooks, Albert N. D. "Education and the Ability to Learn." *The Negro History Bulletin,* November, 1956.

Byrnes, James F. "Guns and Bayonets Cannot Promote Education," *U. S. News and World Report,* Oct. 5, 1956.

Caliver, Ambrose. "Education of Negroes: Successful Transition from Segregated to Unsegregated Schools." *School Life,* April, 1954.

Carter, Hodding. "A Wave of Terror Threatens the South." *Look,* March 22, 1955.

Carter, Hodding. "The South and I." *Look,* June 28, 1955.

Carter, Hodding. "Racial Crisis in the Deep South." *Saturday Evening Post,* Dec. 17, 1955.

"The Case for the South," *Charleston (S.C.) News and Courier,* special edition.

Dabbs, James McBride. "What Is the White South Defending" *The Christian Century,* Feb. 8, 1956.

Dabney, Virginius. "A Frank Talk to North and South About Integration." *U. S. News and World Report,* March 18, 1957.

Dabney, Virginius. "School Crisis in Dixie." *American Magazine,* August, 1956.

"Displaced Negro Teachers in Border States Re-employed." *The Nation's Schools,* December, 1956.

Drewry, Galen N. "The Principal Faces Desegregation," *Educational Leadership,* October, 1955.

Faulkner, William. "A Letter to the North." *Life,* March 5, 1955.

"The Federal School Aid Bill." *Education Summary,* April 20, 1957.

Ford, Nick Aaron. "Consider the Negro Teacher." *The New Republic,* April 15, 1957.

"Four Dixie Governors Join in Call for Interposition." *South,* Feb. 6, 1956.

Garber, Lee O. "Issues Involved in Desegregating Public Schools." *The Nation's Schools,* October, 1954.

Halberstam, David. "The White Citizens Councils," *Commentary,* October, 1956.

Hyman, Herbert H. and Sheatsley, Paul B. "Attitudes Toward Desegregation," *Scientific American,* December, 1956.

"Interposition" editorials and editorial page presentations. *Richmond News Leader,* 1955-1956.

"Is the South Moving 'With All Deliberate Speed?' " *The New Republic,* Feb. 20, 1956.

James, Selwyn. "The Town That Surrendered to Hate." *Redbook,* March, 1955.

Johnson, Charles S. "A Southern Negro's View of the South." *New York Times Magazine,* Sept. 23, 1956.

Killian, Lewis M. "Implications of the Supreme Court Decision on Desegregation," *The Education Digest,* March, 1956.

Kilpatrick, James J. "The Right to Interpose." *Human Events,* Dec. 24, 1955.

King, Martin Luther, Jr. and Hall, Grover, Jr. "Alabama's Bus Boycott: What It's All About." *U. S. News and World Report,* Aug. 3, 1956.

Knebel, Fletcher and Mollenhoff, Clark. "Eight Klans Bring New Terror to the South." *Look,* April 30, 1957.

Leflar, Robert A. "Legal Education: Desegregation in the Law Schools." *American Bar Association Journal,* February, 1957.

Logan, Rayford W. "Is the NAACP Communistic?" *The Christian Century,* July 4, 1956.

Long, Howard Hale. "The Relative Learning Capacities of Negroes and Whites." *Journal of Negro Education,* Spring 1957.

McGurk, Frank C. J. "A Scientist's Report on Race Differences." *U. S. News and World Report,* Sept. 21, 1956.

McKnight, C. A. "The Desegregation Ruling." *The School Executive,* January, 1955.

McKnight, C. A. "Troubled South: Search for a Middle Ground." *Collier's,* June 22, 1956.

McMillan, George. "The Ordeal of Bobby Cain." *Collier's,* Nov. 23, 1956.

McNeill, Rev. Robert B. "A Georgia Minister Offers a Solution for the South." *Look,* May 28, 1957.

Maund, Alfred. "Grass-Roots Racism: White Council at Work." *The Nation,* July 23, 1955.

Miami Herald, Series by Bert Collier, March-April 1956.

Miller, William Lee. "Little Red Schoolhouse in the Middle of the Road." *The Reporter,* Oct. 20, 1955.

Morrow, Robert D., and others. "A Pattern of Integration." *The Nation's Schools,* March, 1956.

Murphy, Jay. "Can Public Schools Be Private?" *Alabama Law Review,* Fall, 1954.

"Negroes on Southern Campuses: What the Editors of Six College Newspapers in the South Think About Desegregation." *The New Republic,* Feb. 27, 1956.

"Negro Teachers for the North?" *U. S. News and World Report,* Aug. 27, 1954.

New York Herald Tribune. Series by Robert S. Bird, April, 1957.

New York Times. "Report on the South: The Integration Issue." March 13, 1956.

New York Times. Series by Dr. Benjamin Fine, September, 1956-May-June, 1957.

Odum, Howard W. "An Approach to Diagnosis and Direction of the Problem of Negro Segregation in the Public Schools of the South." *Journal of Public Law,* Vol. 3, No. 1. Emory University Law School, Emory University, Ga.

"One Plan for Ending Separate Schools" (Louisville, Ky.). *U. S. News and World Report,* Sept. 21, 1956.

"A Pattern for Forcing Mixed Schools in South?" (Clinton, Tenn.) *U. S. News and World Report,* Dec. 14, 1956.

Petal Paper. Editorial reprints and personal comments by P. D. East, Petal, Miss.

Redd, George N. "The Status of Educational Desegregation in Tennessee." *The Journal of Negro Education,* Summer, 1956.

Robinson, Glen. *The Nation's Schools,* August, 1956—January, 1957. Six articles on school segregation-desegregation.

Rowland, Stanley, Jr. "Legal War on the NAACP." *The Nation,* Feb. 9, 1957.

Sass, Herbert Ravenal. "Mixed Schools and Mixed Blood." *Atlantic Monthly,* November, 1956.

Shoemaker, Don. "Desegregation of the Schools." *The School Executive,* January, 1956.

Simon, Paul. "Let's Integrate Our Teachers." *The Christian Century,* Feb. 20, 1957.

"The South Digs in to Fight Mixed Schools." *U. S. News and World Report,* Sept. 7, 1956.

"The South v. the Supreme Court." *Look,* April 3, 1956.

Spence, Ralph B. "Adult Education and Desegregation." *Adult Education,* Autumn, 1954.

Sutherland, Arthur E. "The Supreme Court and Private Schools." *Harvard Educational Review,* Summer, 1955.

Sutherland, Arthur E. "Segregation by Race in Public Schools—Retrospect and Prospect." *Law and Contemporary Problems,* Winter, 1955.

"Teachers in Mixed Schools Size Up the Results." *U. S. News and World Report,* Oct. 5, 1956.

"Teens Show Mixed Feelings on Subject of Integrated Schools." *The Nation's Schools,* February, 1957.

"Virginia's Governor Proposes a Way to Keep Schools in the South from being Mixed." *U. S. News and World Report,* Sept. 7, 1956.

Waring, Thomas R. "The Southern Case Against Desegregation." *Harper's,* January, 1956.

Warren, Robert Penn. "Divided South Searches Its Soul." *Life,* July 9, 1956.

Washington Post and Times-Herald. Series by Alfred Friendly, April 1-4, 1957.

"We Take Our Stand." Collection of editorials from the *Charleston (S.C.) News and Courier,* Thomas R. Waring, editor.

"What Negroes Want Now." An interview with Walter White, *U. S. News and World Report*, May 28, 1954.

"What Three Southern Governors Say About Mixing Schools." *U. S. News and World Report*, Jan. 25, 1957.

Woodward, C. Vann. "The 'New Reconstruction' in the South." *Commentary*, June, 1956.

MAJOR TYPES OF LEGISLATION ADOPTED IN ELEVEN SOUTHERN STATES SINCE 1952 DESIGNED TO PREVENT OR CONTROL DESEGREGATION

Measures Authorizing or Requiring—	Ala.	Ark.	Fla.	Ga.	La.	Miss.	N.C.	S.C.	Tenn.	Tex.	Va.
Abolition of Schools by Local (L)egislation (O)ption	O			L		L O	O	L			O
Grants for Private Education	X			X			X				X
Sale or Lease of School Facilities	X			X		X		X			
Use of Public Funds for Segregated Schools Only				X	X			X			X
Specific Pupil Assignment	X	X	X		X	X	X		X	X	X
Compulsory Attendance (R)epeal (M)odification	M	M		M	M	R		R M			M
Extraordinary Powers for Governor			X	X				X			X
Teacher Employment Laws (R)epeal (M)odification	M		M		M		R	R			
Restriction on or Probe of Pro-Integration and Pro-Segregation Groups	X	X	X		X	X		X	X		X
Interposition, Nullification or Protest	X	X	X	X	X	X	X	X	X	X	X
Use of State Sovereignty or Police Powers		X		X	X	X					
Provision for Legal Counsel to Oppose Desegregation Suits		X	X	X							X
Regulation of Pupil Transfers								X	X		
Guarantee Teacher Benefits in Private Schools				X							X
Elimination of Barratry				X		X		X	X		X
Withholding State Approval of Desegregated Schools					X						
Local Referenda to Determine Desegregation										X	
Prohibition of Interracial Sports Events				X							X
Study Committees to Work on Segregation Issue	X			X	X	X	X	X			X
Separate Schools on Voluntary Basis	X								X		
Segregation by Sex									X		
Specific New Provisions for Segregated Schools	X			X	X	X					X
Teachers to Instruct Own Race Only				X							

UNOFFICIAL FIGURES SHOWING EXTENT OF SEGREGATION AND DESEGREGATION IN REGION AS OF JUNE 30, 1957 [1]

State	School Districts			Total Enrollment			Pupils In Integrated Situations	
	Total	Bi-racial	Deseg.	White	Negro	Pct. Negro	White	Negro
Alabama	111	111	0	471,900	273,200	36.6	0	0
Arkansas	423	228	5	316,709	102,000	24.3	9,000	940
Delaware	106	61	18	53,904	11,411	17.5	25,706	5,145
District of Columbia	1	1	1	34,758	73,723	68.0	34,758	73,723
Florida	67	67	0	594,220	165,957	21.8	0	0
Georgia	200	196	0	644,328	297,672	31.6	0	0
Kentucky	219	180	93	551,771	38,358	6.6	200,000	22,000
Louisiana	67	67	0	375,000	225,000	37.5	0	0
Maryland	24	23	20	397,417	109,720	21.6	384,150	89,668
Mississippi	151	151	0	273,722	268,216	49.5	0	0
Missouri [2]	3,600	244	202	677,500	67,000	9.0		59,000
North Carolina	172	172	0	724,302	301,161	29.3	0	0
Oklahoma	1,639	261	197	489,828	37,367	7.0	243,000	24,500
South Carolina	107	107	0	319,670	243,574	43.2	0	0
Tennessee	152	141	2	626,781	128,164	16.9	16,100	344
Texas	1,800	841	103	1,565,568	248,532	13.7	500,000	25,000
Virginia	114	114	0	566,596	184,417	24.5	0	0
West Virginia	55	43	44	457,807	23,806 [3]	5.2	422,324	24,953 [3]
Total	9,008	3,008	684	9,117,975	2,799,278	23.5	1,835,038 [2]	325,273

[1] Includes official figures for 1955-56 school year or estimates for 1956-57 where actual enrollments for 1956-57 unavailable.

[2] No data available for number of white children in desegregating Missouri school districts.

[3] Actual Negro enrollment as of 1954 used in computing number of West Virginia Negroes in integrated situation while total Negro enrollment for 1956-57 was derived by applying previous percentage total enrollment figures, since statistics in state are no longer kept by race.

INDEX

Set in Baskerville
Format by Joe Vesely
Manufactured by Benson Printing Company
Published by HARPER & BROTHERS, *New York*